700029157343

D1076377

# THIS TIME...
## THE DREAM IS COMING TRUE

# THIS TIME...
## THE DREAM IS COMING TRUE

The Inside Story of England's 2006 World Cup Challenge

HARRY HARRIS

JOHN BLAKE

| WORCESTERSHIRE COUNTY COUNCIL | |
| --- | --- |
| 734 | |
| Bertrams | 01.04.06 |
| 796.334668 | £17.99 |
| RE | |

Published by John Blake Publishing Ltd,
3, Bramber Court, 2 Bramber Road,
London W14 9PB, England

www.blake.co.uk

First published in hardback in 2006

ISBN 1 84454 248 3

All rights reserved. No part of this publication may be reproduced,
stored in a retrieval system, or in any form or by any means, without the prior
permission in writing of the publisher, nor be otherwise circulated in any form of
binding or cover other than that in which it is published and without a similar
condition including this condition being imposed on the subsequent publisher.

British Library Cataloguing-in-Publication Data:

A catalogue record for this book is available from the British Library.

Design by www.envydesign.co.uk

Printed in Great Britain by CPD

1 3 5 7 9 10 8 6 4 2

© Text copyright Harry Harris 2006

Papers used by John Blake Publishing are natural, recyclable products made from
wood grown in sustainable forests. The manufacturing processes conform to the
environmental regulations of the country of origin.

All photographs © Action Images

For the departed Bobby Moore and for the present
England captain David Beckham – let's hope he too can
lift the World Cup for his country

# ACKNOWLEDGEMENTS

Malcolm Padley at NTL is top of my list of acknowledgements in helping to launch This Time. And let's hope that dream of winning in Germany does come true.

Special thanks to Andrew Morris who represents the Boys of '66. Nobok, the legends specialists, and their editor Tom Skippings.

To Harrods for providing the pictures of the launch of the World Cup mascot.

John Blake Publishing deserve recognition for all their efforts, notably John, Rosie, Lucian and Clare.

It has been an absolute pleasure to reminisce about England World Cup triumph with all of the survivors of the team that beat West Germany. I was privileged enough to have been at the old Wembley to see the final, indeed to have had a 'season ticket' to see all of England's games in 1966.

# CONTENTS

# INTRODUCTION

The symmetry is compelling. The Boys of 2006 are off to Germany to repeat the exploits of the Boys of 1966, the team who beat West Germany at Wembley to win the World Cup. Exactly 40 years on, This Time surely England will have their moment in the sun once again. The signs are good.

Last Time – when England won their one and only World Cup – three of the backbone of their side came from the East End. Back then, it was the Hammers trio of skipper Bobby Moore, midfielder Martin Peters and hat-trick hero Geoff Hurst who became legends after helping Alf Ramsey's England beat West Germany 4–2.

This Time, for Moore, Hurst and Peters, read Frank Lampard, Rio Ferdinand and Joe Cole, who grew up and were educated at the East End academy of West Ham. All three, centre-half Ferdinand, midfielders Cole and Lampard, graduated through the ranks at Upton Park before clinching multimillion-pound moves elsewhere.

Defender John Terry, 24, also has East End ties. He was briefly made England captain against the Poles at Old Trafford when Michael Owen came off in the World Cup qualifier – and he is tipped to become permanent skipper one day. The last time England's leader on the pitch came from Barking, as Terry does, he went on to lift the old Jules Rimet trophy. That man was the late, great Moore – full name Robert Frederick CHELSEA Moore!

Terry, the Chelsea central defender, may be touted as the natural successor to David Beckham, but he is adamant that it is the Real Madrid midfielder who will lead England out in Germany, while he sets his sights on completing the dream double of winning the Champions League with his club and the World Cup with his country.

Terry said, 'Everyone can dream, and to lift the Champions League with Chelsea and the World Cup with England would be absolutely unbelievable. It was great winning the Premiership last season, but this is a big year for every footballer and, if I want to do well with England, it's important that I keep on doing well with Chelsea. There's no time to switch off. Qualifying for the World Cup was fantastic, but the big games keep coming thick and fast at club level now in the Premiership and Champions League.

'At the start of the season my main aim was to play for England more regularly. Hopefully, I have got there with the last couple of displays against Austria and Poland and it was something very special when I was asked to captain the team in the final minutes against the Poles. I did captain the side once before, on my debut against Serbia and Montenegro a few years back, but I think everyone apart from the referee was skipper at some stage that night! This time it was really special. I've kept the armband and I will get it framed along with the shirt.

'But I have said time and time again that in David Beckham we have got one of the best captains in the world. Becks is a fantastic player and everyone in the squad believes he is the right man to captain England.'

Terry's outstanding performances for Chelsea have made him England's No.1 centre-back, with Sol Campbell and Rio Ferdinand now fighting for the right to partner him. Terry added, 'I try to improve game by game and it paid off when I was named ahead of Rio for the Austria game. I understood how he felt because it was me who was left out when we played Wales last season, but it was still nice of Rio to come up to me and wish me all the best. It just shows we have a great team spirit. No matter who is playing, the lads are 100 per cent behind each other.'

Jose Mourinho's young Premiership champions form the nucleus of Sven-Goran Eriksson's squad which carries the hopes of the nation in Germany. For an English club who hold the unwelcome distinction of having fielded the first all-foreign first team, against Southampton on Boxing Day 1999, times have changed. Mourinho has a sound backbone of English talent. Joe Cole said, 'It is good to have a lot of your club-mates around you because you know each other's games and it is great.'

In the aftermath of qualification after beating old foes Poland, the Chelsea player added, 'We played some great stuff against Poland, very attacking – we made it like a Premier League game. But it is not important. What is important is that, come the World Cup, we are all fit and everyone is ready. That's when you get the momentum.'

Frank Lampard's scorching volley sealed England's win against the Poles and put them into the World Cup finals draw on 9 December as Group Six winners. The manner of victory helped revive confidence at the end of a patchy qualifying campaign. Eriksson, in his third and final major tournament as boss, has faced flak for failing to get the best out of his squad, but Lampard said, 'We shouldn't criticise too much. We should take the good points out of games. Against Poland, there were a lot of good points. If we play like that in Germany, we can give teams a lot of trouble. You have to remember that, after the previous two games, we criticised ourselves more than anyone. There comes a stage where you don't need criticism from the outside. You can go too far with it. We have great fans. They are behind us. We are going to work hard in the games building up to the World Cup. We showed a bit of what we can do against Poland but we can get better.'

Prior to the World Cup draw in Leipzig, England were seeded only one place below Brazil. Footballing legend Pele reacted by saying that England have a chance of winning if Rooney lives up to his status as 'the most brilliant young player in Europe'. Speaking in the build-up to the draw, the three-time Brazilian World Cup-winner, now 65, said he believed his own nation were clear favourites but picked out Rooney, 20, and England as a serious threat. Pele said, 'Everyone says Brazil are the favourites, but I don't feel comfortable with that because the favourites do not always win World Cups – injuries can make a team weak and, over seven months, a lot can happen. If a team's best player is not in good shape, that can cause many problems. I believe at the moment Brazil are the best team in the world, but England have Rooney, Beckham, Gerrard, Lampard and Owen – five good attacking players – and if they are in good shape for the World Cup, then they will be a strong team. I think Rooney is the most brilliant young player in Europe; I like him very much indeed. France also have good attacking players, such as Zidane and Thierry Henry, while Italy have probably the best defence in the world.'

Wayne Rooney himself believes that, if England can keep progressing at the rate that has helped them to World Cup qualification, as well as that impressive recent win over Argentina, they can lift the trophy. 'We've got the squad and we're capable of going all the way,' he said. 'The friendly against Argentina was a good game for us, but still it was only a friendly and we can't afford to get carried away. We've got three more friendlies. We've got to try to do well and work on the team in those games, and then hopefully at the World Cup we can get the results we need.'

It will be Rooney's first World Cup but, after his exploits at Euro 2004 in Portugal where he scored four goals, the striker will be a marked man in Germany. His first World Cup memories are of the 1998 finals in France, where Michael Owen arrived as England's secret weapon. 'It was Michael's first World Cup when he got in the team, and he did well. He was a young lad, 18, I think. He did brilliantly and has carried on like that ever since,' said Rooney, now firmly established as Owen's partner up front. 'Michael likes to play on the shoulder and I like to drop off, and that works well. We've started to link up well now and obviously Michael's scored a lot of goals for England and he keeps doing that. It allows me to get space in behind because the defenders are always worried about him.'

It was Owen's strike partner at France 98 who was an early hero for Rooney. 'I tried to model my game on Alan Shearer, then I realised I wouldn't be able to do that role as well as Alan. From then I ended up just playing and always wanting to be on the ball. I always want to be on the ball and, if that means dropping 10 yards off the front, that's what I'm going to do.'

Since losing to Northern Ireland in Belfast and facing the backlash that followed, victory over Argentina in Geneva provided an answer to the question of whether the team could compete against heavyweight opposition.

While Eriksson may have taken a huge amount of media criticism when his team spluttered in the friendly with Denmark and then lost to Northern Ireland after a less than impressive display against Wales, the England manager at least succeeded in leading the country to Germany. And that has not always been the case with some of his predecessors. England failed to get to the World Cup finals in 1974 under Sir Alf Ramsey and missed out again in 1978 (Ron Greenwood) and 1994 (Graham Taylor).

Eriksson's latest group of players has been dubbed the 'golden generation', but they didn't look like it until they mastered Poland to top the group.

When the Football Association grasped the nettle and recruited their first foreign coach in November 2000, they had a five-year plan, designed to win the World Cup in 2006. And there must be a chance given the talents of John Terry, Sol Campbell, Rio Ferdinand, David Beckham, Frank Lampard, Steven Gerrard, Wayne Rooney and Michael Owen. To those eight add Gary Neville and Ashley Cole, probably the best pair of full-backs in international football, and it should not be totally unreasonable to think England have a decent chance of coming away from Berlin as champions. The doubts are not down to the quality of the players available so much as whether Eriksson can bring out the best in them.

It is beyond dispute that England ought to have done better at the last World Cup, when Eriksson took the brunt of media criticism; he was accused of being unable to galvanise his players at half-time in Shizuoka. The media suggested Eriksson was as much to blame for the defeat by Brazil as David Seaman was after his misjudgement of Ronaldinho's free-kick. Two years later at Euro 2004, England's first foreign coach again saw his team eliminated at the quarter-final stage in a competition won by Greece.

Eriksson pinned his faith on some promising and outstanding young players, and, while it is a no-brainer that Wayne Rooney should be one of the best young stars of this World Cup, history shows there is always at least one fresh-faced player who appears in the England squad at a major tournament. At the last World Cup in 2002, 21-year-old Darius Vassell was the unforeseen interloper. His debut against Holland, only four months before England kicked off in the finals, featured an audacious goal from an overhead kick that was impressive enough to push him to the forefront of Eriksson's thoughts. Rooney was the breakthrough player in the run-up to Euro 2004. At the 1998 World Cup in France, it was 18-year-old Owen who won his first cap just four months before the tournament. At Euro 96, 21-year-old Gary Neville was Terry Venables's wing-back, even though a year earlier he still had to nail down a place in the Manchester United team.

When the England players accepted a £225,000-a-man bonus to win the World Cup, it is worth remembering that the hat-trick hero of 1966 Sir Geoff Hurst sold his most prized possession – his winner's medal. He accepted a substantial offer from West Ham, thought to be around £150,000, back in 2001. West Ham had already paid £1.45m for the late Bobby Moore's collection of memorabilia, which included his 1966 winner's medal, and they also persuaded Martin Peters, their other member of the World Cup-winning team, to sell them his. The club wanted to show all three medals as the centrepiece of a new £3.5m museum, as part of their £35m stadium redevelopment. West Ham have always been proud of having provided three members of the team which achieved English football's proudest moment. Hurst said at the time, 'I'm happy that future generations of football fans will be able to see the medal. I've had to keep it locked in a bank vault for years because of burglaries. It was always my intention to leave my memorabilia to my three daughters, but how do you divide the medal three ways? As a family we decided the best thing to do was to place it in a museum and invest the proceeds for the girls.'

But money will not be the incentive for the players who make it to Germany in the England squad. Football is about glory and, hopefully, today's England players can live up to the example of the men who brought home the bacon back in 1966.

# ONE

**FROM 1966 TO 2006 – THE PLAYERS:**
HOW DO TODAY'S SUPERSTARS STACK UP AGAINST THEIR
ILLUSTRIOUS PREDECESSORS OF 1966, THE MEN WHO WON
THE WORLD CUP?

**GOALKEEPERS:**
PAUL ROBINSON – GORDON BANKS

### PAUL ROBINSON

Paul Robinson produced his best-ever display in an England shirt
with a five-star performance against Argentina in the friendly game
of 2005. Robinson pulled off a string of stunning saves to help
England to a memorable 3–2 victory. England goalkeeping coach
Ray Clemence gave his educated verdict: 'Paul has more than
shown his worth. He has never let us down. He made three fantastic
saves in the first 10 minutes alone and further excellent saves after
that. If one or two had gone in, it would have made life very difficult
for us. In games against one of the top three teams in the world,
they will create chances no matter how well you play. But, if
defenders feel they've got a keeper who is going to make great
saves to keep them in the game, it breeds confidence in everybody.'

Robinson, 26, has been England's No.1 since taking over from David James. Clemence said, 'His strengths are his agility and speed around his goal.'

Before the Argentina game, the Spurs keeper knew he was far from established. Robinson vowed never to take being England's No.1 for granted as he knows he is 'there to be shot at', especially if he commits the same sort of errors that saw David James portrayed as a donkey in one national newspaper after a massive blunder in last August's friendly with Denmark in Copenhagen.

Robinson has been criticised for a couple of errors with Tottenham, although he claims he was not to blame for Robert Pires's late equaliser in the north-London derby. But the former Leeds player will take pains to study footage of any incident where he feels he may have been at fault to help cement the position handed to him by England coach Sven-Goran Eriksson.

Robinson added, 'Being a keeper is a very lonely position. When you make a mistake, there are not generally many people behind you to help you out. I've been first choice for a year now and I'm pretty pleased with the way things have gone. I feel I have taken to the job pretty well – but you can never take anything for granted.'

David Seaman is a good friend and helps his fellow Yorkshireman out when he can. Robinson said, 'I speak to David a lot, play in his golf tournament and see him now and again. I get the odd call and text message from him, telling me to keep going and giving me some advice and stuff like that. He's been an excellent goalkeeper over the years and, if I can achieve as much as he did over my career, I'll be very happy. But I must admit that getting his hair cut was not before time. And the one thing I can promise is I won't grow a ponytail like that!'

Robinson knows that, just like Seaman before him, his elevation to the top spot means more scrutiny than ever. Seaman was inconsolable after being caught out by Ronaldinho's free-kick in England's last World Cup match in Shizuoka, while his England career ended after 73 caps with another mistake from Artim Sakiri's corner for Macedonia three months later. While he has not made a blunder in England colours, Robinson accepts he is in the line of fire. 'I'm in a position to be shot at and, if I make a mistake, I'll be criticised. I understand that. If you're playing for England, you've just got to make sure it doesn't happen. I've had two isolated incidents recently and, hopefully, it's gone now. But if you are a goalkeeper you have to be mentally strong – and if you're the England No.1, you have to be even harder on yourself and your own biggest critic. The day you start to listen to other people outside your coaches and your manager, that's when you've got a problem. You can't go into a World Cup game thinking about what might go wrong. Every game's got to be positive and I'm confident in my own ability. I know I'm good enough to cope.'

The move to Spurs came at the right time for Robinson. His last season at Leeds, where he had been since joining as a 14-year-old, was a trial he did not enjoy as the cash problems crippling the club saw players sold off and inevitable relegation. 'I felt like I was out there as fodder – every game there were goals going past me and it was really tough,' he recalled. 'I felt I was going stale, too, so I needed the move. Going to Tottenham was a breath of fresh air. It was a new challenge, new faces, new people to impress and it allowed me to focus more on my game and to achieve what I want from it.

'The World Cup is the biggest stage for every footballer, every goalkeeper. Every kid dreams of playing there. I've always wanted to be the No.1 and I've always aspired to be the man in possession. Things can change very quickly in football and no one knows that more than me. But I'm going to work very hard to keep hold of what I've worked a long time for.'

Two decades ago, Robinson was pretending to be Peter Shilton when Diego Maradona scored his 'Hand of God' goal; he was a seven-year-old watching on TV when Maradona cheated England in the 1986 World Cup quarter-finals.

The Spurs stopper said, 'I remember the 1986 game; that was the first World Cup I really remember. I watched it and I was absolutely gutted afterwards.'

Robinson, 26, confessed his delight at his status as England's first-choice goalkeeper, adding, 'It's different class. There's nothing you can say to explain the feeling. To be regarded like that by so many people is a fantastic achievement. But it's also a responsibility to make sure I carry on doing that and keep people happy.'

Foreign goalkeepers rule England's top division, where they once carried a 'Made in the UK' hallmark. Every leading club seemed to boast a homegrown No.1. And if they weren't English, they would almost certainly qualify for one of the other home nations. A generation ago, Gordon Banks was regarded as the world's best and he faced England competition from the likes of Peter Bonetti, Alex Stepney, Jim Montgomery and the rising talents of young Peter Shilton and Ray Clemence. All that is now a fading memory and today's Premiership boasts a surplus of foreign goalkeepers. No single team position has been embraced as warmly by continental newcomers.

Despite the profusion of foreign keepers – and consequently the lack of choice afforded to Eriksson – Peter Shilton backed Paul Robinson to shine at the World Cup finals. Former England keeper Shilton said, 'Paul Robinson looks solid. He came in at a high-pressure time when David James was dropped and handled the situation really well.

'Young keepers need a sound temperament and Robinson appears to have one. The Tottenham fans love him and that's a good sign, too, because they've had some quality keepers over the years at White Hart Lane. His technique is excellent and he appears to be a confident lad. The only question mark is whether he can do it on the biggest stage of all, and we won't know the answer to that until we get to Germany. There isn't a huge amount of competition for the No.1 shirt right now, but I have confidence in him.'

Shilton, 56, starred for England at the 1990 World Cup finals in Italy and was part of the side that eventually crashed out on penalties to

West Germany in the semi-finals. The ex-Nottingham Forest star is convinced Sven-Goran Eriksson's side has a good chance of emulating that success – and even bettering it. 'I played for England over four decades and during that time we had some very strong squads, but sadly we could never repeat the glory of 1966. The current bunch certainly have a chance. But, until the England side gets to Germany, we can't really judge how good they are. All I can say is that Sven-Goran Eriksson is fortunate to have inherited a talented generation of players. I'd certainly say the current group have the best competition for places that I can remember.'

Robinson is now rated very highly, but even four years ago, as soon as England went out of the last World Cup to Brazil, I selected a team that would represent England in the 2006 World Cup finals... and Robinson was my No.1 choice.

Robinson is a gifted keeper who has the potential to justify his newfound status as England's first choice. But, for England, qualifying for the finals in Germany is the easy part, compared to fulfilling the nation's expectations once they get there.

Can Robinson be the man to stop Ronaldinho, Ballack and van Nistelrooy? After David Seaman's performance against Brazil in the quarter-finals, I felt it was imperative to develop a young goalkeeper and would liked to have seen Robinson given many more caps leading up to this World Cup.

For a number of reasons, it never quite worked out until Robinson came forward late on to take over from David 'Calamity' James. James has all the attributes of a world-class keeper but is prone to brain storms, hence Robinson is by far the more secure option. However, none of England's current keepers has any experience of 'international' club football in the form of the Champions League, which Sven-Goran Eriksson has insisted, in the past, is a prerequisite of playing for England.

Robinson moved on from Leeds to a Spurs side currently well placed in the table with every chance of a long-awaited return to

European football. But Robinson's build-up to Germany is more in tune with Wigan than Barcelona, West Brom rather than Real Madrid or Inter Milan.

## GORDON BANKS

Auction prices for items connected with the 1966 final have often been high. Goalkeeper Gordon Banks's medal raised £124,000 at Christie's in 2001, while the shirt worn by Sir Geoff Hurst took the bids up to an impressive £91,750.

Official postcards of the 1966 mascot, World Cup Willie, with a Wembley and Harrow postmark, sell for £30–£40. But what price a Gordon Banks these days? Banks is the most iconic of English goalkeepers. That seemingly impossible plunge to meet Pele's header in the 1970 World Cup finals stands as one of the greatest saves of all time, let alone in the Banks repertoire.

The penalty save from Geoff Hurst in Stoke City's League Cup semi-final win over West Ham in 1972 is another Banks save that lingers long in the memory.

Paul Robinson may be the best of England's keepers at this moment, but he is no Gordon Banks. Well, for that matter he is no Peter Shilton. He's no Ray Clemence either. And he might not even be a David Seaman. Seaman was at the end of his illustrious career when he was made to look a mug by Ronaldinho in the World Cup. But the hero of Euro 96 has not really been adequately replaced yet by England. Robinson has the promise, but the big question is whether he is ready for the biggest stage of all.

Banks did not become a world-class goalkeeper until after England won the World Cup in 1966. England actually had a superior side in 1970, when Banks made that unforgettable save against Pele. When it comes to facing Brazil, or even Germany for that matter, this summer, can England win the World Cup without a world-class goalkeeper?

Unfortunately, once David James lost his way, there were no other options in goal. Eriksson led the way in bringing on young players, but his big mistake was his failure to acknowledge that he should be working to a four-year cycle and not going for glory in the European Championships.

This is what I had to say immediately after England went out of the last World Cup. 'The young players who benefited from Japan and South Korea need to be retained and encouraged as fixtures in the side such as Michael Owen, Rio Ferdinand and Owen Hargreaves. Others need to be groomed by playing regularly right through the European Championship qualifying stages – Paul Robinson of Leeds in goal, a recall for Jonathan Woodgate and an extended run for Joe Cole and Blackburn's England Under-21 skipper David Dunn. Steven Gerrard, a great miss in this tournament, will be welcomed back.'

Banks missed the crucial World Cup quarter-final against West Germany in Mexico because of a tummy upset and his substitute, Peter Bonetti of Chelsea, was no Gordon Banks. It was an illness which cost England a great deal.

## FULL-BACKS:
GEORGE COHEN – GARY NEVILLE

### GEORGE COHEN

George Cohen believes that England's first-choice full-backs – Gary Neville, his opposite number in the England team, and Ashley Cole – compare favourably with himself and Ray Wilson, although they come from such different eras.

George compares his role to that of Gary Neville as he told me, 'I was 26 when I played in the final against the Germans, but Gary is a couple of years older and he has vast amounts of experience.

'I think he defends very, very well, and has improved as he has got older. He also goes forward very well, although, like me, he doesn't score many goals. But full-back was a vastly different proposition in my time: you were expected to defend first and foremost and going forward was a bonus.'

However, George is worried that the stand-in full-backs do not provide the same kind of security he likes to see around an England defence. He explained, 'All right, we have a couple of spare centre-halves, but we are short of full-backs, that's for sure.

'On the left side in particular, we are weak if the team is without Ashley Cole, and we've been without him for some time recently. Jamie Carragher has been tried there, but he is nowhere near as effective as when he stands in at either centre-back or right-back, or even a holding position in midfield.

'Everyone raves about how well we did against Argentina, but I thought they were a magnificent side who outpassed us and the two full-backs lacked experience, which shows they should have been played far more often in some of those so-called meaningless friendlies.

'But Sven has had this annoying habit of giving players little more than cameo roles and that has not been good enough to really try players out. Some of the most influential players throughout the generations, from Johnny Haynes to Glenn Hoddle, were said to be so influential yet they only spent two and a half minutes of the 90 minutes on the ball. So how many seconds would one of Sven's 25-minute substitutes have?

'Gary has great experience and we will need him as well as Ashley. We just won't be able to afford injuries in such key positions, as the back-up looks thin, frighteningly thin, to me. When there was some suggestion that Sven would even bring Gary's brother Phil back into the side to play at right-back, it shows how thin it is!'

Cohen feels that Ray Wilson would compare very favourably with Ashley Cole. Of his full-back partner from '66, George said, 'He was a "knowing" defender. He was brought up like the rest of us on the old WM formation and it wouldn't do modern-day full-backs any harm to study those techniques; they were vitally important for full-backs to understand how to defend and cover properly – and to appreciate why we were never exposed on our blind side – in order to develop a formidable defensive unit. Ray didn't often go forward, but he was a very good defender, very quick over the first 10 yards especially, which came in handy against fast and tricky wingers.

'We didn't give many goals away in '66, but that was no surprise to us because we had been pretty good defensively for some time leading up to the World Cup, more than two years in fact. We had beaten the Germans twice in that time and outplayed Spain in Madrid.

'Alf knew his back four for at least one and a half years leading up to the tournament. Ray and I put together a run of 19 games uninterrupted and Alf based his success on solid defence.

'Perhaps Jack Charlton was a late addition but he did for the England team precisely what he had been doing for Leeds, winning the ball in the air and defending well. Jack used to say it himself, that he wasn't a great player but he wouldn't let anyone play against him; he would never let anything or anybody get past him, no matter what it took to stop them.'

Overall, George has a feeling that England will do well in this tournament. 'I think we have the players to go a long way, but whether we are good enough to win is another matter. I was so impressed when I saw Argentina; you have to fear holders Brazil and you can never rule out the Germans especially when they are at home. I was in Munich with Alan Ball when we beat them 5–1 and everyone was euphoric, and I must say it was the worst German side I had ever seen. But what did they do? They made seven changes and went on to reach the World Cup finals, while we went only as far as the quarter-finals. That's the Germans for you, so don't discount them.

'But England have a reasonable chance themselves, perhaps the best chance since we won it. Rooney, Lampard and Owen are all outstanding players. If we can keep Rooney on the pitch. This boy is a handful all right, but we need to wrap him up in cotton wool and make sure he doesn't miss a game. He is the most potent young player I have seen in a long time.'

## GARY NEVILLE

Gary Neville earned the nickname 'Red Nev' for his part in the England players' dispute with the FA when Rio Ferdinand was banned for failing to take a drugs test.

Neville, 30, is the first local lad to be made Manchester United captain in his lifetime. Sir Alex Ferguson selected Neville to succeed Roy Keane as captain at Old Trafford after the armband had been passed between Ryan Giggs and Ruud van Nistelrooy, among others. But Neville's long service, boyhood links with United and relish for battle resulted in him being handed the honour. 'Gary's attitude has always been 100 per cent,' Ferguson said. 'His service to the club and his character have been so outstanding for the last ten years, it made it easy. Professionalism, good behaviour patterns, strong-mindedness, commitment – all those things you look at with Gary, you come up with ten out of ten. He has improved quicker than anyone at this club in the last two or three years. He is so consistent now.'

Neville suffered a groin injury early in the season but made a successful comeback before Christmas. He accepts that 2006 marks his best chance of winning the World Cup and it will almost certainly be his last attempt. In his *Times* column he observed, 'That knowledge is bound to concentrate your thoughts, particularly after missing the last tournament through injury. I had a few months to prepare for the disappointment but, even so, I remember watching the players after their victory over Argentina in 2002 and longing to be out there with them. Playing in the World Cup finals is something very special and everyone knows that, if we can keep our players fit for next summer, we stand a decent chance.'

He rated the draw in Leipzig as 'pretty kind', although he was keen to avoid Sweden as he explained, 'They always seem so resolute, so hard to break down. The fact that we have not beaten them since 1968 is proof enough of that. We seem to be better against teams that have greater ambitions to beat us but, that aside, we have to be happy overall, particularly when you look at a group such as Italy's. I would expect them to go through but it may not be a comfortable ride. It would be fantastic if we could go into that last group match against Sweden already qualified but, even if that's the case, we would almost certainly want to beat them. We have seen in the past that failing to finish top of the group can bring all sorts of complications. Failing to do that in 1998, when we lost to Romania, meant that we came up against Argentina in the last 16. Conceding those two late goals against France at Euro 2004 meant we faced Portugal before we would have wanted. On both occasions, we went out.'

He concluded, 'People keep saying this is our best chance since 1966, although I don't remember heading into a tournament when people at home didn't expect us to win it. All I think you can say for now is that, if everyone is fit and in form, we have the best opportunity I have known. After that, there are all the unpredictable factors to consider. One thing that will be to our advantage is the number of fans in the stadium. We have had our well-publicised problems, but, at their best, the England supporters would be welcomed to any tournament because they bring such noise, colour and passion.'

ASHLEY COLE – RAY WILSON

## ASHLEY COLE

Ray Wilson once felt like ringing Ashley Cole to pass on some basic full back tips, but he is now convinced that the young Arsenal star has acquired the art of defending.

'You know I have never seen Ashley play, apart from on television but I do watch a lot of games on TV and I haven't seen him for quite a while because of his injuries this season', says Ray. 'He's been missed by his club and by England because he's certainly progressed. He has pace and he plays the game pretty simply which is a hallmark of an outstanding player. If anything that was my gift.'

Ashley Cole has been continually linked with Real Madrid as the most likely successor to Roberto Carlos. While it is highly flattering, it would also be a risky move for Cole who was targeted for racial abuse when he played for England in Spain. FIFA fined Spain's national federation $87,000 for racist taunting by its fans in matches against England.

By his own admission he is sometimes perceived as 'flash and arrogant', but the England left-back claims his reticence in the past has not been arrogance, as some have claimed, but rather comes from a natural shyness that makes him uncomfortable in the limelight. 'I'm quite a shy person, and don't show my emotions too much,' he said in a moment of reflection. 'When I do, then something must be up! I just try to focus on the job at hand and, if it's me playing football, I just want to win things and that's what I try and do. I've spoken to journalists before and they probably thought I was flash and arrogant, but I'm just shy. I think people are starting to understand me now though.'

Cole scored a penalty past Manchester United's Roy Carroll in the penalty shoot-out in the FA Cup final against Manchester United, which might come in handy if England meet Germany in the World Cup! He revealed an interesting approach to penalty taking – driven by fear of failure! 'I don't imagine myself scoring as I walk up, I imagine myself missing – that's the scary part and it makes me more desperate to score,' he said. 'Some players visualise themselves scoring, but I'm not like that – I always think of the worst things that can happen, so that if they don't then it feels even better. But I don't think you can be a loser in a penalty shoot-out because if you miss then you miss, but if you score then you're a hero, so I'm always up for taking a penalty in a shoot-out. You just have to focus and concentrate on where you're going to put the ball and put it there.'

At the start of the season Ashley Cole was hailed as the man who epitomises the new England – by coach Sven-Goran Eriksson. Sven said even before the friendly with Denmark, 'If we get there, I will feel much better equipped for this World Cup than the last. Far better. If all the players are available, I have no doubts whatsoever that we now have the strongest team and strongest squad in the five years that I have been managing England. We are much more confident, much more mature, much more united as a group and more tactically adept too.

'Perhaps a player like Ashley Cole embodies the progress we have made as a team. In the last World Cup he played well but he had very little experience. He'd just come through into the Arsenal first team and got his chance with England very quickly too. These days he's considered one of the best left-backs in the world. He has huge experience, playing every week for Arsenal, tasting big Champions League games and playing regularly with England, including the European Championship. He is typical of our team in that way.'

But the speedy and talented left-back's progress was halted when he unwittingly played with a broken bone in his foot for six weeks before the injury ruled him out until January. Cole had been out of action since early October with a fractured metatarsal in his right foot. 'It's annoying,' he said. 'At the start of the season, I felt really fit and I said to the physios – which probably jinxed it – that I was hoping not to miss a game all season. Then that happened and I was gutted.'

Cole's injury problem showed up in an X-ray ahead of England's World Cup qualifiers against Austria and Poland, having earlier been given the all-clear following a scan. 'In fact, I played with the injury for a month and a half because I didn't really know what it was at first. I was just putting ice on it every day because I thought it was just a knock,' he admitted. 'Then I said to [Arsenal and England physio] Gary Lewin that it was hurting and that night it began to ache. So I had a scan before the Ajax game, but the scan showed it was just bruised, so I thought nothing of it and played. Then I had an X-ray just before I joined up with England and, after that, Gary said I couldn't play because it could break all the way.'

Cole was initially replaced in the Arsenal first team by Clichy, but the France Under-21 international then sustained the same injury in a play-off against England during the European Championships. 'It's unbelievable, just crazy. It's the same foot as me and the surgeon said to me when I did mine that he hadn't seen anything like it in 25 years,' Cole said. 'Then he does the same thing. It's one of those things but I feel so sorry for him. He is just getting his chance in the team and then that happens.'

Ashley finally returned as a substitute during Arsenal's formidable 7–0 demolition of Middlesbrough, watched by a relieved Eriksson. Thierry Henry believed Cole's return to fitness could provide the catalyst for Arsenal's revival in 2006. Henry said, 'Sometimes it's a bit difficult when Ashley isn't there as he knows what to do when he goes up. I just think, and hope, we're going to have a better run in the second half of the season.'

Cole has been the centre of controversy for the best part of a year for his role in the 'tapping-up case' with Chelsea. The player defied manager Arsene Wenger and will take his appeal against the Premier League's guilty verdict in the saga to the Court of Arbitration for Sport. Wenger has warned of the potential 'chaos' if Cole is successful with what is effectively a restraint-of-trade test case.

## RAY WILSON

Ray Wilson is a big Wayne Rooney fan and is inspired by the midfield quality of Frank Lampard, Stephen Gerrard, and David Beckham, but would rather the finals were in England because he fears the hosts will put up a powerful fight to win the tournament.

'I don't see any country in the world with a better midfield than ours, but there is a problem with the Lampard-Gerrard central midfield combination. They don't seem to know which one ought to 'go'. They are both gifted at going forward and their natural instincts is to attack, but one needs to support the other and get back.

Ray is a touch perplexed about the FA's handling of the Sven Goran Eriksson situation.

'The manager has been pretty unpopular for a year before the FA took the decision to replace him after the World Cup, and the press turned on him, and once that stage is reached, when they are trying to trip him up, is time that he ought to go. He should have gone straight away and let somebody else take England to the World Cup. I've got nothing against him being a foreigner, though. I am happy with the best person for the job whether he's from Russia or English.'

Sir Bobby Robson, who managed England to the World Cup semi-finals in 1990, is one of the judges best qualified to speak about England players from different eras. As plain Bobby, he won 20 England caps between 1958 and 1962, and went on to manage his country in two World Cups (1986 and 1990) – his adventures including The Hand of God and a penalty shoot-out against Germany watched by a record UK TV audience of nearly 30 million.

Selecting his best-ever England team, he included Stanley Matthews, Johnny Haynes, Tom Finney and from the modern game Bryan Robson. He went for Gordon Banks in goal, Jimmy Greaves and Bobby Charlton, with Jimmy Armfield his right-back and Bobby Moore alongside Billy Wright. His left-back choice was Ray Wilson.

Wilson oozed class and had been a Wembley winner two months before the World Cup – with Everton in the FA Cup. He started his career as a forward which explains why he usually looked so comfortable on the ball.

Jack Charlton feels that Ray Wilson's contribution to the World Cup winning team should not be underestimated. 'Ray Wilson was very quick and very aggressive and he would like to go forward at times and could produce a great cross with his left foot.

'The press would always say we had four world class players, and that the team virtually picked itself because one was Gordon Banks, two was Bobby Moore, the third was Bobby Charlton and the fourth was Jimmy Greaves. A fifth world class player was Ray Wilson.'

## CENTRE-HALVES:

RIO FERDINAND – BOBBY MOORE

### RIO FERDINAND

No one is better equipped to make sensible comparisons between the legendary Bobby Moore and Rio Ferdinand than Sir Bobby Charlton. Sir Bobby is a leading figure in world football, who not only played alongside Moore but is also a Manchester United director, a man who watches Ferdinand on a regular basis with a detailed eye.

Naturally, there hasn't been a player to compare with Bobby Moore, but Sir Bobby feels that at least Rio comes marginally close. Sir Bobby told me, 'There is no one of the quality of Bobby Moore, and no one should expect that. But Rio has got some of the Bobby Moore talents: he is that good a player with so much ability.

'Rio, though, is a fine player, and under pressure – which is the telling point – he is OK, I don't worry about him.'

Ferdinand has looked class, world class in fact, in previous tournaments, but he had a wobble in form at the start of the season and was dropped for the first time by Eriksson, opening up a debate about who should be the first-choice centre-halves. Sir Bobby's conclusion? 'I'd be very upset if Rio is not one of the first defenders in the team: he has the pace, a facet that even Bobby Moore lacked, and he has the ability. He has good feet which was one of Bobby's big assets, even if he didn't have the pace.

'Bobby had the uncanny knack of being able to calm things down. He was not pretentious, he went about his job, he didn't want to score goals, he wanted to defend. And that was the beauty of Alf Ramsey's team: everybody knew precisely their functions, stuck to their jobs and the team worked. Bobby was an instinctive defender and that is something you just cannot teach.'

Ferdinand, who comes from a tough background in Peckham, suffered a lengthy ban over a controversial failure to take a drugs test, and emerged through the seemingly perpetual crisis at Old Trafford, just as the competition in the heart of England's defence was hotting up. It is the most competitive area of the team.

Jonathan Woodgate was set to return to the England squad after an absence of 20 months for the friendly with Argentina in Geneva, only to pull out through injury. Ferdinand had been dropped for the World Cup-qualifying game against Austria the previous month. He recovered his place only because Sol Campbell pulled a hamstring after an hour's play. But Sven-Goran Eriksson's enthusiasm for him as a footballing centre-half was made clear ahead of the biggest game of the season with Chelsea at Old Trafford, when he said, 'Rio is one of the best central defenders in the world, maybe the most complete central defender we have in this country. He can do everything. Maybe he's not in the best form, which happens to every player. If you take the last World Cup, I think he was the best defender there. And he's still young. So I can't see any reason why he shouldn't reach that level again. I'm not worried about Rio Ferdinand.'

Eriksson admitted that United's game against Chelsea was 'a good test' for him. And, in front of the watching Eriksson, the £30m centre-half was outstanding and shone above John Terry. Along with Sol Campbell and Terry, however, Ferdinand is still in the top three among a cluster of players pushing for a place in England's most oversubscribed position. Jonathan Woodgate is still to prove he is worth the fourth central-defender's berth at the World Cup finals. Real Madrid have shown great faith in him after he missed the whole of the last season through injury following his expensive transfer from Newcastle. First capped by Kevin Keegan as long ago as 1999, he has played for his country only once since appearing in the three opening games of the 2002–03 season.

After the draw in Leipzig, Ferdinand was eagerly looking forward to a reunion with his former Manchester United team-mate Dwight Yorke. 'For Dwight it will be a massive occasion. He'll want to show the people in England he's not forgotten. I'm delighted we got

Trinidad & Tobago. My dad's from St Lucia and I know what a draw like this will mean to the people of the Caribbean. They'll have a few players from the lower leagues in England playing for them who will want to make a name for themselves. It will be like an FA Cup tie against the minnows. They will want our scalp.'

Rio warned, 'We all know how tough Sweden are. We had a hard game against them at the 2002 World Cup to get a draw and they are never an easy side to play against. We haven't beaten them in a competitive match so this would be a great time to start. We beat Paraguay fairly easily in a friendly in the lead-up to Japan but nobody will be reading anything into that. South Americans are always difficult to play against when it comes to the real business. I'm not going to pretend it's the hardest group because you look at the groups Argentina and Italy got and you are thankful you didn't get them. It's been fair to us and now we have to make it count. It's going to be a massive occasion and we're all aware the country expects us to go a long way – and, hopefully, win it.

'And we desperately want to make up for the disappointments of the past. We all thought we could win the trophy in 2002. It was a bitter experience to miss out. I will maintain to my dying day Ronaldinho never meant that 35-yard free-kick – which won the game – to be a shot. I saw him after and he said he meant it but I'm not sure. Nobody disputes he's a brilliant player, but I think that was supposed to be a cross. Who knows what might have happened if that had not gone in? Everybody reckons Brazil are the hot favourites and you have to say that when you read out the names. It's a pretty daunting line-up: Ronaldo, Ronaldinho, Adriano, Kaka and Robinho are all world class. But we've got great players of our own in the likes of Wayne Rooney, Steven Gerrard, Frank Lampard, Michael Owen and David Beckham. We honestly believe we can beat anybody on our day. The country has been waiting 40 years for another World Cup success and it's long overdue.

'Geoff Hurst said it was time the 1966 team stepped into the background and a new victorious England side emerged. He's absolutely right. Here's hoping he gets his wish.'

## BOBBY MOORE

Sir Bobby Charlton feels it is unfair to try to compare anyone in the current England team with Bobby Moore. There has never been a defender like him since. 'There just isn't that kind of quality around any more,' said Sir Bobby. But if there is an equivalent player in the present England side then Sir Bobby would go for Rio Ferdinand as he confirmed: 'Rio has ability, of that there is absolutely no doubt.'

Celtic and Scotland manager Jock Stein once said that Bobby Moore's football intellect was unfair on the opposition. Far from being quick over the ground, he was lightning-fast in reading the game.

The other player who can be compared to Moore is David Beckham, who stressed that his 50th match as captain of England was a matter of unqualified pride. This was a milestone that only three previous English captains have passed. Indeed, Beckham measures himself against previous captains, noting that only Billy Wright (90), Bobby Moore (90) and Bryan Robson (65) had led England on to the field more times, but only Moore won the World Cup.

Moore and Beckham are very different men from very different ages, as James Lawton observed in the *Independent* – 'one which in Moore's case would have made it utterly unthinkable that he would canvass for the job while appearing on a television documentary of his life'.

One of the few journalists around long enough to have known Moore, Lawton added, 'The captaincy of England has been a huge commercial asset to David Beckham. For Moore, it was something he was asked to do, and it just happened that often it seemed it was a chore he might have been able to accomplish in his untroubled sleep.'

Beckham's milestone provoked memories among Moore's team-mates of the man who led them to the nation's only World Cup. Alan Ball, the baby of the team, remembered both the beginning and the end of their relationship. 'The first time I played for England,' Ball recalled, 'I was 18 years old and playing for Blackpool. My club had a game down south at the weekend and Blackpool told me to stay down in London. I had never stayed in London before and I was stuck in a hotel. Mooro heard of my situation and came along and said, "Come with me, little man, I'm going to show you the town."

'I don't want to compare Bobby Moore and David Beckham because they operate in different times with different values and I don't think there is much of a meeting point. All I can say is that, however you define a captain, Bobby was perfect. He had it all. He was magnificently unflappable on the field, but he saw everything and had a quiet word. But most of all he led by example. I never heard an angry word from him, but then I never saw anyone challenge him. He was the captain no one questioned, but he always had a common touch.'

Aware that his battle against bowel cancer was lost, Bobby Moore picked up the phone and called the Boys of '66. He thanked them for the memories he had and spoke of how the days he had spent in their company had been among the best of his life. Ball said, 'I suppose that was an example of Mooro's consistency. He was not a great talker unless he had something to say, and so of course I will always treasure those last few minutes on the phone.'

George Cohen's testament is about the natural touch of a leader. 'Bobby's authority was so easily exerted. He didn't ruffle anyone. He just led the way, as we saw when we went a goal down in the World Cup final. Bobby just took the game to the Germans. When it mattered, he was so urgent.'

Then when the Football Association announced England's winning bonus of £22,000 for the whole squad – the beaten Germans were believed to have received £10,000 a head – Moore's leadership took another form. The FA had suggested that the bonus be shared on a percentage basis depending on the number of match appearances. Moore made a decision. It was for each member of the squad to receive £1,000, irrespective of whether they had played or not.

'One of my first reactions was a professional one,' recalled George Cohen. 'I thought, "Does Jimmy Greaves need £500 of my money?" And then immediately I realised Bobby was right. We had all been in this together and, however it turned out, we were all committed to the same goal.'

Jack Charlton holds Moore in the highest regard, but he wondered about the mystique of captaincy. 'It boils down to example on the field and great teams have more than one captain on the field. Don Revie offered me the captaincy of Leeds, but I told him I was too lanky; I would have felt stupid running out there in front of Billy Bremner. If I was Eriksson, I would consider the claims of John Terry because I've always felt central defence is the best place to lead a side. You see everything from there: you are facing the ball, facing the game. Still, I wish David Beckham all the best in Germany. But he should not worry about his place in history. He should be more concerned about his place on the field.'

In the end, though, Beckham has one chance of emulating the greatest captain in the history of English football, and that is by leading his team to World Cup glory.

## JOHN TERRY – JACK CHARLTON

### JOHN TERRY

Jack Charlton is a great admirer of John Terry. And, it's a measure of the Chelsea captain's stature that Big Jack feels that the decision in central defence is 'Who will play alongside Terry?'

Big Jack says, 'I like a good competitor and I don't think there is a better competitor in the business than John Terry in the last three or four years.'

That is some accolade from the rock on which England's World Cup defence was constructed. 'He is very good in the air, his tackling is also very good, he reads the game, covers very quickly and he is very aware. You never see John Terry standing around, looking at the game. Instead he is constantly adjusting. It all adds up to an extremely good player.'

Sir Trevor Brooking insists the future is bright for England's national team. West Ham legend Brooking was impressed to see eight English players named in the Professional Footballers' Association Team of the Year last season. The Football Association's director of football development is certain homegrown talent is beginning to flourish despite the number of foreign imports in the Premiership. Brooking said, 'While we do have more foreign players playing in the Premier League these days, this is confirmation that the quality of our English players is improving all the time.'

John Terry scooped the PFA Player of the Year award and was joined by England colleagues Gary Neville, Rio Ferdinand, Ashley Cole, Frank Lampard, Steven Gerrard, Shaun Wright-Phillips and Andrew Johnson in the top XI.

Terry's first season as Chelsea skipper could not have gone better. First, he lifted the Carling Cup, then added the PFA Player of the Year award to his trophy cabinet, before raising aloft the Barclays Premiership trophy. Terry was the first Chelsea player to receive the PFA honour. He said, 'It is unbelievable and the ultimate accolade to be voted for by your fellow professionals. It has been a really special season with Chelsea and this just adds to it.'

Terry established himself as a Stamford Bridge legend at the age of 24. When Jose Mourinho took control from Claudio Ranieri, he was quick to pull Terry aside and give him the captain's armband. The Portuguese coach did not think twice, despite having other worthy contenders such as Frank Lampard to choose from.

Terry is the archetypal reformed wild boy. Terry's status as Chelsea's linchpin was underlined when the Blues' captain was handed a new five-year contract. He is currently the only home-bred player in the Chelsea side. His commanding displays are the foundation-stone on which the new Chelsea are building their success. Chelsea already had Terry tied down until summer 2007 after he penned a new four-year deal in July 2003, but they moved to secure his future until summer 2009. Terry hailed the impact of new coach Jose Mourinho as a significant factor in negotiations.

In turn, Mourinho observed long before their title had been assured, 'For me, John Terry is the best central defender in the world. I know Sir Alex would say Rio Ferdinand; I know Ancelotti will say Nesta. For me, it's John Terry. Since the first minute I arrived here, he's played at the same level. Not up and down, no mistakes. Not more committed against Man United and less concentration against West Bromwich. It's not like he prefers to play against tall and strong strikers and has it difficult against fast ones.

'For him, every game is the same, every opponent is the same, the level of his performance is the same. He leads the team. He is an important voice on the pitch. He's absolutely amazing.'

Mourinho has nothing but praise for his skipper who marshals the meanest defence in the Premiership. Mourinho explained, 'We said what we thought of John when we gave him his incredible new contract. He deserves every coin.'

Terry is a key influence within the team, both on the field and in the dressing room where he often gives fiery speeches ahead of games. Mourinho added, 'In some clubs the captain is the captain of the manager. In other clubs he's the captain of the players. In another club he's the captain of the club because he's been at the club for ten years. John Terry is everything here. He's the choice of the players, who respect him and feel he's the best guy to be the captain. He's my man. I trust him completely and I think he has the same relation to me. He's the captain of the club because he is the boy who came from youth football – so, in one person, we have this kind of captain and it's very difficult for a team to be successful without a big voice inside. He can play short and has good vision and a good long ball. He's the perfect player.'

Terry is such a colossus in the Chelsea dressing room, but can he do the same with England? According to former Chelsea captain Marcel Desailly, Terry can make the same impact on world football as legendary Italian defender Paolo Maldini. The French star, who played alongside both, predicted that Terry will give Chelsea the sort of long and distinguished service that Tony Adams once supplied to London rivals Arsenal. Desailly said, 'John can really be the image of the club – he is the one that stands out.'

During Claudio Ranieri's fourth and final season as manager at Stamford Bridge, the Italian coach dubbed Terry the 'man of iron' whom he would not swap for Rio. 'They are both great players, so who do you choose? I am Chelsea manager so I choose John. I know Ferdinand is the most expensive defender in the world, but the money is not important. John is a leader – a leader inside. Some men just have this ability to deal with the responsibility – and in my opinion John is one of them. Franco Baresi in Italy was another who became captain when he was young. But wearing the armband is not important in itself; the key thing is that they are just leaders. John is the iron man – and I've said before that he can be for Chelsea what Tony Adams was for Arsenal. For Chelsea and for the national team...'

When Terry was a 12-year-old, a career as a top-class centre-half was not obvious to the Chelsea staff at the time. 'I hope he doesn't mind me saying this,' said Graham Rix, the club's former youth-team manager and now manager of Hearts, 'but I remember watching him when he was a short, tubby midfielder and he wasn't the most mobile. But he knew what he was doing, saw passes early and embodied the same determination he has now. I remember one match, he injured himself and carried on playing with a pulled hamstring for 20 minutes. That hurts like hell, but he's hard as nails. We took him on and he shot up over the next two years. Everybody was chasing him then, all the clubs, including Manchester United, but thankfully he was happy where he was.'

Terry ended up outshining two central defenders in Marcel Desailly and Frank Leboeuf, who had, in their prime, won the World Cup, men whose technique he studied. Although Terry may not be as elegant, his distribution and drive with the ball at his feet are as vital to his game as the traditional defensive virtues of tracking and tackling, clearing decks and crashing headers – not to mention ruthlessness at set-pieces.

George Graham, who has a specialist's appreciation of defending, is a big fan. 'Some people doubt that defenders can play, but that's a load of crap,' he said. 'Terry can play and he's a born leader. He doesn't have to be beautiful on the ball; he's got qualities the artistic players don't have. I can see him getting better and better.'

Terry has been determined to oust Ferdinand or Campbell from the England side for some time. He was on the bench for the opening qualifiers against Wales and Azerbaijan. Next time it came to a choice between the three for the vital qualifier against Austria at Old Trafford, it was Rio on the bench. Terry would not have believed that possible a year before!

## JACK CHARLTON

Jack Charlton believes that England have an outstanding chance of winning the World Cup. His major reservation is that England can only win the tournament providing Sven Goran Eriksson can finally and quickly establish his best team.

Big Jack argues, 'The public should have a good idea of the best team and they don't. Its always been so different with the Germans. They always knew a year in advance their best team, stuck with them, and developed a hard to beat team pattern.

'When I was picked to play against the Scots a year before the World Cup, it was a surprise for me but once I played in that game, I played in every match and everyone knew where they stood. Alf picked me to play alongside Bobby Moore. Bobby was a very good reader of the game, he would anticipate virtually everything, but he was not the best header of the ball in the world and over distance he lacked a bit of pace.

'I am not so sure that exists with this team. There is still a big debate about who should play in the centre of the defence, between John Terry, Rio Ferdinand and Sol Campbell. There are not too many full back options and there has even been suggestions from time to time that David Beckham has to do more to justify his place in the team. Apart from the two central midfield players there are areas of the team that there is still lingering doubts about the best options.'

Big Jack, an experienced international manager in his own right, is far from sure the FA took the right course in keeping Eriksson on to lead the team in Germany when he is to leave after the World Cup. He argues, 'There are plenty of English coaches around who would have jumped at the chance to take England into the Finals. I just feel the FA are wasting time. If he is going, let him go.'

Gary Neville was so impressed with Rio Ferdinand that a couple of years ago he pronounced him England's best-ever defender. Neville said at the time, 'He's outstanding. He has absolutely everything a defender could want: height, presence, reading of the game, speed, reaction. He's a fantastic player with great composure on the ball. He's probably the best defender England has seen in its history. I'm not being too kind to him there, he's an unbelievable defender. Rio can go on to achieve whatever he wants. There are players around him at this club that can help and work with him, hopefully to give him the trophies that his career will deserve.'

England's 1966 World Cup hero Jack Charlton, who partnered the legendary Bobby Moore in our greatest hour, reacted in typical no-nonsense Geordie style. 'Rio Ferdinand the best ever? No – not at all. There have been a hell of a lot of magnificent defenders in the past 20 years such as Terry Butcher, Sol Campbell and Tony Adams.

There have been lots and lots of good defenders. Gary is entitled to his opinion, but I don't agree with him. Ferdinand is a very good player that is for sure, but to call him the best ever is a total nonsense. What about players like Neil Franklin, Billy Wright, not to mention Bobby Moore? There were some great defenders around in my day.

'Also people forget that in the old days there used to be only one centre-back, and now you have two. So you had twice as much ground to cover back then and we can see how tough it is now when you have two players.'

Jack Charlton – later to manage the Republic of Ireland in two World Cups – remembers the tense quarter-final against Argentina in 1966 almost as well as beating West Germany in the final.

Big Jack was a tall, tough, uncompromising, yet highly dependable defender, who was a trend-setter of his time in that he started the new tactic of standing directly in front of opposing goalkeepers at corners.

He recalls that bruising battle with Argentina that set the tone for England's World Cup success. 'As a centre-half, you spend a lot of time watching the game in front of you – and I couldn't believe what I was seeing,' admitted big Jack. 'From the opening minute, the big guy Rattin was following the referee everywhere. The ref kept telling him to go away, but it made no difference. Finally he couldn't take it any more and ordered Rattin to get off. The only surprise for me was that the ref had tolerated him for so long. Of course it took 10 minutes for him to leave.

'I was standing on the edge of our penalty area watching the arguments on the halfway line. Our manager Alf Ramsey had told us before the game not to get involved if anything like this happened, so we kept out the way until Rattin left. It was a relief to see him finally walk off because he was a really good footballer. Argentina did have a good team but they were happy to sit back that day and go for the draw. The match was tense all round. I remember, at one corner, the goalkeeper fell down and several of the Argentine players surrounded me. It got so bad that my brother Bobby – normally the mild-mannered one – started to shove the Argentine players out the way to protect me!'

A Geoff Hurst goal 13 minutes from time meant England scraped home 1–0 and went on to a semi-final with Portugal. 'But the emotion of the game spilled over even after the final whistle. I was chatting to Nobby Stiles in the dressing room and we could hear all this hammering on our door. After a while, one of the security men came in and said the Argentina players had been trying to come into the dressing room to fight us!'

Big Jack and Rattin met up much later. Jack revealed, 'I had dinner with him during the World Cup in 1986 in Mexico. His English wasn't good enough to have a full conversation but he seemed like a nice, polite man – off the field!'

Jack and brother Bobby each ended up with a World Cup winners' medal of course and in Jack's case it was an example of 'it's never too late'. He was nearly 29 when he made his England debut in 1965. 'I was playing well for Leeds United, but at that age I never really expected to play for my country,' he said.

'Then [Leeds manager] Don Revie came up to me straight after an FA Cup semi-final against Manchester United to say I had been selected for England. I couldn't really believe it. Don said he had told the other England players before the cup tie but didn't tell me because he thought it might have been a distraction! But, although I was surprised to be called up, once in the team I never expected to be dropped.'

Big Jack later became a plain-speaking and highly successful manager, first in club football with Middlesbrough, Sheffield Wednesday and Newcastle – and then famously with the Republic of Ireland. He became a national hero in Ireland by leading them to victory against England in the 1988 European Championship and to two World Cup finals, in 1990 and 1994.

## MIDFIELD:
FRANK LAMPARD – BOBBY CHARLTON

### FRANK LAMPARD

In the absence of the late Bobby Moore and Sir Alf Ramsey, Sir Bobby Charlton is the best ambassador for the 1966 team. Sir Bobby wore the No.9 shirt and evolved into one of the world's most respected and visible representatives of the global game.

Sir Bobby was also a key figure in England's '66 triumph and, although Wayne Rooney does drop deep off the front line, the goalscoring midfield ace of Alf's era has greater affinity to the freescoring spirit of Frank Lampard.

Sir Bobby told me, 'Frank gets around the field the way I used to do in my days, and, although I am not so keen on Frank when he's playing for Chelsea against us, I am more than happy to see him knocking in the goals for England from 20 and 30 yards!

'There is no doubt that Frank plays an important role for England; he has the ability to get forward and score goals and, while that was not so rare in my days, it is rare in the modern game.

'In fact, I am quite flattered to be compared with Frank because he is a fine player, a modern player, and anybody who can score goals at the rate that he does has to be feared and admired in equal proportions. I used to enjoy having a crack at goal from distance and Frank can do that too. For that reason, Frank is one of the people we shall all be looking to to be influential in this World Cup. And, with players like Frank, we have a genuine chance of winning it.'

Of course, there is one essential difference: Sir Bobby was deceptively fast, while Frank doesn't possess such explosive speed. Sir Bobby conceded, 'Over the first few yards, no he doesn't have that pace to get away from people, but make no mistake I am very pleased that he is part of this England team. I wouldn't want to see an England team now without him, absolutely not.'

While Sir Bobby is flattered to be compared to Frank, I suggested it should be Frank who is honoured to be compared with Sir Bobby! Modesty prevented Sir Bobby from commenting!

Modesty, however, is not a word in Jose Mourinho's vocabulary. After his superb performance against Blackburn at Stamford Bridge, the Chelsea manager hailed Lampard as the best player in the world. With two against Rovers, the midfielder took his tally of goals to 100 as Chelsea threw away a two-goal lead and still came back to end a difficult week on a high note with a 4–2 triumph. 'I don't see how he can improve because for me he is the best player in the world at the moment,' declared Mourinho. 'I don't know what the people who organise these world awards do at the weekends because only English people recognise what this player is. He was the best player in the Premiership last season and you have some great players in the world but they play one game a month. This player is top in every game. I would not change him for another player because he does everything. His defence is incredible, he can pass over a long distance, he can pass over short distances; he's professional, he can score goals over long distance – how can he improve?'

Lampard wants to replicate his club success with his country and has become the penalty-taker for England. 'Lamps', 27, is happy at taking over the spot-kick role from David Beckham and said, 'It's a step up taking a penalty for your country. It's a bit different from taking them for Chelsea but I had to take the extra responsibility. For a moment, it is extra pressure but you try to stay calm and composed.'

Lampard has also broken goalkeeper David James's record of 159 consecutive games in the Premiership, and explained the secrets of being football's marathon man. 'I have found the right recipe – hard training and hard rest in between. I have my methods in the way I train, the way I eat and the way I live. I really make sure I don't overexert myself between games.

'With my free time, I go home and get my feet up as much as possible. What I do is I train hard on certain days and take my foot off the gas on other days. That's why there isn't one special thing that has kept me going – a combination of things has made it possible. Diet is important but that would not matter if I didn't get enough sleep. I'm quite experienced now and I know what aspects of my life are important. Of course, I have been lucky with injuries and I thrive on playing regularly. But, when I have time off, I make the most of it and make sure I stay in shape.

'I'm really proud of my appearance record. It's been a long time coming but now I want to extend it as far as possible. The most important thing, though, is to be playing all these games with a team that is winning things. The record is just something special that goes with that.'

Lampard received further confirmation of his status as one of the best players in the world when, two days after finishing second to Ronaldinho in the European Footballer of the Year award, he was named with the Brazilian on a three-man shortlist to be FIFA's World Player of the Year. Sven-Goran Eriksson led the tributes. 'I am absolutely delighted for Frank. We have already seen this week how highly regarded he is in Europe and now this shows what people think of him all over the world. He is one of the best midfielders in the world right now. I can think of almost no weakness in his game. He has tremendous energy, a complete range of passing; he can tackle and scores more goals from midfield than most strikers.'

Lampard observed some time ago, 'Fans and other players are always asking the same thing: What's it like at Chelsea? What is the manager like? What's Roman Abramovich like? Even on England duty, people like David Beckham, Gary Neville and Wayne Rooney all ask about it. They want to talk about Arjen Robben, Damien Duff and John Terry. It just shows the level we have reached now at Chelsea, and it is terrific. There's an amazing buzz about the place – the buzz of a club that's going places, where something big is happening. I think Chelsea is the most exciting club in the world. In the past, you'd look at clubs like United, Real Madrid or AC Milan and wonder what it would be like to be there. Now, people look at Chelsea and so much of that is down to Mourinho.

'People talk about me being the most improved player and that is because I want to get better year on year. My first World Cup in a team that I believe in – both the individuals and the team itself – is something to look forward to. The World Cup is something we believe we have the potential to win. I am very pleased with how this year has gone. I wouldn't say I can't believe it because I have always strived to get to the very top, but it has been a fantastic year. The biggest prize was for the team in winning the league, but to come second in World Player of the Year tops it off on a personal level.'

Jose Mourinho is also clear in his admiration for Lampard. 'Frank is improving every day. He works hard, rarely has injuries and works for the team. Like Steven Gerrard, he is one of the best in the world. It's difficult to say who is the best because some midfield players are more defensive, some more offensive. I would say Frank Lampard and Steven Gerrard can both do things. They are great players.'

Frank Lampard Senior, a stalwart for West Ham among other clubs, paid his son a rare compliment when he compared him to Bobby Moore, a former team-mate. 'Bobby knew how to meet the challenge of big circumstances and take command of them. I'm proud to say I can see a similar quality in Frank.'

His son received a further plaudit when he was voted England Player of the Year for 2005, beating Steven Gerrard and Wayne Rooney. England fans voted via the FA website and the Chelsea midfielder was the clear winner with 29 per cent of the vote. Gerrard and Rooney were second and third with 18 per cent and 16 per cent respectively.

Sven-Goran Eriksson described Lampard as 'one of the most improved players I have seen in the last few years'.

## SIR BOBBY CHARLTON

Sir Bobby Charlton scored some wonderful goals for his country and remains the most prolific player for England with 49 goals. Maybe if Gary Lineker had not been so casual with his penalty against Brazil at Wembley, then Sir Bobby might now be sharing the No.1 goalscoring spot with the *Match of the Day* presenter. Michael Owen is young enough to catch him, and Wayne Rooney's younger still, but Sir Bobby scored his goals from midfield, where Frank Lampard is currently doing his bit for club and country.

Sir Bobby's analysis of the present England team is that, in defence, midfield and attack, there is plenty of room for optimism, and likewise he feels the forwards are capable of making an impact. If he has a slight reservation, it is about the lack of muscle in attack. He said, 'Maybe we do need somebody with a little more power and strength up front. But of course I am talking about the perfect world because I do rate Michael Owen and Wayne Rooney highly. In fact, Wayne is a one-off: he can play behind the front two and is not like anybody else England have at their disposal. But there isn't really a player with the kind of strength up front that we had with Geoff Hurst.'

It was the system Ramsey adopted that aided Sir Bobby in his goalscoring feats. Sir Bobby explained, 'Alf Ramsey devised a 4-3-3 system that was easy for the players to follow, understand and implement. My role was pretty simple: when we were going forward, I was a forward and, when we lost possession, I was a defender. Of course, you had to work hard, and it was physically very demanding. But we didn't mind the hard work because of what went with it – the satisfaction of becoming world champions.

'Frank Lampard is a player who never stops running, never stops playing, which shows he has a really good engine. You need a top-quality midfield to succeed and we had it then, and we have it now.'

**THE NUMBER SEVENS:**

DAVID BECKHAM – ALAN BALL

## DAVID BECKHAM

Alan Ball is convinced that not only is David Beckham worthy of his place in the England team, irrespective of the multitude of media doubters, but also that the captain will play a pivotal role should the nation bring back the World Cup. This would also be an even bigger triumph than '66 since the feat would be achieved on foreign soil.

Ball told me, 'I have the utmost respect and admiration for Beckham. His delivery of the ball in either dead-ball situations or in open play is simply fantastic. I have always been a great believer that, if you supply a service to the strikers, they will definitely score goals. That's what I tried to do in my career, and that is David's great forte. His delivery is fantastic and he can do it on the run. Anything in the last third, in front of the man, is a massive asset for any team and this is key for England because David Beckham is one of the best in the world at producing that kind of outstanding delivery.'

But Ball, who played a more flexible role on the right-hand side of midfield in the World Cup-winning team, had some advice for Beckham: make sacrifices for the sake of the team. Ball, never one to pull his punches, added, 'I want to see David performing to his strengths on that right-hand side and, if that means making sacrifices, then that is what is required if England are going to be successful in Germany.

'That means staying out on the right where the best of his ability will shine through, passing and crossing the ball. He has to take a sharp look at himself and come to the conclusion that England's best chance of winning the World Cup could depend on his attitude as well as his ability. He needs to supply the bullets from out on the right. When you look at him, his body language tells you he wants to be more involved and he comes off the touchline and drifts infield away from that wide area. But, when you have grown up with the right-back Gary Neville and work so well in tandem down that right side, then that is where you become a potent force.

'The priority is to win the World Cup, and, for England to be successful, Beckham has to sacrifice his own wishes and stick to the right side, where he is more effective and which gives England their best chance.'

Beckham watched as a fan when England lost the World Cup semi-finals to Germany in Italia 90. Now he wants to go to Germany with a realistic chance of bringing home the trophy. He said, 'Watching the team get through to the semi-finals and losing out to Germany – that was when we missed the two penalties – that was a memory but it wasn't a good one.'

Beckham has fonder memories of other World Cups. 'My first memory of the World Cup was probably Bryan Robson scoring the tournament's fastest-ever goal in Spain against France in 1982. Robbo was my hero and seeing him play for and captain England, then scoring that goal – that was a dream for me.

'There are a couple of things that make playing in the World Cup so special. One, you're playing for your country and representing England in the biggest football competition in the world. And, two, being part of a tournament like that, with players that you don't necessarily play with week in, week out. But there is such a great team spirit, especially in the England team. It's every young boy's dream to play in the World Cup finals – luckily I've played in two so far.'

Beckham prepared for his 50th game as England captain by rounding on the critics who suggested that he is unworthy to lead the national side. The Real Madrid midfield player maintains that he has the backing of both Sven-Goran Eriksson and his team-mates. He went into the friendly against Argentina in Geneva eager to underline his maturity, seven years after suffering arguably his worst moment in an England shirt, when he was sent off in a match between the countries in the 1998 World Cup finals.

Beckham, 30, led his country out almost five years to the day since Peter Taylor, the caretaker manager at the time, handed him the captain's armband for the first time before a friendly match against Italy. 'Being given the added responsibility of captaincy pushed me on,' he said. 'When I was given the job, I admit it was a surprise. But it was a responsibility that I needed and I wanted to have. When someone gives you an honour like that, it also gives you a great lift. It is a responsibility that I believe I thrived on. Unfortunately, five years on, people say the captaincy should be taken off me to relieve me of that pressure, but I love being England captain and I don't feel any pressure with it at all. To be England captain is one of the greatest honours anyone can have.'

Beckham made it clear that, while there may have been calls from outside the squad for him to pass on the job, those demands have not been echoed inside the dressing room. Eriksson has never lost faith in Beckham's suitability for the job, but Wayne Rooney's outburst during the 1–0 defeat by Northern Ireland in September led to speculation that certain players were unhappy with his leadership. 'It's great, not just to have the support of the manager but also the players,' Beckham said. 'The players have always spoken well of me or stuck up for me when things have gone badly. That is the way I am to them and it's nice that it is like that back. I'm pleased that I definitely have that support.'

His first match as England captain ended in a 1–0 defeat by Italy at the Stadio Delle Alpi in November 2000. Gennaro Gattuso scored the only goal, having two minutes earlier given Beckham a clip round the back of the head behind the referee's back, for which he should have been sent off. Not responding to Gattuso's provocation was an impressive show of self-restraint from the new captain. When Peter Taylor passed on the reins to Eriksson, the Swede kept faith with the man who had become public enemy No.1 after being sent off in the World Cup second-round defeat by Argentina. After that infamous petulant kick at Diego Simeone in 1998, even Beckham said that his rise to the captaincy was 'astonishing'.

Beckham's sending-off against Austria robbed him of the chance to chalk up his half-century of caps against Poland at Old Trafford in England's last World Cup qualifier. He said, 'It's always hard when you are missing out on games, and missing out on that one when we went top of the group was especially tough. I always love playing at Old Trafford and it was disappointing not to be there for a lap of honour. But I was just happy that we got the result and finished top of the group.'

Beckham now goes into his third significant finals as England captain. So far, the best moments have been limited to qualifying games. He acknowledges that it is now or never for him and for England to deliver when it matters most. 'We should go further in big tournaments,' he said. 'In qualifying, when it comes to big games and needing to win, we seem to get the results, but now we have to take that into a World Cup finals and go further than we have done in other tournaments.'

Brazil left-back Roberto Carlos believes his Real Madrid team-mate is still one of the world's best players. Critics have questioned whether the England captain deserves his place in recent months, despite receiving rave reviews for his performances in Spain. Carlos said, 'I think David Beckham is still one of the best players in the world. He's the best passer in the world and also one of the greatest players in his position on the pitch. I would love him to be Brazilian so he could play for Brazil!'

The win over Austria, followed later that night by Holland's win, secured England's place in Germany and brought this observation from the England captain: 'Everyone knows we can play a lot better. We have great individuals but this team is not about individuals: we can play as a strong team. I'm captain but so many other players in the squad are captains of their club sides and we are lucky to have that.

'I believe this team can go a long way – but you get nothing if you don't work hard. Now we have to get down to some more hard work and playing a lot better. People have said the players are against each other in this squad – that some players are more involved in picking the team than others. But the players have always stuck together and people don't realise just what great character we've got in this team. We are all really pleased to have got through. Some of the criticism thrown at the manager is very unfair. He deserves to be taking us to another World Cup.'

Germany 2006 will be Eriksson's final major tournament as England coach, his last attempt at shattering the glass ceiling and taking the team beyond the quarter-finals. Becks added, 'I respect Sven and so does every one of the England players. We're not as close as everyone thinks. One minute, people say I'm thick and the next I'm picking the England team. Sure, I get on with him. But I'm the England captain and you have to get on with the manager. But there is a divide where, if he needs to make a decision and if it's leaving me or another player out of the team, he will make it.'

Wayne Rooney insists his high-profile bust-up with Beckham during England's dismal defeat in Northern Ireland has been forgotten. He believes the fact that words were exchanged proves at least they care about winning. 'David has been a great friend to me. He is a great captain and a terrific player. We speak to each other off the pitch. He is so up for the World Cup finals, probably more than anyone else, because he takes so much more stick. It is very unfair, especially if you look at his performances for England, which have been great.

'I was very frustrated when so much was made of our argument during the Northern Ireland game. Arguments happen on and off the pitch, but they happen because you try and help one another and because you care. I would be more concerned if they didn't happen. Then there would be something wrong. It was blown up out of proportion. We had an argument on the pitch and that was it. The next day we were on the phone talking; we spoke in the dressing room afterwards and everything was sorted out.'

As the hype increased and expectancy levels reached fever pitch, the England captain counselled against complacency after England drew Paraguay, Sweden and Trinidad & Tobago in the group stages. Beckham said, 'It is still a difficult group to play in. We cannot afford to take it lightly and, if we do that, we'll find ourselves in trouble.'

### ALAN BALL

Sir Geoff Hurst would select Alan Ball ahead of David Beckham 'because he was England's Man of the Match in the 1966 final'. That's a measure of Ball's contribution to the '66 triumph. But, when it comes to comparisons, Ball told me, 'Although we both wore No.7 and both play on the right side, Alf had a vastly different formation and it was one that gave me far more flexibility.

'For a start we had a holding player in midfield, and that makes me laugh when everyone start debating whether we should have one now. We had one 40 years ago! We had our own Makelele and he was far better: Nobby Stiles was the best in the world in that role – he guarded the back four, roaming just in front of our defence, and that allowed myself, Bobby Charlton and Martin Peters to be very loose in midfield with plenty of flexibility to interchange and to get forward in search of goals. You would probably say we played 4-1-3-2 with no out-and-out wingers, but with licence to go there if we wanted to.

'So my position contrasts somewhat with David's who is really an up-and-down right-sided midfielder, although I did get to spend quite a lot of time out there myself.'

Ball was a bundle of energy and he could also be tricky and fast, as he explained, 'I went past people more than David does, but his delivery of the ball is better than mine, particularly from the wide areas. I made most of my telling passes from central areas, more than I did when I was out on the right side. But I could put defenders out of the game by going past them.'

Ball was the youngest player in Alf Ramsey's team as well as Man of the Match in the final, so he is perhaps best placed to analyse how young Wayne Rooney is likely to fare in the finals.

Ball told me, 'Again, like David Beckham needs to play to his strengths by staying out wide on the right, Wayne needs to be playing off the front man and not in a wide position. His great strength is running at people; he is terrific with the ball at his feet in full flight. He is excellent at coming from deep positions and taking on the defence with such great ability to go past people. He is also a winner.'

So will Wayne, David et al be winners in Germany in 2006? 'England do have a talented squad, but the big question is whether they have a strong enough "team". We shall find that out soon enough when the World Cup comes along. Talent-wise, we can win it this time, but... there are numerous buts, and one of the buts is whether Rooney can make that colossal leap from being a gifted young player at international level to becoming a world-class one on the biggest stage of all.'

Ball explained further, 'Wayne will be coming into a World Cup at roughly the same age as I did. The only worry for me was whether I could make that giant step upwards in a World Cup, and the same applies to Wayne. He has played in the Premier League, in the Champions League and at international level and nothing seems to have fazed him, but doing it on the world stage is something that Pele, Cruyff and Maradona all accomplished and that isn't going to be easy.

'I made that transition. I played in the Football League with Blackpool; I didn't play in Europe apart from international football and I knew it was going to be a challenge to take the next big step and perform in the World Cup finals. I will be looking for Wayne to do the same. I am sure that he can because he has something special in his locker. If he can, then Wayne Rooney can be the catalyst for a lot of good things in the England team, even the possibility of winning it.

'Yes, I am optimistic. We have a talented group of players but it is whether they can make the sacrifices as individuals to perform for the team. It is teams and not individuals that will bring home the World Cup.'

## STEVEN GERRARD – NOBBY STILES

### STEVEN GERRARD

Steven Gerrard's World Cup butterflies started even before the draw in Leipzig. Gerrard, who missed out on the 2002 finals with injury, commented, 'The butterflies were going a little bit. I don't think it was nerves – more excitement. I just couldn't wait to see who we were getting. You wouldn't say that the draw has been kind to us, but I'm sure that the players and staff are happy with it and confident we can go through to the last 16.'

Gerrard told TheFA.com, 'On paper it looks like Sweden will be the strongest team we will face in our group but it doesn't always work that way. Although I didn't play against Sweden in 2002, being drawn against them brings back memories for me because I captained England against Sweden in Gothenburg [in 2004] which was an extremely proud moment for me. Hopefully, this time we'll get a better result though! It's nice to be playing them in the third game because we will have had the opportunity to put six points on the board by the time we come to play them. If it has gone that way, it could be a case of us battling it out to see who will finish top of the group. I do remember the game we played against Paraguay at Anfield in 2002, but I think their team will have changed and improved quite a lot since. But I'm still confident we can take three points from them. Trinidad & Tobago is a great game but it's also a bit dangerous because we don't know too much about them.'

Gerrard was voted third behind Ronaldinho and Frank Lampard in the 2005 European Player of the Year poll. 'I was expecting to hear that Steven would win,' Rafa Benitez said. 'He played in the Champions League final in three different positions and played well in all of them. He was our inspiration to winning. He is one of the best players in the world...'

Since his debut against Ukraine five years ago, Gerrard has represented England in a range of roles. Against Argentina in the World Cup warm-up friendly, he played left midfield, anchorman and then right-back. 'It's quite good for me, three positions in one game,' smiled Gerrard as he left the thrilling fields of Stade de Geneve. 'It's usually four or five! I'm one of these players the manager will just throw anywhere. The team's more important than myself and I'm happy to sacrifice my strongest position to do my best for the team.'

For all the understandable euphoria generated by this epic 3–2 victory, Sven-Goran Eriksson was left with some significant tinkering to do involving Gerrard. Eriksson must decide whether to continue with Ledley King or adapt his lead midfield quartet – David Beckham, Frank Lampard, Gerrard and Joe Cole – to the differing demands of World Cup opponents. 'I can see the manager changing the midfield depending on who we play against,' added Gerrard. 'If we play against a very dangerous side, he might go for a more disciplined midfield. If it's someone he feels we can beat comfortably, he might go a bit more attacking and play Joe Cole. But it's nice to have that variation.'

Anchoring the midfield tempers Gerrard's swashbuckling instincts and he was fortunate not to concede a penalty for a challenge from behind on Julio Cruz when briefly policing the middle after King's exit. 'Gerrard can do it,' said Eriksson. 'Lampard can do it. But they are not very keen. They want more freedom. I could [persuade Gerrard]. He will do everything.'

Gerrard insisted that he will be fresh for England in Germany, despite his increasingly heavy workload with club and country. The Liverpool captain, speaking at the launch of the FIFA World Club Championship in Japan, had already played 22 senior games with Liverpool and England after returning to action in early July due to his club's involvement in the qualifying stages of the Champions League. The tournament in Japan forced the European champions to rearrange two December Premiership fixtures, prompting fears of a backlog in the second half of the season.

Gerrard missed the last World Cup due to injury and was hampered by fitness problems during England's Euro 2000 campaign. However, the midfielder is confident that plans by manager Rafael Benitez to rest players towards the end of the campaign will ensure he travels to Germany with England in the best possible condition.

Gerrard said, 'I am sure I will go to the World Cup feeling fresh. There are a lot of games this season before the World Cup, but certain numbers of the players at Liverpool will be rested if they have played a lot of football and the manager has already said that, so I'm looking forward to the World Cup. There are a lot of people talking of fatigue, but, if you are winning football matches, then it helps you a lot more than when you are losing, believe me, and I am really enjoying my football at the moment. I watched the last World Cup from home and it was very frustrating, but we've just beaten Argentina 3–2 with England and, six months ago, I won the European Cup with Liverpool, so I couldn't be happier.'

Bryan Robson, the former England skipper, believes Liverpool ace Gerrard is wasted playing wide and has all the tools needed to claim a regular slot in the middle. Gerrard himself says he will play anywhere for England as long as it means more caps. Sven-Goran Eriksson has taken full advantage of Gerrard's willingness by tinkering with his midfield in a bid to solve problems down the left. But West Brom chief Robson said, 'Gerrard has the ideal ability to play central midfield. When he has played there for England, he has turned in terrific performances and does it for Liverpool.

'I don't think there is anybody who can do it better than him. If Gerrard moves over and the manager sticks with 4-4-2, it would present an opportunity for other players to take on the wide role. Kieran Richardson has done well when he played there and Joe Cole of Chelsea has been successful. The carrot is still there for those players to make a regular place their own.'

Eriksson will have to decide whether to deploy Gerrard as his holding player, a role the coach wishes to use against more creative opponents in Germany.

'Gerrard is not keen to do it,' Eriksson said. 'He has too much energy at the moment but in the future he will be a fantastic sitting midfielder. Against Argentina [in last year's friendly], he was outside-left, central and then at right-back, where he put in the cross for Michael Owen. He can play everywhere, absolutely. He can play as the sitter if we want him to, although we often play with him, Beckham, Lampard and Joe Cole, and nobody sitting. They can handle it because they are all clever. Every game we play together is very important.

'If we can improve from the standard we've set so far, I will be very happy. Our midfield is extremely strong.'

## NOBBY STILES

Nobby Stiles was in a confident mood. The 2006 team not only compares to his side of 1966, but he is convinced they have the best chance of winning the World Cup of anyone in the 40 years since England beat West Germany at Wembley.

He told me, 'This side has a great chance of winning it; it has great balance and I will be delighted if they bring home the World Cup. Yes, they really do have one helluva chance.'

Nobby does not believe there is a player in the present set-up whose role compares with the one he was asked to perform under Alf Ramsey. 'I am a big fan of Steven Gerrard's; he is a terrific player. In fact, England's present team have a terrific midfield with Gerrard and Frank Lampard. Wayne Rooney for me can turn a game, and I would say he's the best player I have seen emerge in this country since Duncan Edwards. Michael Owen is still a great goalscorer for his country. So, overall I would say this is the best side since '66 and I hope, please God, that they have a bit of luck and win it.

'There is no comparison between myself and Steven Gerrard, though. I know many people talk about me playing a very similar role to Claude Makelele at Chelsea, and Makelele is a player who lets people get forward. Here we are 40 years later talking about a player in the same role as me! But the game has changed an awful lot, so it's very hard to make such comparisons.

'My job for England was to win the ball and give it to Bobby [Charlton] or Ballie. I had to get back and win it and see if there was any danger and then snuff it out. I wouldn't want to describe me as anything. I played alongside the centre-half at Manchester United, but Alf Ramsey wanted me to play in midfield and I was happy to do anything for my country.

'Whether that kind of player is needed in the World Cup, I don't really know. I am not so sure that they do because there is balance in the team – players like Steven Gerrard and Frank Lampard who can change the course of a match, as well as someone like Rooney.'

So Nobby was reluctant to compare himself with Gerrard. 'He is a great player. I'm pretty sure he can play the holding role in midfield if he has to, but he is a much more accomplished player who can get forward like anything. I would love him to play for Manchester United, but my old mate Tommy Smith says there is no chance he will ever play for United and I can see why he says that!'

Sir Bobby Charlton described Nobby as a 'one-off' and added that there isn't a player in the current England squad to compare him with. 'The closest is Steven Gerrard,' observed Sir Bobby, 'but there is nobody like Nobby in the present squad.' He added, 'He was an instinctive defender; he could sniff out trouble in the same way that Bobby Moore did at the back and he would go in there and nip it in the bud. He had no pretensions about going forward; he just wasn't interested and he was more like Claude Makelele in the modern-day game.'

## JOE COLE – MARTIN PETERS

### JOE COLE

Martin Peters played on the left side of England's midfield and, like Joe Cole, is not naturally left-footed, but he feels his graduation to world-class player came with his tuition under Ron Greenwood at Upton Park when he practised to strengthen his left foot.

Peters told me, 'I played on the left but I am not left-footed; my left was OK, but at West Ham Ron insisted that we worked hard on both flanks and I practised crossing with my left foot a great deal.

'Joe's problem is that, while he sometimes uses his left, more often than not he stops and that gives the defenders a chance to regroup. Joe seems frightened at times to knock the ball in with his left. I never had pace to get past people, while Joe is far superior to me in taking people on. He has more trickery in that department than I did.

'But I am not like Joe Cole, and he's not like me. I was brought up at West Ham to know how to use space and to play the ball in early. I had a great rapport with Geoff Hurst. I knew when he would make his runs to the near post and I would time my cross or pass accordingly. That was perfected under Ron Greenwood and came to good use when that precise manoeuvre carved out the goal in the World Cup quarter-finals that took us past Argentina. It was a perfect example of a West Ham goal.

'Joe was also brought up at West Ham, but I was a goalscoring midfield player. I once managed 20-odd goals in a season, although that year Geoff got more than 30. Frank Lampard is a goalscoring midfield player like Bryan Robson or David Platt, although Frank gets into the box more than I have seen most midfield payers. He's there so often he misses as many as he scores!'

Sir Geoff Hurst's only doubt is about whether England have enough strength in depth to cope with key injures during the tournament, although he was impressed by Joe Cole's contribution when he came on as a substitute in the win over Argentina. 'The England team is capable of winning the World Cup if those 11 can start all six games. But it's also important to have 14 or 15 who can come on, like Joe Cole did against Argentina and made a difference,' said Hurst. 'But in Euro 2004, after Rooney went off, we looked toothless and that's a worry. You need a strong squad to win a tournament. You can't afford to lose a world-class player from any tournament. We lost Gordon Banks in 1970 and he was the best keeper in the world, playing out of his skin. We found out against Germany in Mexico how hard it was to replace him. Who knows what would have happened if he hadn't got injured?

'If we were to lose Rooney, as we did in Euro 2004, then you can patch up but you can't replace him. There are some players who are irreplaceable and in our team they were Bobby Moore and Bobby Charlton.

'I believe there would be disappointment all round if we didn't get into the semi-finals. You have to see progress under a manager. So far he has done a good job with the qualification. Though this team has a lot of experience, none of them is too old. Many of them have played Champions League, which is similar to a World Cup experience. They have been in a World Cup together and a European Championship.'

Hurst was thrilled by England's 3–2 win over Argentina in Geneva. 'We beat Argentina, a top side, and there had been some criticism we hadn't beaten the best teams. Now we've shown we can beat the team who are ranked No.2 in the world.'

But Hurst is convinced England now have the right squad: even today's multimillionaires will have the motivation to try to repeat the glory of 1966 this summer. Hurst added, 'It doesn't matter what sort of money you earn – you can't buy winning the World Cup. It's the same with Tiger Woods in golf and Roger Federer at tennis. The money is immaterial. It's about wanting to be the best player, winning the tournaments, and, for England, it's about wanting to be a World Cup winner and that is priceless.'

Joe Cole is ready for the 'fight of his life' to keep his England place and come of age at the World Cup. The 24-year-old has endured some mixed performances in internationals, but his display in the 2–1 win over Poland should be good enough to keep him in the team. 'It's all down to me to keep producing. But I love that pressure; I thrive on it. I wouldn't want it any other way,' he said. 'It's a long way to the World Cup, but I want to keep my place. It's hard because it all comes down to me really, whichever way you look at it. Whether it's for Chelsea or England, it all boils down to how you perform in the team and, as long as I'm playing well, I don't see that there's a reason to be left out. I think it's in my hands.

'Provided I keep producing I should be all right and that means it's up to me to produce the goods week in and week out. It's a good challenge and I've always been up for a challenge. But it is difficult to perform 100 per cent in every game, especially when the team is not playing well all the time. I'm the sort of player who will feed off other players giving me the ball in the right areas. We've had some tough games – Denmark, Wales and Northern Ireland. I managed to nick a goal against Wales but wasn't firing on all cylinders by any means. I like to think against Austria that I put in a good solid performance and I think I showed my worth to the manager against Poland.'

Eriksson is expected to play Cole in a midfield quartet with David Beckham, Steven Gerrard and Frank Lampard. But, when England come up against the bigger teams in the World Cup, Tottenham

*Top*: Bobby Moore talking to Alf Ramsey during a training session.

*Bottom*: Alf warms up with some golf, watched by trainer Harold Shepperton.

*Top*: Ray Wilson, Geoff Hurst, Jack Charlton and Bobby Moore share a laugh at training.

*Bottom*: Alf Ramsey plots world domination in January 1966.

*Top*: The England team of 1966, with Bobby Moore holding the Jules Rimet trophy.

*Bottom*: The run-up to glory: Bobby Charlton sends the first of England's goals past Ignacio Calderon of Mexico.

Bobby Charlton and Roger Hunt, who scored the second of the two goals against Mexico, leave the pitch.

*Top*: Bobby Charlton
leaps to get the ball as
England take on France.

*Left*: Bobby Moore in
training.

Action between England and Portugal in the semi-finals, featuring the legendary Eusebio being thwarted by Gordon Banks and George Cohen.

*Inset*: Mutual respect. Bobby Charlton congratulated by Eusebio of Portugal on England's victory.

*Top*: In the final against West Germany, Alan Ball gets past the German defence.

*Bottom*: West Germany celebrate their equaliser, scored by Wolfgang Weber.

*Top*: Bobby Charlton and Geoff Hurst play, as England go on the attack.

*Bottom*: Bobby Moore and Nobby Stiles showing intense concentration against West Germany.

captain Ledley King is ready to take his place and play as a holding midfielder. Cole, however, is determined to prove he is worth selection, even though he is ready to stand aside for the good of the team when necessary.

'If we want to go to the World Cup and do well, then it's not just about four midfielders,' he said. 'We need to have variation and the gaffer might want to change things, bring in Ledley, Wrighty [Shaun Wright-Phillips], Michael Carrick or even Scotty Parker. We need options. It would be a desperate shame if we don't fulfil our potential.'

As England mature into a team capable of success, so Cole has developed from being a prodigious talent into a regular for club and country. He is delighted with his achievements as a Premiership title-winner under Jose Mourinho and is equally proud of being part of an England line-up ready to blossom.

'I think we're in a select few who have got a chance and it will all be down to who is fit and who is in good form,' said Cole. 'If our top players are in form at the right moment and are not too knackered or burned-out, then we can go a long way. It's amazing that, when I first went into England squads, there were players like Shearer who I grew up watching as a kid. Now there are players who I played with as a kid, like John Terry, Ashley Cole and Ledley King. It's become a family sort of atmosphere around the squad, whereas before it was like a different generation. Now it's our generation and it's just like how it was in the Under-21s and Under-18s. It's a good togetherness. We're all within three or four years of each other – apart from a few of the old boys!

'I think Frank was the oldest at 28 against Poland. It's just like wanting to see all of your mates do really well, that's the sort of atmosphere we've got now. I still feel like I'm 17 and loving every minute, but you have to make the most of it. I've achieved a lot in my career. I've got nearly 30 caps for England which is probably bordering on the veteran status. I've captained a Premier League side. Winning trophies with Chelsea was fantastic last season and so I've got a lot of experience. I don't feel like a youngster any more. I feel like I have made that step up now to being a proper senior player and I think people within the game – Sven and Jose as well – look at me like that.'

## MARTIN PETERS

Gary Lineker famously said that football is a simple game, played by two teams, 11-a-side, over 90 minutes – then the Germans win. But Martin Peters scored against West Germany back in 1966 and now predicts England can win in Germany.

Peters laughed as he told me, 'Of course the Germans will be one of the favourites as they are in their own back garden, as we were when we won in '66, so you've got to be very cautious in one way when we think of this tournament being in Germany. Then again, why be so cautious because we have every chance of winning if we can achieve the standard we did in beating Argentina in Geneva.

'The secret of Alf's winning side is that we played as a team. We gained the camaraderie from the pre-tournament tour in Scandinavia and I am sure that Sven can get his players united as well. And, if he can, we will then have a real opportunity of winning after so long; it's hard to believe it was 40 years ago.

'Of course, those memories will never leave me and, while it all ended in glory, it didn't begin very well in our qualifying group. The first game against Uruguay was ordinary; the truth is we actually struggled to get a 0–0. Alf changed the side around and gave me my opportunity to come in and – again I must be honest – we struggled against France just three days later until Bobby Charlton's wonderful goal, a goal that we all still have fond memories of. It showed Bobby at his best, hitting the ball on the run – a fantastic strike – and we beat them 2–0. Again Alf changed the team, and we seemed to get better each time that he did.

'The quarter-finals were against our arch-rivals Argentina, and that was some game until Rattin got sent off for arguing with the referee. After beating Argentina, our confidence soared; we beat Portugal in the semi-final in a fantastic contest against a side that possessed the best player in the world at that time, Eusebio.

'And it was a great final against the Germans. When it went to extra-time, Alf told us all to stand up as we watched a team of masseurs come on to the pitch and the Germans have their legs massaged. But Alf just told us that we had won it once, go out and win it again. We all believed in Alf and we believed we could do it.'

Peters helped Gillette launch their FIFA-authorised Best Young Player award, along with David Platt and me, and there was a retrospective list of those who would have won that award in all the previous World Cups. Franz Beckenbauer was named Best Young Player of 1966, but Peters felt that honour could have gone to Alan Ball.

Peters, now one of the high-profile former players on matchday duty at White Hart Lane, declines to name any of the present England side who might have earned a place in his beloved 1966 line-up. He explained, 'I dare not because we are such big buddies still, and I have to keep meeting up with them at reunions.'

He went on, 'It is very difficult to make comparisons in any case, particularly with a team that actually won the World Cup. Let's see if this team win it first. Rather than say who would get into the team, let's look at the squad.

'Players of the calibre of Gerrard and Lampard would be in there, so too would Michael Owen, but I am not sure about David Beckham. Yes, David is a fantastic player, but we had Alan Ball on that right side and he was Man of the Match in the final. He was the youngest player at only 20 as well. Ashley Cole is a fabulous player at left-back but nothing got past Ray Wilson. They certainly have a lot to live up to if you want to make comparison with the '66 team.

'England will win the World Cup again and, after 40 years, it might as well be sooner rather than much later. I do feel they have a great opportunity this time.'

## STRIKERS:
THE NUMBER TENS:
MICHAEL OWEN – SIR GEOFF HURST

### MICHAEL OWEN

Sir Geoff Hurst predicts Michael Owen can help bring about a repeat of the World Cup glory days of 1966 in Germany. Hurst believes Owen will prove he is the world's greatest striker by helping England bring football's Holy Grail back from Germany.

Hurst, who scored a hat-trick in England's finest footballing hour in the 1966 World Cup final, believes Liverpool, Manchester United and Arsenal will regret not signing Owen from Real Madrid. Owen went to Newcastle for £16m, a price which before his injury looked a bargain after Liverpool boss Rafael Benitez stalled, United went cold and Arsenal decided not to bid.

He was stunned that none of the major Premiership clubs signed Owen. 'It does surprise me other clubs didn't come in because goals are such a valuable commodity. But £16m is a big fee and it will restrict it to only a small number of clubs. His record is incredible. If you buy Michael Owen, then you buy goals. That's what Newcastle have done and he will be a brilliant signing for them.'

Hurst said, 'If the chances are there, Michael is probably the best player in the world at putting them away. He's got this unbelievable knack of scoring goals wherever it comes from – his foot, his head, side of his head, his knee and whichever angle or pace. He is an unbelievable predator. His record is second to none: he's still only 25, has won 74 caps and it's only a matter of time before he beats Bobby Charlton's record.'

Hurst expects Owen to become England's greatest goalscorer by the age of 30. Owen's two late headers in Geneva against Argentina took his statistics to 35 goals in 74 games, only 14 goals behind leading scorer Bobby Charlton, who finished his career on 49. Now Hurst can see Owen overtaking Charlton's record and challenging Peter Shilton's total of 125 caps. He said, 'I look back and, when I was 25, I had played just 10 games for England and scored five goals. So what he can achieve is unbelievable. With Owen scoring goals and Wayne Rooney, who is a wonderful player, alongside him, there's no doubt in my mind we have an opportunity to win the World Cup.

'I would say that, if Michael keeps fit, there's a strong possibility he could become England's record goalscorer. The decision will be Michael's. He started very young, so it's about whether he wants to retire young as well. That's a decision only he can make. But he loves football and I would assume he will continue until the manager no longer picks him. If he wanted to play on until he's 30, for instance, that's five more years and another 50 caps. Probably another 25 goals as well. So he'd be the leading goalscorer. It's all in his hands.'

Gary Lineker, the man second only to Bobby Charlton in the all-time goalscoring charts, is backing Owen to take the World Cup by storm. Owen equalled Lineker's record tally of 22 competitive goals for his country when he scored in England's 2–1 victory over Poland. After England qualified from their group, Lineker, who won the Golden Boot after bagging six goals in the 1986 World Cup finals in Mexico, backed the Newcastle striker to hit even greater heights. He said, 'Congratulations to Michael. I never knew the record existed until a couple of games ago – so I didn't even have a chance to enjoy it! But it's fine by me that Michael has caught up. The more goals he scores for England, the better for everyone. People needed a lift against Poland and he's given them it. The great thing about Michael is he's a proven scorer. If you get the ball in the box, he will score. He is our most reliable scorer and it won't be any different at the World Cup. He relishes those types of occasions and always does well.'

Lineker is one goal behind Bobby Charlton for England, with 48 in all. He expected to be passed by Owen and said, 'He's clearly going to break this competitive goals record quickly and I'm sure he will be after the rest of them after that.'

Owen will inevitably be one of the favourites to claim the Golden Boot for top marksman at Germany. But he has set his sights on an even bigger prize. 'You'd treasure it if you got it, but I wouldn't set out to win the Golden Boot – I'd prefer to win the golden trophy by a long way. I'd love to be the man to score the goals to help us win it, but the main thing is the World Cup. I wouldn't settle for getting knocked out in the last four. The aim is certainly to get as far as the semi-finals – but it wouldn't stop there. We will go there with a squad that, apart from Brazil maybe, I'm sure is not bettered.'

Owen reckons his strike partnership with Wayne Rooney can help him become the first English player to win the Golden Boot since Gary Lineker claimed the prize in Mexico. Brazil have a team full of *Galacticos*, including Ronaldinho, Robinho, Ronaldo and Roberto Carlos, but Owen, 25, feels England have their own superstars – especially Rooney.

Owen said, 'I remember being in the players' lounge at Real Madrid looking up at the telly and seeing him score a hat-trick on his Manchester United debut. He's so effective. People can do all those turns and flicks and look good, but not really create or score many. But Wayne is a fantastic player in that he does create and score goals.'

Owen, captain for the final qualifier against Poland at Old Trafford in the absence of the suspended Beckham, believes we will see a totally different England once the tournament kicks off. He believes Eriksson's men will suddenly raise their game. Despite a thumping by Denmark, a shock loss to Northern Ireland and narrow victories over Wales and Austria, Newcastle striker Owen says there is nothing to worry about. 'You can't tell me we will be taking this form of the last few games into a game against Brazil, Italy or Germany in a World Cup. You can't tell me, because we are playing like this now, that they will beat us 3–0. We've got proper players who will raise their game for those games. Maybe there's a little bit of lack of confidence because we haven't set the world alight over all the last few games. But, if we were playing against Brazil in the World Cup tomorrow, you wouldn't expect us to be playing at the level we are playing at right now. The actual World Cup is virtually a different sport. It's so different to going away to a small country in Europe where it's freezing cold, with a bad pitch and a hostile crowd. There's no lack of effort or passion, but it's what football is like these days. It's far harder than it was. It will be a different game you are watching in the World Cup. They fancy themselves against you. You fancy yourselves against them.

'You only have to look at the players we have to know that they are not going to lie down and die in front of anyone. The last World Cup was a first tournament for a lot of players. You look at the squad now and no one is too inexperienced or past their best. We've got a squad full of players who can all perform in a World Cup.'

And you never know, Michael Owen's metatarsal injury might have come at the right time for England if not Newcastle: if recovery goes to schedule, he should be fighting fit for the World Cup, with just enough match practice to be in top condition.

## SIR GEOFF HURST

Sir Geoff Hurst has spent almost 40 years revelling in the role of England's World Cup hero and he has seen hundreds of players fail to emulate the achievements of 1966. But he was encouraged by the performance of Sven-Goran Eriksson's side against Argentina and said, 'Naturally the country is very buoyant. I think we're all feeling this is the time for the current side. They have been together a long while and most are playing regular Champions League football. The experience and the youth combined is a lovely combination.'

Sir Geoff, the only man to score a World Cup final hat-trick, was delighted with the draw in Leipzig even though it once again paired England with Sweden, a team they haven't beaten since this country were world champions.

He said, 'It's a pretty good group for us because, on balance, there were some tougher groups. But Sweden is always a tough one. We haven't beaten them since 1968.'

Sir Geoff added, 'What I'd like to see is England play a team that uses the same diamond formation as Sweden in one of the friendly matches before the tournament. In most groups, you have a No.3 team who, if you do not approach the match in the right manner, could be a potential banana skin. Paraguay could be that team for us. However, I would expect us to go through from the group stages.'

## SIR GEOFF HURST'S ENGLAND WORLD CUP TEAM:

Paul Robinson; Gary Neville, John Terry, Rio Ferdinand, Ashley Cole; Ledley King, David Beckham, Steven Gerrard, Frank Lampard; Wayne Rooney, Michael Owen

WAYNE ROONEY – ROGER HUNT

### WAYNE ROONEY

Roger Hunt felt it was a huge 'compliment' when I suggested to him that, for the purposes of this 2006 and 1996 comparison, I had paired him up with Wayne Rooney.

The Liverpool goalscoring ace told me, 'He's one of the most naturally gifted footballers I've ever seen, and he is a big-occasion player and because of that – even at the age of 20 – I feel he will make a massive impact in this World Cup.

'One of his greatest assets is his ability to have enormous confidence in himself, as he just loves playing football on any stage. He might only be 20, but he's already played more than 20 times for England and scored goals into double figures. That's really just incredible for someone of his age.

'With Wayne Rooney in the England team, we have a great chance in Germany. Remember in the European Championship, once Wayne was injured, we were not quite as good. Yes, I have every reason to be optimistic about England's chances this time. We have a good squad and a good team; we just need to steer clear of injuries, particularly Wayne, and then we have a great chance of winning it.'

Sir Geoff Hurst believes that, in Rooney, Michael Owen now has the perfect strike partner. Sir Geoff reached this conclusion after the pair destroyed Argentina and his feeling is that this England team has the best chance since 1966 of winning the World Cup.

'It is definitely our best chance since 1966,' said Hurst. 'They have experience in the squad; they have been together for such a long time. Rooney is the best individual player we've had since Paul Gascoigne. Even in 1966, if you analyse our team, we weren't blessed with that many naturally gifted players, outside of, say, Bobby Charlton or Jimmy Greaves. Rooney's such a talent and is now fully focused on his game and nothing else. His temperament was a distraction and yet he seems to have overcome it.

'If you get sent off, you're the worst player in the world, not the best. He is still playing the game unbelievably aggressively, but now doing it within the boundaries of being sensible. He's an undoubted talent. You need an outstanding player who can turn a game. Rooney is comfortable in those sorts of surroundings. He's brilliant, exciting to watch and plays it aggressively.

'That can be the biggest quality of English players – aggression. But the best players have always had it. Pele, Maradona and even Bobby Charlton had a mental toughness which top sportsmen always need. There's a difference between losing your rag and having an edge. Even in boxing you can't afford to lose your temper. You need to be cool, calm and calculating. You need to get on with it whatever the opponents are doing to you. So you mustn't take away the fire within Rooney, it just needs channelling. That is what makes him a great player, but you are not a great player if you are in the dressing room having been sent off or suspended for two yellow cards.

'Owen and Rooney are individuals more than a partnership, but they are both so good at what they do that it means they're fantastic together.'

Sir Geoff felt Bobby Moore and Bobby Charlton were 'irreplaceable' in 1966. Now the same goes for Rooney. He said, 'Once every generation, a kid comes along. Paul Gascoigne was special but, before that, you have to go back to Bobby Charlton.'

Sir Bobby Charlton believes Rooney can eventually follow in the footsteps of George Best. However, Charlton, who won the European Cup for United alongside Best in 1968, believes Rooney still has much to prove. He said, 'Wayne has a long way to go to be classed as the new George Best. But he has it inside him, in his heart, to do it. He's liable to score a goal from nothing and I'm really relieved he plays for us. It remains to be seen if anyone can ever play the way George did.'

Rooney ran West Ham ragged in a stunning virtuoso performance at Upton Park last year as United came from a goal down to win 2–1 in a game that turned into a celebration for Best. Charlton, who played at Old Trafford for 17 years, added, 'Wayne gets the old ticker going when he plays like that; he is a very exciting player. People seem to be surprised at his performances but he is a natural footballer who loves the game. He has a great touch and an enthusiasm for the game that makes him so exciting.'

Rooney also showed the darker side to his undoubted talents at Upton Park. Referee Steve Bennett booked him for kicking out at defender Danny Gabbidon. Rooney, though, said in mitigation, 'I thought it was a foul on me which the referee never gave me. Stupidly, I kicked out at the lad, which I shouldn't have done, and it was a deserved yellow card. I am learning all the time and realise what I have got to cut out.'

England skipper David Beckham observed, 'Wayne goes out on a pitch not worrying about anything. He's like my son Brooklyn, who goes out in the garden to play and have fun. He tries to do different things and that's why people love him so much. Wayne is proving what a great player he is week in, week out.

'There are good players at United, but he's winning games single-handed. He's getting better every game without a doubt. His confidence is high and, when it is high, you believe you can do anything. That's what George Best was like: he had a huge amount of confidence. He went into games believing he could do anything and he could. We would all like to have the George Best legacy and be mentioned in the same breath as him. One of the things George said to me was to make sure I enjoyed playing because that's what he did. He was happiest on a pitch and so is Wayne.'

Speaking at the launch of his new football academy in Greenwich, Beckham joked, 'Is Wayne still young enough for the academy?'

Few sporting teenagers have earned more money, made more headlines, been faced with greater expectations and had more demands placed on them than the boy from Croxteth. But, after turning 20, Rooney is England's big hope in Germany.

Argentina legend Diego Maradona predicts that Rooney will make a huge impact in Germany and that he could return to England with the ultimate prize. 'Back in 1986, I helped Argentina win the World Cup. Can Wayne Rooney do the same for England next year? Yes, no doubt. He has the same characteristics as me both as a player and a person. He is a great player, a powerful player, but I do think he needs more guidance, more leadership.'

Rio Ferdinand, Rooney's closest friend at Old Trafford and with England, insists the mate he calls 'Wazza' is moving towards manhood and maturity. Ferdinand said, 'He's just adapting to life as such a famous footballer. He was thrust into the spotlight at a young age and he's had to deal with that – not easy for any young player. I've been through the mill myself as a young kid and I know what it's like to suddenly come into the spotlight. But Wayne has been under double, triple, quadruple the pressure I was under. He's had his ups and downs in terms of his relationship with the press and the way certain things have been reported about him – some true, some not – but as a player you have to deal with that and at the moment I think he's dealing with that admirably. What's more, I think his disciplinary record since he came to United has stepped up unbelievably, and that's something that doesn't often get talked about.'

United manager Sir Alex Ferguson has encouraged Rio to provide guidance to Rooney after the prodigy's £27m move. But Rio insisted, 'I don't need to give Wayne advice any more. I don't say, "Wazza, I think you should do this or do that," but I think he learns by example. On the pitch you may say, "Chill out," to get him to take it easy and let the game flow and not argue about decisions. But Wazza is a great player and he's got that fire in his belly.

'I know it's a cliche when they say, "If you take it away, he's not going to be the same player," but it's very true. When he's out there playing, the emotion gets to him sometimes, but I'm sure with experience he'll be able to curb that and channel it in a positive manner – something he's getting towards now. He's never been a nervous person from the first day he came here – that's just the way he is. He's one of the lads. It's easy to forget how young Wayne is because of the things he does with a football and the way he carries himself. But he's making progress and he's not just someone who sits there as a young lad and accepts things.

'He is not frightened to air his views on the pitch and to be heard. Wayne's doing just fine, believe me.'

Wayne Rooney himself insisted England can lift the World Cup after his return from suspension helped Sven-Goran Eriksson's men turn in their much-improved display against Poland at Old Trafford.

It was the perfect way to silence the critics who virtually ignored the fact England had sealed their place in the finals the previous weekend, and it only confirmed Rooney's belief this side are capable of emulating Sir Alf Ramsey's historic 1966 heroes. 'I have said many times before that we have a squad good enough to win it and nothing has changed,' he said. 'Hopefully, we get a good draw and go on to win it.'

He added, 'We have had a lot of criticism over the last few months, some of it deserved, some of it not. But we have done well to bounce back and finish top and, hopefully, we can carry on that form over the next few games.'

Although Rooney was far too hot for Poland to handle, the teenager was forced to take a backseat in the goalscoring stakes as Michael Owen put England ahead before Frank Lampard sealed victory with an acrobatic strike 10 minutes from time. On the Old Trafford pitch where Rooney has scored so many sensational goals himself, it was an effort to savour and one even the then precocious 19-year-old admitted he wished belonged to his own portfolio. 'I would have been proud of that one,' he said. 'Frank has scored some brilliant goals for Chelsea and that was another fantastic one.'

Without Rooney, it has been suggested, England do not have a prayer of winning the World Cup. The striker himself said, 'Sometimes you watch Brazil and think how are you going to stop them? The forward players they've got are frightening. For me, Ronaldinho is the best footballer in the world. He is a great player. He's strong, quick, has good feet and scores goals as well. That's all you can ask. They have had a great team for the last 20 years. They will be the team to beat and, in my opinion, we have to try and be as good as Brazil. If we can beat them, we can hopefully go far and win it.'

England's hopes of winning Euro 2004 disappeared when Rooney limped off with a broken toe during the quarter-final defeat to Portugal. Memories of that day have made Rooney doubly determined to succeed this time. Having turned 20, he wants to prove he has grown up as a footballer. 'I think I've improved since Euro 2004. Signing for Manchester United has made me a better player. I will go into the World Cup with a lot more experience than I had at the Euros. I believe in myself and I believe in the team. There is a lot of expectation. We were close in Portugal and got knocked out. There is pressure on all of us. I'm confident, excited and I think we've got a very good chance. We've got some great players who can win us the tournament.

'I never really imagined playing in a World Cup. To do it is a dream come true. Everyone who goes to the World Cup wants to prove themselves and I'm no different. I want to score, make goals and try to do the best I can. I was gutted that I had to go off at Euro 2004. That makes me even more hungry to go to the World Cup and win it. I don't know if we could have won Euro 2004 if I had stayed on. If I don't play, there are players who can come in and score goals.'

Despite Rooney's improved behaviour against Poland, FIFA president Sepp Blatter feels the Manchester United striker must be 'called to order' by his managers. He said, 'Wayne is a No.9, like I was. I also had discipline problems from time to time in my career. When you play at such a high level, you need to be called to order.'

Blatter wants Ferguson and Eriksson to get involved in helping Rooney. 'His manager should be tougher on him. His manager should tell him, "You are so talented but now keep the right way otherwise it is not good for the game." He has such a good career in front of him and can go on for 15 years – but he needs self-discipline. One day he should be brought to the FIFA offices – he's invited. I would show him the pictures of me and he could see that I was also a centre-forward like him.'

Manchester United manager Sir Alex Ferguson believes Rooney's aggressive streak is a rare and vital asset among young players. 'Wayne is an exceptional young player. He has a competitive edge about him few players of his age have. He has not exceeded my expectations because, even before I signed him, I felt he was the best young player England have produced for decades – better than

Paul Gascoigne. The desire to get him was obvious and I am just so delighted we managed it.'

Persistent concern with his dress sense, his temper, Colleen's taste in shopping and whether he will end up 'like Gazza' preoccupies this nation, whereas the rest of Europe sees Rooney as England's big hope in Germany.

When Rooney turned 20, he already boasted 27 full England caps and 10 goals. At Rooney's age, Gascoigne had zero caps. And Gazza only won his 26th cap after his 26th birthday, which suggests that, in terms of footballing development, he was a full six years behind. In fact, Rooney compares favourably with just about anybody who has played the game before him. At this stage of his career, only Pele could be said to be ahead of Rooney – and, even then, he had won three fewer caps. The Brazilian had 23 caps and an outrageous 25 goals before his 20th birthday. Diego Maradona's 20 caps and eight goals come close to Rooney, as do Norman Whiteside's (21 caps, seven goals) and Robbie Keane's (18 caps, six goals).

Pele won a starting spot in the side that became world champions in 1958, the first of his four World Cup tournaments. Maradona forced his way into the team that, months earlier, had won the 1978 World Cup.

Rooney started in 24 of those 27 internationals, hardly a beneficiary of too many cheap substitute caps. Rooney walks all over his contemporaries – Cristiano Ronaldo (11 caps, five goals), Ronaldinho (14 caps, eight goals) and Fernando Torres (six caps, one goal); the generation before – Ronaldo (13 caps, five goals), Patrick Kluivert (10 caps, four goals), Raul (seven caps, one goal); and the all-time greats, regardless of whether they are British – Duncan Edwards (nine caps, one goal), Denis Law (six caps, one goal), Stanley Matthews (two caps, one goal); or foreign – Marco van Basten (four caps, two goals), Franz Beckenbauer (two caps, no goals) and Johan Cruyff (two caps, one goal).

At his present rate of progress, he will win his 100th cap around his 28th birthday and beat Peter Shilton's record of England appearances (125) just after he turns 31. If he keeps going, he'll win his 150th cap, breaking Lothar Matthaus's record for European players. He can do that before he turns 34. Breaking the all-time record of 173 caps – held by Mohamed Al-Deayea, of Saudi Arabia – will be somewhat more challenging, but, if he really wants to do it, he is due to catch him by 2022, when he will be 37. Maybe by that point, he will be partnering a young England forward named Brooklyn Beckham, who will be 23 by then.

Rooney could break all England records by the age of 31. He said, 'I don't think about that at the moment but if it happens in the future it will be nice.'

Brazilian maestro Ronaldinho predicted that Rooney would be one of his major rivals for the Player of the Tournament award at the World Cup. Ronaldinho said, 'Rooney is still young but he has a great future and will be one of the big players in the World Cup and beyond. I like seeing him play and watching the way he approaches the game. The world will see him and talk about him at the World Cup. When I look at him, I think that maybe he has enough ability to be a Brazilian... but not quite!'

England's victory over Argentina and the draw have added to the confidence in Eriksson's team. Ronaldinho, whose cross-cum-shot fooled David Seaman and knocked England out of the 2002 World Cup, acknowledged the threat a Rooney-inspired England pose. 'I think England have a really great team and they will be serious opponents. They have great players and I have huge respect for them. I think everybody in the England team is of the highest level.'

## ROGER HUNT

Roger Hunt was handed the No.21 shirt when Sir Alf Ramsey announced his 22-man squad for the World Cup finals. Although not first choice initially, he ended up playing in every one of the World Cup games.

He explained, 'When I started my career as a junior, I was what we used to call in those days an inside forward. The usual style was to play with two wingers and two inside forwards who would link up with the attack but play a bit deeper than a striker, so maybe I played in the sort of role that suits Wayne Rooney.

'But as Alf's formation and tactics altered we became known as the "wingless wonders", and so it became more like the 4-4-2 that is commonplace in the modern game: I ended up playing more as an out-and-out striker rather than coming from deep. It was a change in style for me with England because with Liverpool we were still playing with the two-winger system.

'So Alf named his 1–22 and I was No.21 and it was generally expected that the 1–11 would be Alf's first choice, but John Connelly was No.11, and Jimmy Greaves No.8. As it got closer to the tournament, so there were a few adjustments to the team.

'Jimmy Greaves had been missing for a while with an illness and I played with Geoff Hurst for quite a few games in Jimmy's absence, but generally it was accepted that the first choice 8, 9, 10 attacking formation would be Jimmy, Geoff Hurst and Bobby Charlton. I'd been in and out of the side for quite a few years, but the longest run I had in the team was during Jimmy's illness.

'Then we toured Scandinavia and Portugal to play four games before the World Cup and one or two changes started to evolve. I got into the team and Geoff was the one left out, and that's how we started the World Cup. But as we all know Geoff came into the side for the quarter-finals and kept his place instead of Alf bringing back Jimmy, so anything can happen...'

# TWO

**MEMORIES OF '66:**

ENGLAND'S FINEST HOUR

For Gordon Banks, the memories of 1966 are all-consuming. 'It was just a wonderful time,' he told me. 'We went into the competition with hopes high, but you never really know how it's going to turn out. But it turned out wonderfully: it is something I will never forget for the rest of my life.'

World Cup final day, 30 July 1966, is etched into English football history: a mark set down 40 years ago when the high streets of the nation emptied as folk rushed home to watch – or listen to – England win the Jules Rimet trophy.

'Nobby for Prime Minister' read a banner as the England bus found a way through the throng. Alan Ball pointed it out to Nobby Stiles and they laughed. Three hours later, they would be dancing their memorable jig on the turf, exhausted and elated at the same time with West Germany beaten 4–2 in extra-time.

There are moments frozen in history where we are always asked, 'Where were you when...?' – such as when Kennedy was assassinated or man landed on the moon, and when England won the World Cup.

Sebastian Coe, a Chelsea fan, recalled, 'I was nine when England won the World Cup and I can remember exactly where I was – I'm reminded every time I go to Stamford Bridge because the house where I watched the game is opposite the main entrance to the ground on the Fulham Road. My parents were born and brought up in west London. My parents' range of friends crossed many boundaries, artistic and social, and was exemplified in our host the day England's footballers won their last international trophy.

'He was a Russian Scot – a painter whose collection of football canvases captured an era long past of football rattles, flat caps and Woodbines, scenes he observed from his large picture window. His labour in the Fulham Road was one of love and it was subsidised by commercial work which, among other things, included painting backdrops for early James Bond movies. I can remember his mental contortions that day – as a Scot, he was not entirely at home with the thought of the World Cup going to Lancaster Gate, but, as a Russian, he was acutely conscious of the deprivations inflicted by England's foe on his maternal family only 20 or so years earlier. By five o'clock, he was convinced we had all witnessed a miracle – the divine hand of God in the form of the Soviet linesman who gave England their third goal and the momentum to lift the Jules Rimet trophy.'

Sir Geoff Hurst knows precisely where he was. As the only man ever to score a hat-trick in the World Cup finals, he naturally retains special memories of England's sole major triumph in 1966.

He recalled, 'We won it because of the self-belief that had been building over that period of time. My memory of that squad was that they were all hardnosed professionals. One of Alf Ramsey's favourite sayings was "I want players who won't let me down." Frankly, we never felt like we were going to get beaten and, in fact, we very rarely did.'

The moment England clinched the 1966 World Cup is *the* footballing scene engraved on so many minds in this country. Of course, the triumph of Bobby Moore's team against West Germany might have had a lot to do with home advantage and, when FIFA gave the finals to the FA, it was in effect a decision made by an internal committee at a time when England had a greater presence in football's corridors of power: Stanley Rous became FIFA president in 1962. England faced Germany in the final round of voting, which took place at the FIFA congress in Rome in 1960. Spain dropped out before the final vote, which we won by 37 votes to Germany's 28.

Hurst's third goal ended the match at Wembley as Kenneth Wolstenholme coined the most famous commentary phrase of all time: 'They Think It's All Over – It Is Now.' Yet, until Hurst completed England's 4–2 triumph over West Germany, English supporters were plagued by misgivings, as Ramsey's England had not gone into the 1966 tournament widely regarded as favourites. Far from it. The smart money was on Brazil, Portugal and Hungary who were highly fancied, and Argentina were the dark horses. Most expected England to reach the quarter-finals from an easy group, but few thought they could win it and Ramsey's solemn declaration that they would triumph was regarded as a typical 'Alfism'.

When they met Argentina, it didn't look good until the sending-off of Antonio Rattin. The great football rivalry that has so far involved the Hand of God, the sending-off of David Beckham and even a booking for Bobby Charlton for dissent can be traced back to Rattin's dismissal at Wembley in 1966. 'I suppose that is when it all began,' Rattin said, 'although Alf Ramsey called us "animals" without justification.'

The 1986 encounter, the first after the Falklands war, was by far the most dramatic, and entertaining, of all the games between the two nations, but 1966 was the most brutal. Rattin has his special place in history thanks to his refusal to leave the pitch after his sending-off in the World Cup quarter-final. The tackles were flying in from both teams when, after 35 minutes, Rattin was ordered off by Rudolph Kreitlein. The German referee was later to say that he 'did not like the look' on the face of the towering midfield player who was also Argentina's captain.

The Argentina players jostled Kreitlein, as Rattin became increasingly exasperated and Ray Wilson, the England full-back, shouted,: 'I hope he sends 'em all off.' Rattin was eventually persuaded by police and other officials to depart, but, during the long trudge to the dressing room, he stopped to wipe his dirty hand on one of the corner flags. There was a Union Jack on it. 'It was a tough game, but no one had been complaining about the tackles,' Rattin recalled. 'Both sides were giving as good as they got. We were big players, but England had some tough characters like Nobby Stiles. The sending-off should never have happened and it wouldn't have done if I could speak a word of German. I hadn't even made a foul. All I wanted to do was talk to the referee, but the next thing I knew he was pointing off the pitch.

'*Quiero a un interprete.* [I want an interpreter.] I must have said it 20 or 30 times, pointing to my armband, but he couldn't understand a word I said. My voice is loud by nature and I am a big guy, but I was sent off simply for a misunderstanding. If I became heated, it was only after he had sent me off, but I think there were other forces at work behind this.'

As a politician in the Peronist party *Justicialista*, Rattin suspected some sort of conspiracy to ensure England progressed. He cites a meeting to allot referees to games that took place an hour before the scheduled time. 'There was an apology [to our FA], but it was too late then.' He added, 'It wouldn't happen like that now, with live television cameras all over the world, but all the home teams were helped in those days.'

Rattin's sending-off inspired the introduction of red and yellow cards. Ken Aston, working for FIFA, world football's governing body, was a supervisor that day and one of those who helped persuade Rattin to leave the pitch, but, struck by the confusion, he would later dream up the idea of cards to show players and public. The mayhem at Wembley also meant that Charlton's booking by Kreitlein went undetected. It is commonly believed that gentleman Bobby Charlton was never cautioned in his 106 international appearances; it only came to light when Charlton was on a trip eight years ago with Keith Cooper, FIFA director of communications at the time. 'I mentioned to Bobby that he had never been booked and he looked a bit sheepish,' Cooper said. 'He told me he thought that he had been booked against Argentina, but had never checked up on it. I went away and found the minutes of the 1966 organising committee and there, in black and white, it mentioned cautions for Charlton J and Charlton R. I wrote to Bobby to inform him that he could not claim a clean record and that, obviously, I would never mention it to anyone. Gary Lineker has one up on him.'

Rattin, now 68, is happy that his sending-off brought about something positive. 'I feel proud of the fact that I have helped to change the game for the better,' he said. 'It is just a shame for me that red and yellow cards came one World Cup too late. The England team was good enough to go all the way in 1966 – they beat Argentina 1–0 – but it had been an even game until my dismissal. That is why I didn't want to leave the pitch because I felt that I, the captain, was abandoning my team-mates to their fate.

'I was sent off for no reason, for nothing, but it taught me one thing and that is the importance of languages. I have three daughters and I told them that I wanted them to learn German and English.'

After the brilliant but belligerent Rattin took 10 minutes to leave the field of play following his dismissal, Sir Alf Ramsey described the Argentina team as animals and physically prevented full-back George Cohen from swapping shirts with one of them.

Once Portugal had been beaten in the semi-finals, optimism strengthened, but when Helmut Haller put the Germans in front after 13 minutes of the final, following a rare unforced error by Ray Wilson, old doubts crept back.

Previous World Cups had served merely to confirm the insularity of the English game. They had lost to the United States in 1950, gone out to Uruguay in 1954, the Soviet Union in 1958 and Brazil in 1962 without making a serious impact on any of these tournaments. The West German side which faced England at Wembley was in transition – strong in attack with Uwe Seeler supported by Siegfried Held and Lothar Emmerich, who had helped Borussia Dortmund beat Liverpool in the Cup Winners' Cup final at Hampden Park that spring, but uncertain in defence with their goalkeeper, Hans Tilkowski, weak on high balls.

Nevertheless, Haller's early goal gave them confidence and, although Hurst soon equalised, England's football was fitful, not helped by the young Franz Beckenbauer's marking of Bobby Charlton. The fussy interventions of the Swiss referee, Gottfried Dienst, did not enhance the spectacle either.

In the last minute of normal time, England led 2–1, courtesy of Martin Peters. Uwe Seeler made a back for Jack Charlton, but Dienst awarded Germany a free-kick, which was taken by Emmerich and handled in the goalmouth by Haller before Wolfgang Weber beat Gordon Banks. 'You've won it once, now win it again,' was Alf Ramsey's famous message to his players as they faced extra-time.

The image that forces its way into memories of '66 is the moment when Hurst's shot hit the bar before bouncing down towards the line and the roof of the net seemed to bulge slightly. Certainly the nod of assent from the Soviet linesman, Tofik Bakhramov, appeared to confirm the obvious.

Franz Beckenbauer won 103 caps with West Germany between 1965 and 1977. He took part in three World Cup finals as a player, gaining victory as captain in 1974; he was European Footballer of the Year in 1972 and 1976 and won three European Cups with Bayern Munich, 1974–76. In 1990 he was voted European Player of the Century.

Beckenbauer is also the only man to win the World Cup as player and then as manager. What are his most treasured memories against England? 'Above all, 1966 – my first World Cup, as a young player. Fantastic. Personally meeting players like Pele, Eusebio and Bobby Moore. It was a dream. We played a superb tournament; it was a wonderful final against England, even though my job was to shadow Bobby Charlton. They deserved to win the title, whether or not Geoff Hurst's second goal was a goal.

'I remember, too, our first win over England, a friendly in Hanover, after seven previous defeats – and not just because I scored the only goal, with a deflection! In 1970, England had their best team; they totally outplayed us for 60 minutes, and we had never had even a small chance. Then I scored our first goal, an average shot that went under Peter Bonetti. Everyone was surprised, even us. Was it a mistake then by Alf Ramsey to substitute Bobby Charlton? It seemed so. I don't remember much about our winning the European quarter-final at Wembley in 1972, where Netzer ran the game. The 1990 World Cup semi-final? We were a little lucky with the penalty shoot-out. It was the best match of the tournament, very exciting, both hitting a post. I think we deserved to win the title.'

But does he remember what Wembley was singing at the end of the 1966 final? Not 'Land of Hope and Glory' or 'Abide With Me', still less 'God Save The Queen'. It was 'When The Reds Go Marching In' and Nobby Stiles, socks down with his gap-toothed grin, summed up the nation's joy as he tripped jauntily across the pitch holding aloft the little Jules Rimet trophy.

For England such moments are rare. They occur roughly once every 40 years!

Football remains the hottest property on television but it can never again achieve the kind of fantasy viewing figures of the halcyon TV years when England's World Cup win set an all-time British record of 32.3m viewers, or when Chelsea's FA Cup final replay win over Leeds in 1970 was pipped in that decade's ratings only by news of Apollo 13's splashdown.

It was English football's finest hour as the competition gripped hearts and minds from the opening goalless draw against Uruguay through to quarter-final victory over the 'animals' of Argentina, with Bobby Charlton's two semi-final goals against Portugal and the win over Germany with Geoff Hurst's hat-trick. For winning the World Cup, the England players were awarded a £1,000 bonus. Most of them were paying tax at 80 per cent and as Alan Ball said, 'I've told me dad never to tell me to vote Labour again.'

As Sir Geoff Hurst weighed up the merits of the '66 team against the present-day version, it was the lack of quality back-up which concerned him most. As he explained, 'There was certainly a lot of competition for my place with Jimmy Greaves and Roger Hunt around. There just isn't that same threat to the places of Rooney and Michael Owen. We did well in Portugal in Euro 2004 until Rooney was injured, but we went out with a whimper against a Brazilian side down to 10 men in 2002. The downside is the [lack of] strength in depth. More and more people are talking about it. The pundits, the journalists and I have been saying it for some time, particularly in the key areas. Players have to come on and make a contribution. It is not just 11 players who win a World Cup. Others have to be ready to play their part.

'In 1966, there was the feeling that the two Bobbys – Moore and Charlton – were permanent fixtures in the side, but that was not how they saw it. I talked a lot to Mooro about it and he said he always had the feeling with Alf Ramsey that a poor game would put your selection in jeopardy. Contrast that with Beckham's guarantee that, if he can walk, he will be chosen. But I also think he's done a good job as captain. The players clearly respect him and that is the most important aspect of being a leader. David can get frustrated when things are not going right and he could perhaps be a little more cool-headed but you know he cares and wants to win.'

Hurst scored a World Cup final hat-trick, the only man ever to do so, but his name would never have become legend, he would never have been knighted and he would never have spent the next 40 years as one of the game's ambassadors if it hadn't been for Alf Ramsey's decision not to select Jimmy Greaves for the final. Immortality awaited Hurst. It was to be perpetual misery for Greaves.

No one would have guessed before the 1966 tournament began that Greaves would not end it as first choice. It is an issue that will never leave him, although the passing of 40 years has put it into perspective.

The tragic loss of his four-month-old son, Jimmy Jr, to pneumonia in 1961 was followed by his brutally honest admission of his descent into alcoholism. 'Jimmy's death devastated my wife, Irene, and myself. It nearly drove us out of our minds. We were inconsolable. If ever there was a time in my life I wanted to call back yesterday, it was the day young Jimmy died. Though we had our daughter Lynn [to be followed in later years by Mitzi, Andy and Danny], our grief suffocated us. You grieve for the loss of any loved one but, when it is your own child, no words can describe that grief. As parents, you expect your children to outlive you and, when that doesn't happen, you become an empty shell. Jimmy was a beautiful boy and his time on this earth was all too brief. It kind of puts losing my World Cup winner's medal to Geoff into perspective, doesn't it? But you don't go through life without having some really bad times, and I've had some great times, too.'

For a man who famously surrendered his No.10 shirt through injury 10 days before the World Cup final, then sat in the back row of the Wembley grandstand to witness his replacement scoring a hat-trick in England's 4–2 defeat of West Germany, he remains remarkably cheery. Greaves admits he turned to booze to blot out the memory of this tragic episode. 'But there were other "reasons", too, like trying to cope with retirement, though I now see them not so much as reasons as excuses. That said, I have no excuse for what I became and for the hell I put Irene and the children through.'

When his onscreen sidekick Ian St John replied 'Bill Shankly' to the question 'Who was the biggest influence on your career?', Greaves quipped, 'Vladimir Smirnoff.'

Greaves was so influential with the Three Lions of England that, by the time of the '66 finals, he had scored 43 goals in 52 international appearances. After playing in the opening three group games against Uruguay, Mexico and France, he sat out the ill-tempered match against Argentina because of a leg injury and, although he was fit to play in the final, was omitted in favour of the in-form Hurst. 'It's something I honestly never think about until people like you bring it up. So, no, I'm not haunted by the memory or anything like that. Of course, it was a huge disappointment, but I knew in my heart Alf [Ramsey] would not change a winning team, so it was no great surprise when he read out Geoff's name.

'I'd always been one of the few players – and there were only two or three of us plus the manager – who really believed we were going to win the World Cup in '66. The rest of the country was highly sceptical. But I truly believed it was our destiny. What I didn't believe was that I wouldn't be a part of the final. It's unfortunate because, had it been now, I'd have probably been at least a substitute and been involved from the bench. What I found hard to take was to be one of the "forgotten XI" because we lived with the rest of the team in the hotel and trained together but after that you weren't involved.

'Even on the great day itself, we sat up in the back of the stand in our civvies; these days even the water-carrier would receive a medal, but there was no such honour for us. Actually, even Alf didn't get a medal; it was the 11 players on the pitch and those 11 players only. It was a very difficult period of my life, but I like to think I put it behind me pretty quickly because the following season I scored 37 goals for Spurs and we won the FA Cup, so it wasn't as though I was down in the dumps. But it was the chance of a lifetime and I lost it.'

As a goalscorer Greaves has few equals; he was the greatest

goalscorer of his generation. Greaves specialised in debut goals ever since making a scoring debut for Chelsea as a 17-year-old in 1957 under the unique managerial skills of Ted Drake.

Greaves stopped drinking a long time go; he would be dead if he hadn't. He has got his life together. He is a contented, genial man. 'When I'm allowed to, I play a bit of golf, do a bit of gardening, walk the dogs. I try very hard to make as much space for myself as possible. I live in a beautiful village, Little Baddow. Got 200 acres of woodland at the bottom of the road, golf course beyond. If you were parachuted into there, you wouldn't know you were in Essex – because everyone has a weird idea about Essex. I love it. Been there since 1981.'

Greaves does not blame football for his alcoholism. 'I'm not sure we had what you could call pressure. I look back at George Best, I look back at myself, same problem as George, same as Gazza. I think, in a funny way, why we succumbed was due to a lack of pressure. I think we missed football. I missed it. It wasn't the pressure of playing that made me start drinking heavily; it was the emptiness of not playing. And I think that's probably true of George and Paul. I don't think they felt that much pressure playing. They loved it too much.'

He cannot understand why players now complain about stress, about being tired, about their very well-paid lot. 'I'm sorry, I cannot see that earning fifty grand, a hundred grand a week, doing what you enjoy and can do naturally... I can't see where the pressures are.'

He sympathises to some extent with Wayne Rooney's situation, because he is young. And he knows how cruel the media can be if you slip up in public. 'But really, a professional footballer goes to work, doesn't have to be in until 10 o'clock, does a bit of training, usually gets fed, looked after, cosseted, doesn't have to travel anywhere under his own steam. If he's married, he's living in a big house somewhere; if he's not, he's got some nice-looking women around him probably. He can go to all the best places in the country, he's a celebrity, he's welcome anywhere. He trains three or four days a week and on Saturday he does what he loves to do: plays a game of football... How can that be pressure? Bollocks.'

And they could never get enough games into a week. 'Players being tired? No, I can't work that out. At Tottenham, Bill [Nicholson] used to organise the odd game midweek against non-league clubs, get two or three thousand people in, to give 'em a few quid – and most of us used to volunteer to play, rather than train. Training was a pain.

'It's all about money, I suppose. Clubs keep them away from everyone, with a Big Brother attitude. It's sad. We didn't have all those agents and minders. I mean, we earned good money, compared with the average wage-earner, but it wasn't fantastic, nowhere near what it is now. I think Wayne Rooney is a very good footballer. He's raw, but he's got lots of natural ability. The thing about Wayne is he doesn't look like Michael Owen or David Beckham, does he, unfortunately? I mean he hasn't got the glamour look. The press pick up on that. But he can play, and he should be allowed to. Like George and myself, and Gazza, he can do it without thinking.

'I'm not sure any of my type of player – including George and Gazza – could do that, stand up in front of a blackboard and teach others how to do it.

'I never listened to Bill Nick. Not at all. Bobby was the same, Bobby Moore. You're talking about the best defender we've ever had by a million miles. Bobby never thought about the game. Never listened to Alf. He didn't need advice. And, to be fair to Alf, I never heard Alf give him any.'

Greaves feels Sven-Goran Eriksson has overcomplicated his job as England manager. 'Sven picking all those players – he's just making excuses for himself. I don't see any sense in it. He's much better off identifying his best team and picking them every time. That would be my way of doing things, but I'd be called old-fashioned. To change 11, which he did in one game, crazy.'

For a while in the 1960s, Greaves was one of the finest footballers in the world. Greaves reviewed his club career: 'I had a good few years at Chelsea and joined them straight from school – they are very much part of my life as are Tottenham, and I have a great affection for both clubs in equal amounts. I had seven years at Chelsea and nine years at Tottenham. I had great times at Chelsea, and that club was very much part of my young life.'

Greaves The Goal rose through the Chelsea ranks and commanded media attention even before his debut in 1957. In his first full season in the youth side, he scored 114 goals. Chelsea had won the title for the first time in 1955, but the following season finished 16th! But along came Greaves to lessen the sense of frustration, scoring on his debut against Spurs on the opening day of the 1957–58 season, at the age of 17. He scored six in his first nine games, then took a break back in the reserves, before returning at Christmas to smash four past Portsmouth.

Chelsea's average gate rose by 7,000 as they flocked to see the new goalscoring sensation of his generation, with average attendances hitting 38,000 that season during which he struck 22 goals in 37 games including a hat-trick in the 3–2 win over Sheffield Wednesday. Yet, Chelsea finished only 11th.

Still the fans kept flocking to the Bridge, the gate rising by another 1,500 to nearly 40,000 average as Greaves amassed 37 goals in 47 games. He made his debut for England scoring in the 4–1 defeat in Peru. In his third season, he scored 30 in 42 games and Chelsea still finished 18th! By the time he was 21, Greaves had already collected a century of league goals, the youngest player ever to do so.

Greaves scored five goals in a game on three occasions. He collected 13 hat-tricks. In December 1959, he scored all five at Preston in a 5–4 win. He didn't stop scoring until his final game for the Blues at home to Nottingham Forest in 1961, when he scored four times; as the club knew he was leaving they made him captain for the day. He was carried from the pitch on supporters' shoulders. It ranks as one of the biggest errors in the club's history that he was allowed to leave for AC Milan.

Greaves scored 127 goals in 167 games. Unfortunately, the defence let in more goals than even Greaves could manage at the other end! In his final season, Chelsea finished 12th, having scored 98 goals only to concede 100. In that season, Greaves also scored 13 for his country, including two hat-tricks.

In his final season Greaves created a record of 41 league goals which, of course, still stands today. He only played 40 games. In consecutive home games he scored three against Manchester City, five against West Brom and two against Aston Villa. The end of the Greaves reign also marked the end of the Drake era.

At the time, the game was gripped by the battle to end the maximum wage of £20 a week and Milan moved in with fortunes to offer. Greaves scored regularly for AC Milan, but did not like the move and, despite Chelsea's attempts to buy him back, he moved to Spurs where he became part of the side that made history as the first British club to win a European trophy.

Greaves enjoyed two decades of goalscoring success, but also some astonishing lows, such as being left out of the World Cup-winning side in '66, and then steadily declined into alcoholism. He overcame his addiction to become a popular TV presenter – the *Saint & Greavise* show was the peak – and he continues to write an established newspaper column in the *Sun*.

Greaves would like an English manager for England, which hardly comes as a surprise to anyone who's read his excellent column in the *Sun* over the years, but he still thinks they can win the World Cup in 2006 – despite Sven. 'I think we've got an outstanding squad of players. Terry had a great side, Terry Venables in '96, and we should have won the European Championship. He was a great manager for England. Other than that side, I'd say this is the best team we've had in 30 years.'

# THREE

**HOW ENGLAND GOT THERE:**
THE GAMES THAT COUNTED

Sven-Goran Eriksson was proud and delighted when England marched on to Germany as Group Six winners, having beaten Poland and Austria in their final two qualifiers at Old Trafford to transform a doubting nation. Sven declared, 'We can win the World Cup. With a little bit of luck, I believe that we are one of six teams who can.'

The Swede's makeshift line-up against the Poles, who led the group going into the game, turned out to have 'saved the best until last' as they turned round a run of dismal performances by beating their main group rivals comfortably. Eriksson added, 'I think the fans can be convinced we can triumph from that performance. I am sure, with the players and squad we have, that we have a very good team and a good chance. Tonight it was very good, excellent. The lads did a very good job, won the group and I'm very pleased for the squad, the fans and the staff. We have lost very few points over 10 games. I am extremely happy.'

Stand-in skipper Michael Owen gave England a 43rd-minute lead, only for the Poles to level on the stroke of half-time with a volley from Tomasz Frankowski – their one real strike on goal. But then Frank Lampard produced a stunning winning volley 10 minutes from time to send the 65,000 fans at Old Trafford home with renewed belief in the England team and their chances of World Cup glory.

Wayne Rooney also added some magic on a night England fans were able to forget previous dire displays against the likes of Denmark and Northern Ireland. Rookies Shaun Wright-Phillips, in for suspended skipper David Beckham, and Ledley King also added a breath of fresh air. Eriksson said, 'In Wayne Rooney we are talking about a young talent of 19 with 27 caps. Incredible. But he is not just a talent, he is now a world-class player. There were players coming in here who don't normally play for England and they did a great job. Ledley King was excellent and so was Wright-Phillips in the first half. But he got a bad knock and was not 100 per cent right, so I had to take him off.'

England had actually qualified a few days before when they defeated Austria, and then, a few hours later, Holland's 2–0 win over the Czech Republic confirmed they would at least finish as one of the best runners-up. Eriksson observed, 'We got the result of the Holland game when we were sitting and eating. The players, staff and myself were delighted. We've qualified three or four days before we thought we would. I'm very excited. The big aim for the last two years has been to qualify for the World Cup. There has been a lot of discussion about whether England were going or not – especially after the Northern Ireland game. Our critics started to say maybe not. Now the big aim is to have our preparation right for the World Cup. We will play better and be much better in Germany next summer. If we have all the players fit, I'm very, very confident. I've said for two years that we would qualify and have a very good World Cup. I will go on saying it. But, to win it, we must play better than we have done this season.'

BBC pundits and ex-England captains Alan Shearer and Gary

Lineker had accused Sven's players of lacking passion. Eriksson blasted, 'Those names who were talking about the game, I don't agree with them at all. Shearer has his opinion, but I don't share it. There were far more positives than negatives from this game. I think the passion was there. We also worked very well as a team after David Beckham was sent off. I can't agree with them. England are one of the four or five teams that can win the World Cup. If we're lucky with few or no injuries, we can do it.'

Beckham walked up the ramp through the players' tunnel and towards the team bus, looking drained, a man put through the emotional wringer. Even by the standards of the crazy world he inhabits, it had been a strange week. He called it 'one of the worst of my life', referring to concerns over the health of his three-year-old son, Romeo.

Though it was to end in smiles a few hours later when he and his England team-mates received confirmation that their place in this year's World Cup finals was secure, he did not need the indignity of a red card against Austria. Perversely, he had left the field to a standing ovation, but results – the one in Prague as well as the one in Manchester – meant his indiscretions would prove far less costly than the one in St Etienne five long years before, when he was sent off for kicking Argentina's Diego Simeone at France 98.

He mustered a smile and said, 'We'll see,' when asked if he feared the reaction to his second red card for England might be as extreme as the first. Though one man urged the media at Old Trafford to 'bury him', it seemed that this time Beckham was fortunate that the tide of public and media opinion, not to mention their sympathy, was with him.

Beckham was irresponsible to chase after Andreas Ibertsberger less than a minute after his first booking, even if contact with his opponent seemed to be minimal on both occasions. His act of petulance left England to play the final half-hour with 10 men in a match they could not afford to draw. If they had failed to hold on to their lead, he would unquestionably have been to blame, his guilt doubled by suspension for what would have been a crucial final match against Poland. But, in the end, recriminations were not needed. It is ironic that Beckham showed such a lack of self-control after lecturing Wayne Rooney on the subject in Belfast a month earlier, but he denied that this was a case of the red mist descending. 'It wasn't that at all,' he said. 'I was disappointed to get the first yellow card because I knew I was out of the next game, but, even with the second challenge, I've got the ball. There are other people who are saying on the television I shouldn't be doing things like that, but every player does that.'

Beckham talked of having 'some history' with the referee, Luis Medina Cantalejo, who sent him off in a Copa del Rey match between Real Madrid and Valencia the previous season, and showed his contempt by offering a sarcastic handshake to Ibertsberger, who suggested his opponent had simply 'lost his temper and got a bit angry'. Beckham, though, resisted the temptation to blame either of them and tried instead to find positives to draw on. This proved easier at the end of the evening, by which time England had qualified and he was able to celebrate with his family, including Romeo, who was now out of hospital after suffering convulsions during the week. 'It's turned into a nice celebration because we can all enjoy the night and have a bit of fun,' he said. 'When I woke up this morning, I was hoping we could qualify, but it's been a long rollercoaster of a day for me personally. I'm happy because we're there. It's been a tough week for the whole family – it's worrying when your son goes into hospital twice in three days. It makes it very hard to concentrate on anything else, but he is on medication now and is feeling a lot better. What a day, what a week really. But it's ended on a high.'

## GAME 1
# 4 SEPTEMBER 2004
### AUSTRIA 2, ENGLAND 2 (VIENNA)

The Faria Alam scandal and Mark Palios's resignation as chief executive of the Football Association, dictated the mood as Sven-Goran Eriksson, the affair's great survivor, launched his third qualification campaign for a major tournament, little knowing his own departure was in fact imminent. While Soho Square was still recovering from one of its most bitter internal power struggles, Eriksson's side contrived to increase the pressure on their manager by squandering a two-goal lead in Vienna. When Andreas Ivanschitz's shot went straight through him for the equaliser, the blame fell upon David James, who has not played in a competitive international since. That was not the only aspect of the game that seemed to go wrong – Ashley Cole and Wayne Bridge's partnership down the left no longer looked viable. There was confusion when substitutions were made, with Bridge coming off instead of the injured Steven Gerrard, and suddenly Eriksson was under pressure again. Most of all, the game signalled the return of the 'Untouchables' theory – that there were players in Eriksson's side who would be selected regardless of form, an accusation that has plagued the Swede ever since.

Earlier, everything looked to be going to plan as Gerrard looped in a belter midway through the second half, after comical defending had left Lampard with an open goal from Beckham's direction-switching free-kick. England should have coasted home against supine opponents even when substitute Roland Kollmann cracked a free-kick over the wall and beyond the slow-moving James. But then the keeper made the mother of all cock-ups to let Andreas Ivanschitz's weak deflected shot squirm under his body and roll over the line.

This was the first time England had squandered a two-goal lead since the 3–2 defeat by Portugal at Euro 2000. Gary Neville, Beckham and Michael Owen were all survivors of that.

**Goals**: Lampard (24) 0–1; Gerrard (63) 0–2; Kollmann (70) 1–2; Ivanschitz (73) 2–2

**England**: James; Neville, Terry, King, A Cole; Beckham, Gerrard (Carragher, 82), Lampard, Bridge (J Cole, 84); Smith (Defoe, 76), Owen.

**Subs not used**: Robinson, Dyer, Wright-Phillips, Vassell

**Booked**: Pogatetz; Beckham

**Man of the Match**: Lampard

Sven said, 'I think the worst thing I could do at this moment is to panic, changing five players for Wednesday, taking out Owen, Beckham or whoever else. I will not panic. I will stick to more or less the same formation.'

### GAME 2
# 8 SEPTEMBER 2004
## POLAND 1, ENGLAND 2 (KATOWICE)

Sven swung the axe, chopping James and Alan Smith and bringing in Spurs duo Paul Robinson and Jermain Defoe. Neither let him down, with Defoe marking his first England start with a sweet turn and finish to put Eriksson's side ahead.

The ghosts of Katowice, where Alf Ramsey experienced the beginning of the end in 1973, threatened to haunt their modern-day successors when Zurawski gave Robinson no chance and England had to dig deep. While Owen claimed the final touch to Ashley Cole's low cross, the own goal was rightly credited to Glowacki.

England extended their unbeaten run against the Poles to 13 games and 31 years. Defoe looked, for one half at least, like a natural England striker. Given the ball, he swivelled in the area and beat Jerzy Dudek from close range, although this match was famous for the *omerta* the players had agreed to keep after what they perceived as unjustifiably harsh media treatment following the defeat to Austria. It was a shame the England players spoiled things by their petulant silent protest afterwards.

This was Defoe's first goal for England, and Robinson's first start, but the newcomers were not permitted to do anything more than wave at reporters who faced an unprecedented media blackout from the squad. Sad really because it was a gritty performance against a team who came back after half-time with an equaliser.

England lost Gary Neville after 31 minutes to a thigh injury and got their winner when Ashley Cole's cross was turned in at the near post by Arkadiusz Glowacki. Their complaints about the press coverage centred on the criticism of James. Yet, by all accounts, the senior players, although sympathetic to the veteran goalkeeper, agreed it was time for him to go.

---

**Goals**: Defoe (37) 0–1; Zurawski (48) 1–1; Glowacki og (58) 1–2
**England**: Robinson; Neville (Carragher, 32), Terry, King, A Cole; Beckham, Lampard, Gerrard, Bridge; Defoe (Dyer, 87), Owen.
**Subs not used**: James, Wright-Phillips, Smith, Vassell
**Booked**: Glowacki, Kukielka; Owen
**Man of the Match**: Defoe

---

Sven said, 'I can understand it [the media blackout after criticism of David James]. There should be a limit to the criticism of individual players. They don't agree with it and are trying to defend the group.'

### GAME 3
## 9 OCTOBER 2004
### ENGLAND 2, WALES 0 (OLD TRAFFORD)

Back on track, back on course and back with a bang for Beckham as he hogged the headlines for the right and wrong reasons.

Owen again tried and failed to claim a goal, this time Lampard's early strike, and, with Wales weak and woeful, England were always in command with the fit again Wayne Rooney a constant menace. Beckham sealed victory with a beauty of a curler into the top corner, but then lost his head with two stupid challenges on full-back Ben Thatcher. Getting booked and suspended was bad enough, but boasting that he 'had the brains' to do it deliberately saw FIFA president Sepp Blatter leading the attack dogs against him.

This was the first home game against the Welsh in 21 years. It was also Beckham's first goal in open play since Macedonia, October 2002 and marked the return of Rooney, possibly in the role he should always play for England – behind the two strikers. Defoe's goal against Poland – and Gerrard's injury – meant that Eriksson played the Tottenham striker in a 4-3-3 formation, with Nicky Butt as holding midfielder. The teenager, playing for England for the first time since breaking that metatarsal at Euro 2004, was as good as Wales were poor.

It should have been straightforward. England looked solid and Lampard scored after four minutes, but Beckham intervened with his own sub-plot. Soon after he scored with a brilliant, swooping shot from the left side of the box, Beckham cracked a rib in a challenge with Ben Thatcher – and then he sought retribution, picking up a booking which ruled him out of the visit to Azerbaijan. The England captain's temper was questioned once again, but the real drama did not unfold until his team-mates were in Baku.

---

**Goals**: Lampard (4) 1–0; Beckham (76) 2–0
**England**: Robinson; G Neville, Campbell, Ferdinand, A Cole; Beckham (Hargreaves, 85), Butt, Lampard; Defoe (Smith, 70), Owen, Rooney (King, 86).
**Subs not used**: James, Terry, J Cole, Wright-Phillips
**Booked**: Beckham; Pembridge
**Man of the Match**: Rooney

Sven said, 'It wasn't easy. Wales defended very well. They didn't let our full-backs play at all. They went back with a lot of players and closed all the spaces. I think we did a good professional performance. We won and that was fair.'

**GAME 4**

## 13 OCTOBER 2004

**AZERBAIJAN 0, ENGLAND 1 (BAKU)**

The Black Sea city of Baku is the furthest from home England have ever played a World Cup qualifier. It was Jermaine Jenas's first and only competitive start to date.

As the team prepared in Azerbaijan – with a horrendous evening's rain forecast for the evening of the match – Beckham went seriously off message by calling up a reporter to tell him that he had not been foolish in picking up the Thatcher booking in the game against Wales: he had done it on purpose. Beckham claimed that, knowing the rib injury would rule him out of the Azerbaijan game anyway, he 'took a yellow' to clear his suspension.

Damned for his honesty, the criticism that Beckham took for admitting his motives reached a ludicrous pitch. Geoff Hurst hyperventilated about how aghast Sir Alf Ramsey would have been about the whole affair, although no one was sure what the former England manager had to do with it. Those of a less hysterical disposition pointed out that this was common practice in football.

Beckham picked a good game to miss – torrential rain, a howling gale and a terrible pitch made any sort of normal football impossible.

Jermaine Jenas was handed Beckham's No.7 shirt as well as his slot on the right as Eriksson stuck with the front trio of Rooney, Defoe and stand-in skipper Owen.

It was Owen who claimed the vital goal, rising in the box to trickle home a header from Ashley Cole's cross and cast aside the despondency of his early struggles to make an impact for Real Madrid.

After that, it was a case of making sure the defence stayed as watertight as possible in the conditions. Job achieved, England were in pole position.

---

**Goal**: Owen (22) 0–1

**England**: Robinson; G Neville, Ferdinand, Campbell, A Cole; Butt, Jenas (Wright-Phillips, 72), Lampard; Rooney (J Cole, 85), Owen, Defoe (Smith, 55). **Subs not used**: King, James, Terry, Hargreaves

**Booked**: Gulivev, Sadygov; Butt, Cole, Rooney

**Man of the Match**: Owen

---

Sven said, 'It was difficult to play good football in these conditions because the wind was blowing in all directions. We did a very professional job, and that means in our last two games we have got six points and did not concede a goal. This is very good. I would blame the conditions for the fact we didn't kill the game off.'

## GAME 5
# 26 MARCH 2005
### ENGLAND 4, NORTHERN IRELAND 0 (OLD TRAFFORD)

Two disastrous performances in friendlies – against Spain and the Netherlands – preceded Eriksson's 50th match in charge of England. After Rooney had to be substituted at the Bernabeu Stadium the previous November, so he wouldn't be sent off, the teenager was the saviour for Eriksson once again at Old Trafford.

The game was not as easy as the scoreline suggests, but it was very comfortable in the end once Joe Cole broke the deadlock straight after half-time.

Owen stole the second off Lampard's toe and a fabulous Rooney run ended in a Chris Baird own goal as the Old Trafford crowd bayed for more. Lampard provided it, claiming another deflected strike and, with England in total command, it could have been more as Owen closed to within one goal of Lineker's England competitive record of 22.

To Lawrie Sanchez's side, Rooney was untameable – he bulldozed past two defenders to cross the ball for Chris Baird's own goal. At the very least, Eriksson had won this landmark game, but this time there was no hint of what lay in wait for England at Windsor Park six months ahead.

---

**Goals**: J Cole (47) 1–0; Owen (51) 2–0; Baird og (53) 3–0; Lampard (62) 4–0
**England**: Robinson; G Neville, Ferdinand, Terry, A Cole; Beckham (Dyer, 72), Lampard, Gerrard (Hargreaves, 73), J Cole; Rooney (Defoe, 80), Owen. **Subs not used**: James, Carragher, King, Heskey
**Booked**: Johnson
**Man of the Match**: Rooney

---

Sven said, 'He [Joe Cole] can be the answer if he carries on like this. He was excellent and I don't think he lost the ball in a stupid way once, which he has before. He has finally learned that football is not only about making tricks. It is about choosing when to do it and when not to.'

### GAME 6
## 30 MARCH 2005
### ENGLAND 2, AZERBAIJAN 0 (ST JAMES' PARK)

England were unchanged for the first time in the campaign. Beckham's booking was his 12th on international duty – only Paul Ince (15) has picked up more than the skipper.

After four goals against the Irish, expectations were for double figures against a side smashed for eight by the Poles four days earlier but instead England stuttered. Owen had a night to forget, missing a hatful of chances and picking up a booking that ruled him out of the game in Cardiff.

It was not until six minutes into the second period that Gerrard's volley bounced its way over the line to ease the tensions that were beginning to accumulate. Then Beckham, timing his run from halfway to perfection, killed it off with the second.

Beforehand, it all looked like a simple stroll down the road to Germany. It turned out not to be the avalanche of goals that the St James' Park crowd had hoped for, but, typically for England, not enough about this performance was poor enough to invite outright condemnation. They played just about well enough to eclipse an unremarkable team and Beckham's goal was a source of relief for the England captain, who took a long ball from Lampard on his chest just after the hour and ran in on goal to score.

The match was only really memorable for a rant at Michael Owen from Azerbaijan coach – and Brazil's 1970 World Cup-winning captain – Carlos Alberto, which was as baffling as it was unexpected. Alberto claimed he had read that Owen had promised to score five against Azerbaijan – he never did – and was outraged. So much so that he described England's current highest goalscorer as a 'midget'.

---

**Goals**: Gerrard (51) 1–0; Beckham (62) 2–0
**England**: Robinson; G Neville, Ferdinand (King, 77), Terry, A Cole; Beckham (Defoe, 84), Gerrard, Lampard, J Cole; Rooney (Dyer, 77), Owen. **Subs not used**: Carragher, James, Jenas, Heskey
**Booked**: Beckham, Owen; Vugar, Guliyev
**Man of the Match**: Rooney

---

Sven said, 'We created a lot of chances, but we were patient and didn't lose confidence, which is the sign of a mature team. I don't know how many goals we could have scored, but we're happy to win.'

## GAME 7
# 3 SEPTEMBER 2005
### WALES 0, ENGLAND 1 (MILLENNIUM STADIUM)

A sixth straight competitive win represented England's best run since 1985 under Bobby Robson as England partially erased the memory of their battering in Denmark two weeks earlier, but all the problems were still there.

Beckham played as the 'quarterback' in a 4-5-1 formation that left lone striker Rooney isolated, struggling to bring Lampard and Gerrard into the game. Only Robinson's Banks-like save from John Hartson's first-half header kept England on terms at the break. Even Cole's deflected opener at the start of the second half failed to bring the confidence back.

Rooney was denied by the outstanding Danny Coyne, but the longer it went on, the more pressure England were under, leaving John Toshack to predict they might well end up behind the Poles. The seeds of England's demise against Northern Ireland were sown in Cardiff. The 4-5-1 formation was implemented in order to accommodate Joe Cole and Shaun Wright-Phillips as well as Beckham, Lampard and Gerrard, who had all been consulted by Eriksson about what line-up they should play. The players did not want Defoe in the side – he had been ineffective in a dreadful 4–1 friendly defeat by Denmark in Copenhagen the previous month.

In attack, only Rooney's endless adaptability made the 4-5-1 formation look effective – he can, of course, make any role work. Beckham was much more comfortable in the holding midfield role, although the same could not be said of those around him. There was mild criticism of Lampard from Eriksson – uncharacteristic of him – but most of all the England coach was desperate to deny suggestions that he was giving in to player power in the selection of his team.

**Goal**: J Cole (53) 0–1

**England**: Robinson; Young, Carragher, Ferdinand, A Cole; Beckham, Lampard, Gerrard (Richardson, 84), Wright-Phillips (Defoe, 67), J Cole (Hargreaves, 76); Rooney. **Subs not used**: Upson, Kirkland, Neville, Bent

**Booked**: Hartson

**Man of the Match**: Beckham

Sven said, 'I think the midfield, for most of the game, was pretty solid. We're professionals and, if you're asked to play in different positions and different styles, you should be able to do it.'

## GAME 8
# 7 SEPTEMBER 2005
### NORTHERN IRELAND 1, ENGLAND 0 (WINDSOR PARK)

This was Eriksson's first defeat in 22 qualifiers and England's first loss in Belfast since 1927. It was the ultimate indignity for Eriksson and his shell-shocked team as they slumped to arguably the worst defeat since the 1–0 World Cup humiliation by the USA in 1950.

Rooney was a liability in waiting. He was booked and came so close to being sent off as England descended into a shapeless, hopeless rabble. Beckham's first-half free-kick hit the bar with Maik Taylor a spectator, but from then on Ireland's sheer spirit found Eriksson's complacent side fractious and without thought.

Even so, England would probably have got away with a point only for Rio Ferdinand's concentration to drop and play David Healy onside for the goal that guarantees the winger will never have to buy a drink in Ulster for the rest of his life. Eriksson admitted, 'It was a disaster.' He was right.

It was the darkest day of Eriksson's regime and one of the most humiliating defeats in the 143-year history of the FA. Looking for what had gone wrong, it seemed that every one of England's weaknesses showed up that night at Windsor Park. Rooney lost his temper and Owen was isolated in the 4-5-1 formation, while Ferdinand displayed one of his least assured performances against a team below Rwanda in the FIFA rankings. Beckham, in the holding midfield role, was not disastrous but the long balls that he swept forward rendered the roles of Gerrard and Lampard redundant. They simply could not keep up with the attacks he launched.

As things fell apart, Eriksson looked lost on the touchline – a man seemingly without anger but also without authority. He took off Lampard and brought on Owen Hargreaves and, by then, with their team a goal down, the nation realised that this was far from a World Cup-winning side. David Healy's fine finish ensured Eriksson's first defeat in a qualifying game for a major tournament. He could not afford another.

---

**Goal**: Healy (74) 1–0
**England**: Robinson; Young, Ferdinand, Carragher, A Cole; Wright-Phillips (J Cole, 54), Lampard (Hargreaves, 80), Beckham, Gerrard (Defoe, 75), Rooney; Owen. **Subs not used**: Upson, Kirkland, Neville, Bent
**Booked**: Baird, Capaldi, Johnson; Rooney
**Man of the Match**: Robinson

---

Sven said, 'If anyone doubts I am in charge of this team, they are badly wrong. My relationship with David Beckham is very good. That is important, he is the captain. But if people think he has other favours, they are absolutely wrong.'

### GAME 9
# 8 OCTOBER 2005
## ENGLAND 1, AUSTRIA 0 (OLD TRAFFORD)

Beckham's decision to hand the spot-kick duties to Lampard was vindicated when the Chelsea midfielder drilled home after Owen was held in the box and then the striker was denied another cast-iron penalty soon after. But England failed to turn their advantage into goals and, when Beckham became the first England captain to be sent off after three rash challenges in as many minutes, it became a backs-to-the-wall exercise.

The 10 men held on in a nervy finish at Old Trafford, although there were no celebrations – until the news came in from Wenceslas Square. Beckham was the first England skipper to be dismissed – although Ray Wilkins had Bryan Robson's armband on in 1986. Beckham also became the first player to be sent off twice in an England shirt, yet he still saw his side reach the World Cup finals after Holland's 2–0 victory in Prague rendered Wednesday's final game against Poland irrelevant.

Both teams at the top of Group Six had qualified, one as winners and the other as one of the two best runners-up. The players were dining at the Lowry Hotel in Manchester when news of their place in Germany was confirmed. The important bottom line was that three hard-earned points against Austria courtesy of a Frank Lampard penalty had put them through. 'It's the best we've played this season, but I know we can play a lot better,' observed Eriksson. Tough, but with Wayne Rooney, Ashley Cole and Gary Neville to come back there was no reason for pessimism. Tournament form tends to bear little relation to the struggles involved in qualifying, as anyone who watched Brazil and Germany all the way through the last World Cup cycle would confirm.

As for the sending off, Beckham was unlucky in that Andreas Ibertsberger exaggerated the extent of the contact when brought down on the edge of the England area, and a different referee might even have penalised a theatrical dive. Yet Beckham did contact man and not ball, and his second yellow card came barely two minutes later. 'I thought both bookings were harsh. David was unlucky twice,' Eriksson said, stopping short of blaming the referee.

For this game, England reverted to 4-4-4-2 with Beckham back on the wing. Had Michael Owen's finishing been anywhere near its usual standard, England could have been two or three goals to the good before Beckham's removal. Peter Crouch showed his capabilities, linking well and playing some clever ground passes. Crouch's height seems to invite cliches, but he was only standing in for the suspended Rooney, and he poses an entirely different set of questions for defences. This is a Plan B that might work. For England's Plan A to work, Beckham and Rooney need to be on top form.

**Goals**: Lampard (25) 1
**England**: Robinson; Young, Terry, Campbell (Ferdinand, 64), Carragher; Beckham, Gerrard, Lampard, J Cole (King, 61); Crouch, Owen (Richardson, 81). **Subs not used**: Kirkland, Wright-Phillips, Bent, Defoe
**Sent off**: Beckham (two cautions)
**Booked**: J Cole, Beckham; Ivanschitz, Schopp, Kiesenebner
**Man of the Match**: Lampard

Sven said, 'I think in the second half we defended brilliantly, we were all together and fighting. I don't think they had a chance to score in the second half. I thought the sending off was harsh. We kept the same formation after David was sent off, and we let Michael Owen drop a little bit. As a performance I think we played very well.'

**GAME 10**
# 12 OCTOBER 2005
**ENGLAND 2, POLAND 1**

Lampard sent England through to the World Cup finals at the top of Group Six with a brilliant winner. He struck a superb volley 10 minutes from time to give a vastly improved, Rooney-inspired

England the victory they deserved. 'We've answered a few questions,' said the Chelsea midfielder. 'We wanted to play with a lot of pace and we did.'

Michael Owen opened the scoring to equal Gary Lineker's England record of 22 competitive goals. The entire mood surrounding Eriksson and his team changed as Owen scored with the instinctive flick. Behind him, Ledley King proved that England are a better side with a holding midfielder, the Spurs captain bringing focus and shape to the middle of the park, the anchor that gave Lampard the freedom which brought his deserved late winner.

Like King, replacing the injured Gerrard, Wright-Phillips stepped into the absent Beckham's boots. At the heart of everything, Rooney dazzled. While Eriksson bristled at the criticism, the fans and the country saw what they had been waiting for, an excellent display of football. Rooney demonstrated his ability to beat players and even to stay on the right side of referee Kim Milton Nielsen.

It took until two minutes before the break for England to go in front. The goal came, when Terry won the fight for Lampard's corner. Cole, 18 yards out, drilled the ball goalwards and Owen's clever touch produced a poacher's goal. Then disaster struck. Rio Ferdinand and Luke Young were sucked to the ball and that left substitute Tomasz Frankowski with the space to ram a volley past Paul Robinson.

England, though, stepped up the pace after the break and Rooney went close when he turned Ferdinand's downward header over the bar. Cole had an effort disallowed for offside and Owen had a header well saved. By this stage, Peter Crouch had come on – his arrival was met by a chorus of jeers which were followed by guilty applause soon afterwards – but, when the keeper denied Owen and then kept out Young's deflected cross, it looked like England would be frustrated.

Finally Crouch collected the ball in his own six-yard box and, when the ball reached the other end of the pitch, Lampard fed Cole and kept going as the ball was transferred to Owen whose chip was met by a thunderous Lampard volley.

Eriksson insisted England were world-beaters after an 'absolutely excellent' performance from a team missing the suspended Beckham, the injured Gerrard, Ashley Cole and Gary Neville, and which raised expectations among the England faithful.

'I am very pleased for the players and the fans,' said Eriksson. 'We did a good job on Saturday and went on to do another good job today. We have won the group and that is excellent. You can say what you like but this is the best squad and the best team we have ever had.'

---

**Goals**: Owen (43) 1–0; Frankowski (45) 1–1; Lampard (80) 2–1
**England**: Robinson; Young, Ferdinand, Terry, Carragher; King; Wright-Phillips (Crouch, 67), Lampard, J Cole (Smith, 86); Rooney; Owen (Jenas, 83). **Subs not used**: P Neville, Kirkland, Bent, Defoe
**Booked**: Baszczynski, Sobolewski
**Man of the Match**: Rooney

---

Sven said, 'When we play like this then there are very few teams that can cope with us. This was excellent. I'm very, very happy for the fans. They travelled to Denmark, they travelled to Northern Ireland and I know they were as disappointed as we were, but here we are after two very good performances. I am looking forward to playing in Germany.'

# FOUR

**THE EXPERTS:**

YES, ENGLAND CAN WIN... THIS TIME

Jose Mourinho believes Sven-Goran Eriksson's side – four Chelsea players were included in the starting line-up that faced Poland, a match that finished with John Terry as captain – can win the World Cup.

Suggestions that he might want to manage the national team in the future have infuriated him, but the strong Chelsea element in Eriksson's team has inevitably drawn him into the debate. 'I think England can [win the World Cup],' Mourinho said. 'I think it will be a World Cup where it will be very difficult to spot a team much better than all the others. I don't see a team as good as France when they won the World Cup. I see teams on the same level. I think the difference is not about the quality of the team, it's about the future after the World Cup. You look at Germany and the Netherlands – when this World Cup is finished, they have a team for the next World Cup. Then look at Portugal, France, England, almost every team especially in Europe – they have the same team they had in Euro 2004; they change one of the names but the players are very similar. But when the World Cup is finished, they will say, "We need a new team for the next World Cup.'"

Frank Lampard, John Terry, Shaun Wright-Phillips and Joe Cole will all be central to Eriksson's plans, but Mourinho warned his players that any suggestion they were saving themselves for the World Cup would be heavily punished by their manager. 'The players know me well. We have worked together enough for them to know me well,' he said. 'And, when I have just a little, very little feeling they are not thinking about Chelsea, they know they have a problem because they are not playing for Chelsea. They know me so I don't have this kind of fear. I'd love to have 11 [players in the national team]. You always want to get the best from your players. I want all my players to be successful and play for their countries and win competitions.'

Diego Maradona and Ossie Ardiles are footballing legends who back Wayne Rooney and Steven Gerrard to lead England to World Cup glory. Maradona inspired Argentina to a World Cup triumph in 1986, while former Tottenham favourite Ardiles masterminded his country's triumph eight years earlier.

'England have some really great players like Beckham, Owen, Gerrard and Ferdinand and, for me, they have the best chance of all the European teams at next summer's finals,' said Maradona. 'But Wayne Rooney is the English player with the most natural talent and desire. His temperament is a positive, not a negative. It will make him fight on the field and conquer adversity. You can't be a saint and still be successful in football. It's a tough, physical game and nobody gives you anything for free.'

Ardiles expects Rooney to make a major impact in Germany, but he picked out Liverpool skipper Gerrard as the man to watch. 'England will be a force because defensively they are strong thanks to them having Sol Campbell, John Terry and Rio Ferdinand – I am sure Rio will come good for the World Cup,' said Ardiles.

'In midfield England are very strong too, with Gerrard who is my favourite player. I like him very much and, if there is one player I would have liked to have played alongside, then it would be him. I like everything about him – he is a winner. He can go forward; he can hold. He scores goals. He has everything. Frank Lampard is another one; he seems to be getting better all the time and he has similar attributes to Gerrard. Then there is Rooney, who was wonderful at the last European Championship and people will expect a lot from him. If Michael Owen can stay free of injury, then he can be really hot, too. If England have a weakness, then maybe it is the fact they don't have a holding midfielder in the mould of Claude Makelele.'

Former England boss Glenn Hoddle also believes Wayne Rooney can inspire his team-mates at the World Cup in the same way Diego Maradona did when Argentina won the trophy in 1986. Rooney has been tipped to be one of the stars of this year's finals in Germany, with Hoddle insisting the Manchester United striker needs to be on top form if England are to take the crown from favourites Brazil. Hoddle said, 'Rooney's an extra-special player. What he does is raise the standard, that's what Platini did for France and Maradona for Argentina. If you look at every team to win the World Cup, they have an extra-special player who can lift the team. We had Bobby Charlton in 1966, a player who could lift us to another level.'

Rooney returned from suspension for England's final qualifying game, the youngster starring in an impressive 2–1 win over Poland. 'It doesn't matter if he plays against Brazil or anyone else,' Hoddle added on BBC Radio Five Live. 'When he plays, other players score and find space because defenders are on him. It's always good to have a player like that.'

When asked if England can win the World Cup, Hoddle said, 'Personally, [I think] they could – but, if you pushed me, I think Brazil will win. There's a good chance, though, we'll have a good World Cup.'

With his 22nd competitive international goal against Poland in the final qualifier at Old Trafford which helped England to top their group, Michael Owen equalled Gary Lineker's record. Owen insists it is only a question of time, however, before Rooney beats them both. When Rooney's goal against Macedonia in September 2003 made him England's youngest-ever scorer, he asked his team-mates to sign a photo of the momentous strike. Owen infamously wrote, 'That's another of my records you've taken, Ugly A\*\*e!' The former Liverpool and Real Madrid hitman later admitted, 'I'd better get used to Wayne rewriting history.'

Owen, 25, was the Premiership's youngest scorer for five years until Rooney's wonder strike against Arsenal in 2002. And he was also England's youngest international in the modern era until Rooney burst on to the scene against Australia in February 2003, aged 17 years 111 days. Owen added, 'Wayne came into the England team at an even younger age than I did. If you play well and keep your form, you are going to play a lot of games for your country. And, with the ability Wayne has, that means many more goals and many more records to be broken.'

Owen is backing the teenage phenomenon to take the World Cup by storm after lighting up Euro 2004 in Portugal. 'You could see the lift Wayne gave to the whole team and he would scare any defence in the world when he plays like that. He is a top player who really enjoys playing in that role just behind me. I just try to give him as much room as possible because he only needs half a yard to make things happen. Everyone saw what he did at Euro 2004 and, with two more years' experience, hopefully he'll be even more potent next summer in Germany. It was a big, big blow when Wayne was injured and had to go off in that quarter-final against Portugal at a time when we were playing really well. I was feeling really sharp that day and Wayne was on top form. We created a lot of chances and then he got injured and everything changed. You can never legislate for a blow like that and it's why you can never predict with great certainty who is going to do well at these tournaments. Because you only need one dodgy sending-off or an injury to a big player like Wayne and it can really break your stride. But, if England can keep everyone fit towards the end of the season, I'd be confident of our squad going to Germany and doing very well.'

Owen believes the morale-boosting 2–1 victory over the Poles will be a turning point for Eriksson's side after unconvincing displays in their four previous games. 'We've been as disappointed as anyone with some of our performances this season, but I'm sure the fans are back on our side now. You can't blame the opposition but the fact is we played four games against teams who regard a draw against England as a fantastic result. Even at home they string five across the midfield and get everyone behind the ball. No one likes it when a team is playing for a boring 0–0 draw, so it was much more enjoyable because Poland came out and tried to play. When the opposition do that, it allows us to show what a good team we can be. It was an English performance if you like, with lots of energy and tackles, lots of running and plenty of attacks.'

Owen was still readjusting to the pace of the Premiership following his £16m move to Tyneside from Real Madrid, so he was delighted to be back in the groove for England. His 33rd goal in 74 games collected against Poland left him fourth in the list of all-time England scorers behind Bobby Charlton, Gary Lineker and Jimmy Greaves.

And equalling Lineker's record for goals in competitive matches was a moment for Owen to savour. He said, 'Gary was probably my biggest hero as a kid, so it's a nice feeling to match his achievement.'

The trouble is, it won't last for long with Rooney around. The whizzkid himself said, 'I've not scored a competitive goal [for England] since Euro 2004 – I'm storing them up for next summer's World Cup. It's a massive tournament for me and I want to go there and show I can score goals at that level.' Rooney was top scorer at the European Championships with four, but he limped out of the event with a broken foot as England lost a quarter-final shoot-out to Portugal.

Owen is sure England are going to Germany with a squad

loaded with match-winners; they are not just a one-man team. 'I can see why people want Wayne to be England's answer to Ronaldino, but I would like to think we have a few players in that mould. Frank Lampard has proved he can come up with important goals. Then there's Steven Gerrard and, of course, we have also got Wayne. That's the great thing about this England team – you look all over the pitch and we have plenty of players who can become match-winners. All the players realise that Wayne is one of our gems, but when you go to the World Cup you need more than one. I believe we have a few players capable of delivering. I love working with Wayne and I think we have a decent understanding. He doesn't really enjoy getting in behind the last man by running in behind defenders, but that is one of my strengths. I try to drag defenders back towards their own goal and that gives Wayne time and space to do the things he is so good at. We complement each other really well.'

Tottenham's Dutch coach Martin Jol is adamant that England will be contenders for World Cup glory and says Sven-Goran Eriksson's men are better than his home nation. Holland rendered England's final group game against Poland something of an anti-climax following their victory over the Czech Republic. It meant England had already qualified for the finals in Germany this summer, although England made doubly certain by beating the Poles 2–1 at Old Trafford to finish top of their group. Eriksson and his side had been heavily criticised during their qualifying campaign, particularly after the shock 1–0 defeat at the hands of Northern Ireland, but the manner of their victory over Poland has put the smile back on the faces of the nation.

Now Jol believes Eriksson's side will be major contenders for success in Germany and considers that they are better than the current Dutch side – a team which had won 10 out of their last 12 internationals when Jol declared, 'They are still moaning in Holland because we had two draws against Macedonia. But that is good. If you want to create top players, you have to be very critical and honest and that is a good mentality. But you can only judge how good they are against the likes of Brazil, Argentina and England because we were the same as England. We didn't play in the best group. I think, if England play at the top of their game, they are a better side than Holland. Even in Holland they say that we don't have the best players but they play as a team.'

Jol went on to explain that Holland's main hopes rest on the shoulders of Chelsea's wing wizard Arjen Robben. The Dutch ace has been on top form for his club and country, but, when he does not perform at his best at international level, then the Dutch struggle. 'If Robben is not there, we are still very vulnerable,' admitted Jol. 'When he is not there, we don't seem to play well. If he is in the team, he is always scoring the first goal or giving us that extra spark and you need that.'

Like former England manager Glenn Hoddle, the Dutchman believes Manchester United's Wayne Rooney provides the same kind of inspiration. He added, 'Rooney has the same kind of spark for England. But we play the same formation all the time and, if England get the chance to do that, I think they will be one of the contenders in Germany.'

Terry Butcher had been an outspoken critic of the current England coach and his methods, but after qualification he observed, 'I'm amazed how the doom and gloom engulfing England's final two World Cup-qualifying games can suddenly give way to ludicrous claims that we can win the World Cup in Germany next summer. What possessed players like Michael Owen, David Beckham, Wayne Rooney and manager Sven-Goran Eriksson to make such ludicrous public declarations is beyond me. I can only assume Eriksson wasn't standing on the grass in the dugout at Old Trafford on Wednesday – he was smoking the stuff!

'Only joking, Sven. In defence of the players they are clearly paying lip-service to their manager having limped over the qualifying line in a group so weak I would have tipped my local pub side to qualify from it.

'When the draw was made, I can only assume FIFA's hierarchy must have ventured out of their cuckoo clocks in the Swiss mountains and delivered a gift-wrapped box containing England's Group Six opponents with a message that read: "Here's your Get To Germany Free card, try messing this up." And let's be honest, we nearly did, dropping five points in a qualifying programme from which we should have expected to have taken all 30. After the humiliating performances against Denmark, Wales and Northern Ireland, we have qualified with a mediocre display against Austria and one of our better ones against Poland.

'Does anyone really believe that this England will win the World Cup next summer? Even the supporters who are normally carried away on a wave of unrealistic expectation are beginning to question the team's true potential under an inflexible manager like Eriksson.

'Those who have witnessed recent performances cannot possibly believe England present any threat to the main challengers. The problem is that, when players start to make bold statements about England's chances, all it does is bring needless pressure to bear. To suggest that we are second only to Brazil is astonishing. I know from past experience that the best way to go about a World Cup campaign is quietly because, once you start shouting your mouth off about how good you are, there is no escape route from your critics.

'I have never questioned the individual talent England have at their disposal but individuals don't win trophies – teams do. Eriksson claims he has 10 world-class players in the world's top 50 but his entire squad could be in the top 50 for all I care – it's no guarantee of success. That said, if I was the FA, I would try to make a deal with Manchester United and stop Wayne Rooney playing for the rest of the season. If there is one player in this England team capable of inspiring the nation, it's Rooney – and without him we are doomed. I would go as far as to say that, if anything happens to him prior to the finals, I'd be of a mind to not even go to Germany because we wouldn't have a chance, believe me. Even so, I doubt if England's opponents are trembling in their boots ahead of the finals. We have worrying weaknesses – not least because we concede sloppy goals and rely on an inflexible manager who picks out-of-form players because he's worried it might affect their delicate egos. England's shape against Poland was the best in a long while and on that basis Eriksson should employ a midfield anchorman in his side – which means one of his star midfielders has to go. It's likely that, if Ledley King was to take up the role, then Eriksson would axe Joe Cole and employ David Beckham, Steven Gerrard and Frank Lampard, and I'm not sure that is the answer because the balance isn't right. It's there for all to see.

'It's no coincidence that world champions like France and Brazil all employed a midfield sweeper system on their way to success. But I suspect Eriksson will now stick rigidly to a 4-4-2 system after his disastrous attempts to tamper with the side against Wales and Northern Ireland. I remember when I played in the World Cup finals in 1986 and 1990 and Bobby Robson was forced to make sweeping changes to survive. During the 1986 competition, we went into the final group game with Poland on one point – we were on the brink of elimination. Robson dropped players with big reputations and drafted in others to employ a completely different formation and we went on to win the game comfortably.

'In the previous two major competitions Eriksson has seemed incapable of making changes. I suspect we all know the team that will begin the World Cup – and I fear it will be the same team that comes home early.'

Colin Bell is convinced England's hopes will suffer from Chelsea's domination of the Premiership. Bell won the title, two League Cups and one FA Cup with Manchester City. In 1999 he was selected as one of the 100 best footballers of the 20th century. Bell, who won 48 caps during an illustrious career cut short by knee injury, was part of Sir Alf Ramsey's underachieving side that failed to reach the 1974 World Cup after a draw with Poland. Yet, despite the present England team beating the Poles this time round to end their qualification campaign with a bang, he believes the lack of strength in depth will scupper their chances in Germany. Bell, 59, said, 'Because of the huge gap between Chelsea and most of the rest, and the fact there are so many foreign players, there is a lack of quality Englishmen. The England squad is selected from the top three mainly. Whoever's English is automatically in the squad – even if they are in the reserves. Sven-Goran Eriksson thinks whoever is English at Chelsea should be selected – but in my day we never had anyone from the reserves in the national set-up. You could put a list on the wall of the great players of the 1970s who never even got close to a cap. Nowadays they'd have walked in. There was quality in defending, goalkeeping, midfield and attack. Every team had stars. Pick any game out of the First Division and you'd see a quality match, even if it was the bottom two. Today we've got the bare XI, but if anyone gets injured there's no quality cover. If Bobby Moore or Bobby Charlton – true world stars – got injured it wasn't an issue. You had four or five players in any position who came in. It will be a big issue, though, if, say, Rooney, Lampard or Gerrard is injured.'

Tony Adams feels Eriksson should take the captain's armband away from David Beckham and award it to John Terry. The former Arsenal and England captain also urged Eriksson to build the team and tactics around Wayne Rooney, permitting him to attack from deep as Paul Gascoigne once did. Adams used a media session at the Swindon headquarters of England sponsors Nationwide to dismiss Alan Smith as a disaster in midfield and Mikael Silvestre as a poor defender whose selection by France for the World Cup would do England a favour. 'Beckham is needed in the England team,' he said. 'His distribution is fantastic. There is not a better crosser of the ball in the world. But, as a leader, Terry would be the man. From his position you can see the pitch; you can drive the team. He has inbuilt leadership. He gives everything, and other players see that and it rubs off. That sort of player can lift a team, make other people great. That's what I tried to do. So Sven has got another big call, but if it benefits the team he has to do it. I would definitely like to see John Terry as England captain.

'You can see the aura of the guy. I know it's a cliche, but he's a winner. You can see the way he drives the team and it is the little moments like set-plays when the game goes dead when those players can lift the team. You make other people great. It's little things: you're telling Gary Neville to get a yard forward, letting Ashley Cole know his man's free. The statistics are that 33 per cent of all goals come from set-plays in World Cups. If you have somebody in there making sure the marking is right, it's a big help. If you have a player in your team who is going to head the ball away and organise it so other people do their jobs in both boxes, you will win games.'

Terry Venables pulled off a major shock in the build-up to Euro 96 by stripping David Platt of the captaincy and making Adams his leader – and it nearly paid off as England reached the semi-finals only to lose to Germany on penalties. Adams, who is convinced England can go all the way in the World Cup, added, 'I think JT has grown. It comes with being in the Chelsea team. You need good players around you and high standards. If you are working at one level and somebody sets the bar higher, it makes a difference. I remember somebody getting into training before me. I couldn't have that so I started getting in at nine o'clock. Then it was eight. You push yourself and you are preparing properly. If somebody has better standards, you have to raise the game. He's had that kind of day-to-day stuff at Chelsea. I would imagine John's own standards are going up and up and he's gone to another level.

'Being handed the captaincy has lifted him too. Some players accept it. I would imagine every team John Terry has ever played for has made him the captain. I think some people just grow from that and the team grows from it, more importantly. Terry Venables took a big decision before Euro 96 when he made me captain. He knew the effect I had on other players, and I think Sven has got the same big call to make.'

Adams claims Terry's success with Chelsea has made him captain material, even reviving memories of his own glory days. 'Do I see something of myself in him? I was taller and better,' smiled Adams. 'But he reads the game well so he gains a yard and his pace is no problem. He's good in the air. Tactically, he knows how to play the system. His distribution is very good, but it is more than that. He has this added bonus of being a leader. It's nothing to do with individuals. We need Becks to play; he's one of the best in the world on the right side. But sometimes David might need to be rested because we need Shaun Wright-Phillips in the last 10 minutes. OK, he can throw the armband to someone else. But I just feel John gives the whole team a lift. If you could put John in now as captain, it may show a sign for the future. I hope the manager is strong enough to make that decision. I hope that personalities don't stand in the way of a decision that's got to be made for the sake of the country.'

Another contentious idea is for Ferdinand to operate in front of England's back four, as Ledley King did so efficiently against Poland. 'This is not new; we did it to good effect with Gareth Southgate when I was playing. Rio can't do that at Manchester United – at the moment they haven't got two other centre-halves. But he could do it for England because behind him we've got Sol [Campbell] and Terry. We've made massive tactical progress in this country. Let's not go back to 4-4-2, straight up and down, no rotation, no movement, or we're going to get a good hiding again. Rio is a big player, we need him. If I was the manager, I would want to know whether he could do it or not. It would take guts, but I hope Sven is strong enough to say that he knows he needs different teams for different situations.'

Describing Rooney as 'Gazza with a better finish', Adams borrowed a notebook to sketch the positions he thought Rooney

*Top*: Geoff Hurst outjumps the German defence.

*Bottom*: The referee has a word with Nobby Stiles with Alan Ball at the far left. Franz Bechenbauer can be seen behind them, in the centre of the picture.

*Top*: Martin Peters scores for England close to full time.

*Middle*: George Cohen and Jack Charlton in action.

*Right*: They think it's all over … Geoff Hurst scores England's fourth goal, becoming the first player to score a hat trick in a World Cup Final.

Bobby Moore with the Jules Rimet trophy.

*Top*: Germany leave the pitch.

*Bottom*: Bobby Moore kisses the trophy.

*Top*: Bobby Moore shows Alf Ramsey the trophy.

*Bottom*: The team share their triumph with the fans. Bobby Charlton (*far right*) is close to tears.

**More celebrations on the pitch.**

The Queen presents proud captain Bobby Moore with the World Cup at
Wembley Stadium.

should be operating in and from, collecting and striking from inside his own half. 'You need Rooney to get the ball and run from wide positions.' As for United's recent lapses, Adams commented, 'If I was Fergie, I'd be worried about Alan Smith. I don't see Alan doing what Keane did, box to box, and there is always going to be the comparison because he's in Roy's position.' Adams thinks England can go the distance in Germany with 16 or 17 top-quality players. 'But,' he cautioned, 'we need them in their best positions.'

Northern Ireland's assistant manager Gerry Armstrong has experience of playing against Sven's men and argues, 'England will be among the favourites to win the World Cup, but, while they have the players, they don't have the mentality. Just look at the class that oozes from that squad – David Beckham, Steven Gerrard, Frank Lampard, Michael Owen and Wayne Rooney to name but a few. The biggest problem, however, is that you're never sure which England is going to turn up. Sven-Goran Eriksson's men are just not consistent enough, and that's crazy with the talent they have on parade. But that's also where the root of the problem lies. They are not a team, just a bunch of world-class individuals. England need to believe in themselves if they are to win a World Cup. Such is the attitude of Argentina and Brazil, they wouldn't come to Belfast and lose to Northern Ireland. Just look at one of England's biggest assets. Forget the likes of Brazil, Argentina, France and Germany – England have the most technically gifted defence in the world. John Terry, Sol Campbell and Rio Ferdinand are world class. Jamie Carragher is so solid and then there's the likes of Ashley Cole. No other team can beat that defence for quality.

'Even in midfield, Eriksson has the likes of Lampard, Becks and Gerrard. But again there are big questions. England can't afford to fire on just one midfield cylinder. Lampard has been awesome for Chelsea and is scoring goals for fun, but his world-class mates Gerrard and Becks have struggled to find any consistency this season. Where Sven decides to play Wayne Rooney will be a key factor. Rooney could be the star man, the one whose brilliance makes or breaks England. But will Sven play him in midfield, in the hole or up front? The one place he doesn't want to stick him is out on the left, as Sven has done in previous games. The Manchester United star looks like a fish out of water there; he gets frustrated and it proved it doesn't work. Rooney will shine, but I think the real star for England in Germany will come out of the woodwork, a player who is on fire for his club and not part of the regular set-up. It could be a Jonathan Woodgate – he's been playing brilliantly for Real Madrid – or maybe Spurs lethal striker Jermain Defoe. What would help England is if Sven stopped playing his players out of position and in the roles they excel in for their clubs.

'England are not versatile enough tactically to cope with positional quirks. There's no way they could cope with the onslaught of Ronaldo, Robinho and Ronaldinho in their current formation. It's my belief that world-class players do not automatically make a world-class team. England must become more determined, be more flexible, have bags more belief and play as a team if they are to win the World Cup.'

England have a strong chance. I'd love to see them bring back the trophy but obviously there are a lot of very good teams in there like Brazil and France and Italy. And I wouldn't rule out the hosts, either. We have a lot of quality in the side, though, and one of the strongest defences in the world. That is a big advantage. Sven is already doing a good job and there is no doubt that England have one of the best squads in the tournament. All everybody wants is for us to fulfil our potential.

# FIVE

## 12 NOVEMBER 2005
### ARGENTINA 2, ENGLAND 3

Michael Owen scored twice in the final three minutes to give David Beckham victory in his 50th game as England captain, a finale that sent out a message to the rest of the world that England had finally established their credentials as potential World Cup winners.

Argentina, still brooding about defeat by England in Japan at the 2002 World Cup, seemed intent on making a statement ahead of Germany. But Owen displayed his priceless predatory skills to score two late goals and clinch England's thrilling victory. Four minutes from time and England were losing to their arch-rivals in this prestigious pre-World Cup friendly when the Newcastle striker did what comes naturally to him: he stole in to grab two vital headers and win it. England fans inside the stadium in Geneva were euphoric as they watched Sven-Goran Eriksson's team pull off a spectacular fightback against one of the favourites for Germany.

Owen admitted England had given their confidence a massive boost after twice fighting back from behind. Owen said, 'To come back twice was great and that is what these World Cup warm-up games are for. Results like this are definitely good for our confidence, but even when we lost to Northern Ireland it didn't really shake our belief that we can go on and do well in the World Cup. There's no doubt we are in with a shout, no more, no less. There are four or five teams who can go to Germany and win it. It was a cracking game, with so much more excitement than a normal friendly.

'Our fans were brilliant. Even when they scored, the supporters stuck behind us; the atmosphere was great. Before the game we thought we could win it and, when you lose a goal, then it is a setback. But the important thing was that we showed we have got the character to come back from something like that. We created a lot of chances. We hit the post and I had a goal disallowed – but they also created plenty of chances and always looked dangerous when they were going forward. It could have gone either way today and that just shows there is not too much difference between the top teams in the world. When we lost to Northern Ireland, people were saying we had no chance. Now everyone will be saying we can win it. But the players don't really buy into that sort of stuff. We know we have a chance and, with results like this, it is always nice to increase your confidence. We have a good chance and no less than that. There are a few other teams who have got a chance and results like this help to give you confidence. But, if we hadn't won today, we would still go there thinking we can win it.'

Eriksson sent on much-maligned striker Peter Crouch, and the Liverpool star's aerial presence seemed to terrify the Argentineans. England captain David Beckham said, 'We are very happy, more happy with the performance than the result. It was tough at times. They are the second-best team in the world and they made it really hard, but we showed tremendous character. We can't get carried away, but we can enjoy the night and the performance. We can take a lot of confidence from the game.'

The Argentina players arrived by coach singing songs that branded the England players 'whores' and 'poofs'. But David Beckham responded, 'We don't mind them singing before the game as long as they're not singing after it. We'll take that every time we come up against them.' Argentina's behaviour was condemned by the United Nations, who had organised the match in Switzerland to promote sportsmanship. UN peace envoy Adolf Ogi said, 'This is totally unacceptable. I will be asking the Argentine authorities to explain this incident.'

But England refused to rise to the bait, which included taunts from the Argentinean backroom staff as the teams lined up. Beckham added, 'The same sort of thing happened on their coach after they beat us at the 1998 World Cup. But whatever happens outside the game doesn't really interest our players. We're just going to enjoy this performance and result. We have shown the togetherness you need to be a big team and I hope we've sent a message to the rest of the world that this England team never knows when it is beaten. Celebrating my 50th game as captain like this is special. There's no such thing as a friendly between England and Argentina.'

Rio Ferdinand said, 'If that's the way Argentina want to get themselves worked up, then so be it. All I know is that it was a great game. There were some strong tackles, but they were all fair and there were no problems between the players on the pitch.'

Now Beckham challenged the England players to maintain equally high standards all the way to the finals in Germany. 'This was the perfect game to begin our preparations. We have to play like this in every friendly because we still need to work on our performances. There is a special togetherness about this team. People will see how we came back from a goal down in the final minutes. But even at 2–2 we never settled for the draw. We had the same spirit at Manchester United.'

Wayne Rooney, who tormented their defence throughout, scored England's opener six minutes before the interval to level the scores after Hernan Crespo had put Argentina ahead. Argentina went in front in the second half through Walter Samuel's header. But he only set the scene for Owen's moments of magic.

Eriksson returned to a diamond formation; Rooney was given the free role that his genius demands and the 20-year-old looked ready to take on the world against Argentina. His contribution featured a gloriously taken equaliser, another effort which hit the post and an all-round performance that was quite simply mesmeric.

The Argentina coach detailed the uncompromising Martin Demichelis to follow Rooney all over the pitch. In the early exchanges, captain Roberto Ayala managed to scrape his studs down the back of Rooney's calf in one challenge, before Demichelis was punished for barging him in the back.

In Madrid or Belfast, Rooney would have reacted with a glare that promised retribution. This time, he kept his composure. One clipped cross into the box was perfect for Michael Owen to head home, but the celebrations were silenced by an offside flag. One moment Rooney was beating three players on the edge of his own box before relieving the pressure with a pass out to Wayne Bridge, the next he was sweeping a pass to Gerrard at the other end of the field.

In the 30th minute, Rooney was the width of a post from scoring, racing on to Gerrard's pass before lifting a shot over Roberto Abbondanzieri which bounced back off the woodwork. Sixty seconds later, he came up with a blistering solo dash which was only halted by a crude Ayala bodycheck. Even when Chelsea's striker Hernan Crespo put Argentina ahead on 34 minutes, it was Rooney who came up with an instant response.

David Beckham's header was perfect and Rooney produced a predatory finish, anticipating that the England skipper would win the ball and knock it forward into the box. In the second half, it was

Ayala who was asked to cope with him, particularly after Argentina's skipper had put his team back in front in the 54th minute. Rooney would certainly have scored again had Gerrard spotted him unmarked six yards out instead of pulling the ball back for Frank Lampard to fire over.

In the final ten minutes, Rooney was asked to drop deeper into midfield when Eriksson's search for an equaliser prompted the introduction of Peter Crouch. It still needed a world-class save to keep out Rooney's chip four minutes from time before Owen levelled from the subsequent corner and then scored an amazing injury-time winner.

It was the old-ish master Michael Owen who earned a spectacular victory against the old foes with two dramatic late headers, but this was an occasion that also highlighted the fact that England cannot do without Rooney. They were left directionless when he limped off on that fateful evening against Portugal in Lisbon at Euro 2004. Rooney's genius is the bedrock for genuine optimism going into the 2006 World Cup.

It was not a flawless performance by any means. Most of the trouble came down England's left-hand side. This was hardly surprising seeing as left-back Wayne Bridge had barely kicked a ball in eight months. But, with Luke Young's inexperience painfully uncovered on the opposite flank, the evening underlined what was already pretty obvious: England need their first-choice stars and Gary Neville and Ashley Cole were missed.

Sure enough, Rodriguez breezed past Bridge and sent over a cross that brushed Rio Ferdinand's leg before providing Crespo with a tap-in. If Rooney felt any guilt about his involvement in the Crespo goal, he soon banished it in the only way he knows how. Gerrard's flick found its way to Beckham and his intelligent header invited Rooney to swagger into the box for his 11th international goal, which he duly despatched into the bottom corner.

Eriksson soon realised the folly of his selection and sent on Paul

Konchesky for the second half. Ledley King was another player who was not entirely at ease. Having looked imperious in his last game against a poor Poland, he was made to look the squarest of pegs by the outstanding Riquelme. King gave away the free-kick that led to Argentina restoring their lead. Konchesky was as culpable, though, somehow ignoring the presence of Samuel who headed goalwards from a suspiciously offside position. Ayala ensured it crossed the paint but it was already all but in. Once again, Eriksson held his hands up by ending King's involvement. England's subsequent response was impressive.

Eriksson had to rethink King as his No.1 holding player following his inability to cope with Riquelme. Centre-half King had already expressed his own reservations about his midfield role after the World Cup-qualifying win over Poland. Now he had even more doubts and admitted, 'Argentina are a world-class side and it was very difficult for me. Riquelme, in particular, is a top-class player and he would drift out wide, drag me with him and leave spaces in the middle for other players to come into. I've never come up against a player like him before, at least not when I've been playing in midfield. I knew before the game that he was top quality. He seems to play at his own pace but you still can't get near him which is strange. Coming up against players of Argentina's calibre was a real lesson for me. That's what these games are all about.'

But overall Eriksson was delighted as he beamed, 'I am extremely happy with what I have. It seems our squad is much more mature every time it comes together. If we don't have injuries it's the best squad I ever had. I hope we can bring everyone to the World Cup.'

He was particularly impressed with his attacking pair. 'They play very well together. They are both top-class players. I hope they are fit and in decent shape for the World Cup. Michael Owen is 25 and has been in the game for seven or eight years. Wayne is only become 20 and he's got 28 caps. I don't know any other players at the age of 20 who've done that in the world.'

Eriksson declined to claim the Owen–Rooney partnership is the best in the world. 'There are a lot of good strikers in the world. France is not bad when they have Thierry Henry and David Trezeguet!'

Rooney reckoned the match turned when goal-shy Peter Crouch came on as an 80th-minute substitute for Charlton defender Luke Young. Beanpole Crouch, 6ft 7in, had not scored since his £7m summer move from Southampton to Liverpool – and was jeered by England fans during the previous month's victory over Poland. But Rooney said, 'Crouchie was brilliant when he came on. He was probably the main influence on us winning. He's had to take a bit of stick but he's worked hard, played well for Liverpool and come on against Argentina and changed the game. We were 2–1 down and he gave us a different option up front. For the equaliser, their defenders were so worried about Crouchie getting on the end of Stevie Gerrard's cross, they left space for Michael to get a free header. Michael's probably the smallest in the side and somehow he still manages to score so many with his head. Beating Argentina like that has done wonders for our confidence and, if we can keep playing like that, we can do really well at the World Cup.'

This was Rooney's first taste of South American opposition and, for the first 15 minutes against the team currently occupying fourth place in the FIFA world rankings, he could only watch in awe. Rooney added, 'Argentina are a great passing team. They had a lot of possession early on and penned us into our own half. But we knew that was going to happen as they're such technically gifted players – and luckily Paul Robinson made some great saves. After a while, we got more of the ball and that let us raise the tempo and play at a pace that suited us.

'We wanted to run at their defenders and commit them to making tackles in areas they didn't want to. We really piled on the pressure after we went 2–1 down and, once we did, I don't think they could live with us.'

Owen, who took his international goal haul to 35, insisted his partnership with Rooney was not a one-off. 'I'll never lose my finishing touch and there is no one in the England team quite like me. I am always on my toes for the entire 90 minutes. That's why my partnership with Wayne is developing so well. Every one of his strengths is totally opposite to my strengths. We showed that at Euro 2004. I had a slow start but then started picking up, while Wayne was on fire from the first minute. That's why we dovetail so well. The first time I was picked with Wayne I was thinking, "Who couldn't play with him?" Now we're really gelling as a pair.

'Wayne plays differently to anyone else. He has got virtually everything and it's important that other players understand his strengths so we don't knock long balls to him. My job is to keep out of his way. He is better than me playing in that hole, so why do I want to drag defenders into his space? My game is not Wayne Rooney's game. My strengths aren't coming off and linking the play and all the rest of it. My strength is seeing opportunities, knowing where a ball is going to go, sniffing out a chance and, obviously, scoring goals. I have to know what Wayne is best at and he understands where I'm strongest. We've now been playing together for more than a year and our appreciation of each other is getting better all the time.'

While Owen is closing in all the time on Bobby Charlton's 49-goal England scoring record, Rooney is pushing him all the way for the honour of becoming his country's finest finisher. Rooney had already scored 11 and he only turned 20 last year. Owen said, 'It doesn't matter who Wayne plays against, he always sends a message out. You like to think everyone in your team is capable of rising to the occasion but there is no doubt Wayne is a big-game player. That's what you need in a World Cup. You don't want someone who only scores against smaller nations; you need someone who can put in a performance like that against the proper teams like Argentina. Even if Wayne has a quiet first 10 or 15 minutes, you just know he is going to pull a rabbit out of the hat at some stage.'

Owen found it tough to keep his own emotions in check following his dramatic stoppage-time winner. 'It was the most competitive friendly I've ever played in. The excitement, the opposition, the standard of play – Argentina could have gone in two up at half-time; we hit a post, had a goal disallowed. Maybe if we'd lost, it might have left a sour taste but this was a huge morale boost to everyone. The whole country was down after we lost to Northern Ireland. Now they're on a high because we've beaten Argentina. But neither result really changes anything. Argentina, Brazil, Spain, Holland and Italy – we know we're in among that pack.'

Frank Lampard savoured his first taste of action against one of the South American giants. He enthused, 'We treated this as a qualifying game or a World Cup finals match, and we wanted to win it to make a big statement of what we are about. For us to beat one of the best teams in the world was huge. We went out with a fantastic attitude and carried that through the game.

'We knew it would be a valuable experience and that certainly turned out to be the case. We had to contend with a different style of play to what we are used to – we didn't come up against anything like that in qualifying. Their technical ability and the use of the player in the hole who can move the ball around you and hurt you were a challenge we had to deal with, and I thought we coped well. We will need to do the same at the finals because we are going to come up against that style of play from the likes of Brazil, and Argentina of course if we meet them again. I think we are learning to play against teams like this. Playing Champions League football has certainly helped me personally. When you come up against players like Juan Riquelme in the hole, who are a bit special, you learn that you cannot play the straight four across midfield. You need a bit of depth to cover players like that. Riquelme is a great player and very influential, but we did really well in terms of keeping him at bay.'

King's inclusion was designed to restrict Riquelme's influence, but the Villarreal schemer was the game's outstanding performer for the first hour. Lampard added, 'You have to be prepared to change for different parts of the game and I thought it went well with Ledley in the first half. But, when we went behind for the second time, we needed to add more of an attacking influence to get back in the game, and we did. I played with Stevie Gerrard in the centre of midfield for a while, and then at the end of the game it was Wayne Rooney alongside me. They are all good players and that makes it easy. But it showed the versatility in the squad, and the fact that we can change things round if necessary. When you play against teams of that quality, you know that you will be under pressure at times.

'You have to keep going and play to your strengths, and our strengths shone through. When the tempo rose, we matched it. We pushed on, stepped up and created chances. I know they had a few chances as well, but I still think we had the best ones. We were disappointed to be 2–1 down because we thought we were good enough to win. But we persisted and created the chances which saw us pull it off.'

Rio Ferdinand admitted his surprise omission for the World Cup qualifier against Austria had provided him with a boot up the backside. 'It was a shock to find myself on the bench. Nobody wants to be out of the team. It tears your head apart. But you have to deal with it in the best way possible and I hope my disappointment didn't show when I was sitting in the dugout against Austria. I tried to be one of the lads and give my support to the guys who were in the starting team and I think that's what makes this group different to previous England squads I've been involved with. In the past, I've seen people reacting a lot differently when they were told they weren't playing and it was important I didn't do that. Being left out of the team is part and parcel of international football these days. Of course you want to be in the team. But first and foremost you are there to support the group and this squad has a fantastic camaraderie.'

Ferdinand went on as a substitute for the injured Sol Campbell against Austria but he did not know if he had done enough to merit a return. 'It was unfortunate for Sol and probably fortunate for me that he picked up that injury. I knew I had to take my chance and I think I've done that. But what counts more than anything about Saturday's win was the fact that we have beaten Argentina. There have been so many things that have happened between our countries in the past on and off the pitch. And now we have added our own chapter to that history with a fantastic match. But there is a danger of going over the top, so it's important we don't get carried away and try to keep a lid on some of the euphoria which will follow this result. It was a great match to be involved in and everyone walked off the pitch in Geneva with their head held high. I was happy enough with my own performance but there is always room for improvement and we will take a lot of useful lessons from this game. Unlike European teams, the South American sides tend to be far more fluid when it comes to their formations, so the experience of dealing with that will stand us in good stead for the World Cup.

'I've rarely come up against a player as good as Riquelme. His movement and awareness were unbelievable and you couldn't allow your concentration to waver for a moment against him. The way he manipulates the ball and puts in the killer pass makes him a player you could watch for hours. Maybe we switched off for their second goal and that's something we'll have to take a look at. But Riquelme was so clever to chip it to the back post when everyone was expecting him to shoot. Yet we reacted so well to come back from behind to snatch the victory. And hopefully that will play on Argentina's minds if we come up against them again in Germany next year. Even more important is the confidence we can take from this result. We know we are capable of overcoming one of the best teams in the world and that will do wonders for our self-belief.'

Against Argentina, Paul Robinson turned in his best performance at international level, making three world-class stops in the first 10 minutes to deny Juan Riquelme, Carlos Tevez and Maxi Rodriguez. But none was better than his 49th-minute reaction save to keep out Juan Pablo Sorin's point-blank header. The jury had been out on Robinson but he said, 'Hopefully, I've proved I can do the job. As England goalkeeper, you are always there to be shot at, but it's all about limiting your mistakes and putting in consistent performances. That was probably my best game yet for England and certainly my most pleasing considering the final result.

'I was probably busier than I would have liked, especially in the first 20 minutes and I do prefer it when I don't have so much to do. Argentina caught us cold. We were all over the place in the first 20 minutes and they really put us under the cosh. There were a few saves I was pleased with, particularly that one from Sorin, but that's what I'm there to do. I know it's a cliche, but I was just doing my job. I've been pleased with my form for the past 18 months. Right now it just feels great to have been part of such a great game. They are the second-best team in the world and it's a fantastic result for us. Yes, they created some chances against us but we gave them even more problems and that is something we must not lose sight of.

'We were aware that they weren't so strong at the back. Our game plan was always to get at them and let Michael Owen and Wayne Rooney do what they do best. And the fact that we opened them up so many times shows just how far we have come as a team.'

Steven Gerrard started in left midfield, then briefly moved into a central role with Lampard when King made way for Joe Cole. He ended up at right-back when Young came off. Gerrard is used to filling a variety of midfield roles at Liverpool as well as playing just behind the front man and even as an out-and-out striker. 'I'm one of these players the manager will just throw anywhere out of the way. Three positions in one game? That's good for me – it's usually four or five! But I don't mind, the team's more important and, wherever the manager wants to put me, I'll give it my best shot. It's very difficult even at domestic level to play out of position and, at this level, it's a step up. But I was well happy with my performance.'

Gerrard even supplied the pinpoint cross from full-back that allowed Owen to head the first of his last-gasp goals. He said, 'That's Michael Owen and that's why he's one of the best in the world. He can be quiet for a long time and then kill teams off like that. It was a great victory. We had belief we could beat them and it was a great game to play in. We'll take a lot of confidence from it. In friendly games, we haven't really been producing but we played very well this time. The never-say-die attitude has been missing lately in the friendlies but it came back here. This was the game when we had to prove to people across the world we are a good side and we can go to the World Cup full of confidence. We know on our day we can beat anyone. On this evidence, we can mix it with anyone.'

Frank Lampard would love to square up to the Brazilians. 'If you look at the players in our squad, we believe we can compete against the best, and Argentina are definitely one of those sides. Brazil are the ultimate benchmark, and it is hard to compare yourselves against them because they have such fantastic individuals.'

Club colleague Hernan Crespo suggested England are good enough to win the World Cup after seeing them clinch a dramatic victory over his Argentina side. 'I was impressed by everybody in the England team. And, when I saw Joe Cole coming on as a substitute, I realised how many great players England have. They played their best and it was a good match. England are good enough to win the World Cup, not just for this game but because they have the players. They are one of the favourites to win the World Cup.'

But an aggrieved Crespo claimed referee Philippe Leuba deliberately denied the Argies a penalty at 2–2 so it would end a draw. 'It was a clear penalty for us, yet the referee didn't give it and they took the ball downfield and scored. In the World Cup they will whistle in those situations. But the referee didn't whistle this time because he thought a draw would be good for everybody – he was wrong.

'It was a great match, one we didn't deserve to lose. But when you play against a great team there is always the risk that it can go wrong for you.'

Coach Jose Pekerman insists his team will get revenge if the countries meet again at the World Cup finals. 'It is always sad to lose in the last three minutes like we did. But we didn't lose this match – we lost the last three minutes. We were technically superior in midfield to England and, if we meet them again in the World Cup, we will win, for sure.'

Alan Shearer, reunited with Owen as a strike partner at Newcastle United, was a BBC studio pundit as his team-mate struck in Geneva. He observed, 'It didn't surprise me to see Michael Owen score twice. I've always said that, if you give Michael chances, he will score goals. His record is phenomenal. He's a top-drawer striker, and he and Wayne Rooney make a very dangerous partnership. Michael is a brilliant finisher and you know that, if you give him chances, then he will score, which is great news for England and Newcastle.'

Sir Alex Ferguson backed Wayne Rooney to lead England to World Cup glory. 'Wayne is getting better all the time and will be maturing nicely come next summer. He took his goal against Argentina really well. England will have a great chance next summer. Everybody expects England to do well and they'll be in with a real chance.'

In his *Sunday Telegraph* column, Gary Lineker observed, 'This was more like it, an England side playing to their full potential and most importantly in an attacking style which comes naturally to them.'

Lineker knows that the media and the public will get carried away and we will go from believing England have a team who have no chance of winning the World Cup to regarding them as favourites. But Lineker provided a balanced view when he added, 'The truth is we have a team with a genuine chance of winning the competition – what's more, our best chance since 1990 – but then most of us already knew that before this game. In fact, this England team might have a better chance than mine had in 1990 because they have more world-class players. And it's in Europe, in a climate in which we can actually compete and play our normal game, so, yes, we have a chance, a good one, but no more than that.'

Lineker also pointed out that England need their best players to stay fit after an arduous season. He pinpointed the importance of Rooney: 'Above all, we have to have Wayne Rooney fit. Yet again yesterday he was magnificent for England. What a star!'

Alan Hansen observed in his *Daily Telegraph* column, 'As Michael Owen demonstrated against Argentina, you can be anonymous for 88 minutes but a couple of inspired pieces of play will make all the headlines. I have always believed that Rio Ferdinand is a remarkable talent and, of the three top-class central defenders available to Sven-Goran Eriksson, he has more natural ability than either John Terry or Sol Campbell. But too often recently, Ferdinand has fallen the wrong side of mediocre. When England beat Argentina in Japan three years ago, Campbell and Ferdinand were an awesome partnership, and now it seems one of them will have to make way. Campbell has done nothing wrong and is entitled to question why he is suddenly third choice. However, to win any major trophy a manager has to be completely single-minded and there is no room for sentiment in international football. The best partnerships are ones where each player brings different qualities to the mix. One of the reasons Ferdinand attracts so much criticism is that his play is very elegant and casual and sometimes it looks as if he could not care less – which is the opposite of the truth. Terry is completely different; he flings himself around the area in a way Ferdinand does not. In Euro 2004 it seemed his biggest weakness was a lack of pace; he kept getting pushed further and further back. Although pace is still an issue, he is a far better and more confident player now than he was then, especially when it comes to his positional play.'

Trevor Brooking, the FA's director of development, is confident that, if they can show the same resilience, they can have a major say in the tournament. 'Within the dressing room afterwards, there was a sense of satisfaction with the level and the quality of the match, but one or two chances either way and the game could have been different. They [Argentina] did create chances and they are a good attacking side and there are issues that you have got to learn from. What everyone has tried to say involved with England is we think we are capable of winning the tournament. We had a little spell where we went from no-hopers to world-beaters and we are somewhere in between towards that top end. But the big plus is, against a side like Argentina, we can claw our way back; we have got great fight, we have got great skill, options going forward, so I think we can go into the tournament now. You could see how chuffed the lads were afterwards. They were absolutely delighted to get the win – and, psychologically, that's a big issue now. Whatever happens next summer in any game, they know they are quite capable of getting back into matches against quality opposition.'

The win over Argentina erased memories of embarrassing defeats by Denmark and Northern Ireland earlier in the year and – at least for a while – eased the pressure on Eriksson, whose future had already been the subject of intense speculation. However, at the time Brooking insists the Swede has never wavered. 'It was pretty intense, you have got to say, but I think Sven understands it goes with the job.'

The dazzling victory over Argentina brought an unprecedented rush for seats at the new Wembley Stadium and a betting bonanza on England winning in Germany. Fans have bet more than £500m on England winning the competition, making Sven-Goran Eriksson's team joint third-favourites. Bookmakers were overwhelmed by England supporters putting so much money on their team and they stand to lose vast sums of money should the fans be proved right.

Within two hours of opening for business, Wembley National Stadium Ltd received £1m in ticket applications (or confirmations of orders) and, by the end of the day, £2m had been taken, the highest since the 2004 European Championship finals and equivalent to the average takings for a week. All 160 corporate boxes at the £757m stadium have been taken and recently WNSL have been concentrating on selling the different levels of seats. The most expensive are the Corinthian, which require a £16,100 licence fee (a type of membership) and a ten-year season ticket costing £5,400, which works out at £588 per event, although this includes full corporate-hospitality facilities. The cheapest reserved seats are Club, which cost £3,900 for a licence fee and then £1,350 a year, worth £145 for each match.

The match in Geneva was also a vindication for the FA, who went ahead with the fixture despite warnings that it was foolhardy holding the match against such intense rivals on the same day that Turkey – another country with whom there has been a history of antagonism – were playing Switzerland in a World Cup play-off fixture in Berne.

To add to the buoyant mood after the Argentina game, the World Cup went on show in London as speculation about the FA bidding to host the 2018 competition increased.

# SIX

**DAVID BECKHAM:**
ENGLAND CAPTAIN AND PROUD OF IT

Ahead of the friendly with Argentina in November 2005, David Beckham admitted it was an 'amazing' feeling to be preparing for his 50th game as England captain, particularly since he idolised Diego Maradona when he was a kid – a time when he also dreamed of captaining his country.

In fact, Beckham picks out Maradona as his favourite player of all time. 'I think there is always going to be one. [It was] Maradona for me. Some of the things he has done in the World Cup finals have been incredible. He was a great, great player for his country and the clubs he played for. Lothar Matthaus was a great player for Germany. Some of the goals and performances he put into the German national team in the World Cup finals were incredible.'

Prior to the World Cup warm-up game in Geneva, Beckham was surfing the internet to find out exactly where he stood in the all-time list of England captains. He currently lies fourth but has his sights on pushing into the top three. Bobby Moore, the World Cup-winning captain of 1966, skippered England 90 times, the same number as Billy Wright. Next comes Bryan Robson on 65. Beckham said, 'I had my computer in my room. Somebody had mentioned about me being fourth-highest and I wondered what the other players were on, and whether I could catch them. I saw Bryan Robson and thought that was possible, then I saw the other two and thought, "We'll see!" It would be nice to catch them because the three players in front of me are players I have always looked up to. You dream of being mentioned in the same sentence as these guys.'

Becks inadvertently knighted the legendary Moore when he added, 'Even to be mentioned in the same breath as Sir Bobby Moore is an amazing honour. If that is in the history books, then I would be more than happy.'

Beckham loves being captain of England so much that he is prepared to put up with all the pressures that go with it. As he explained, 'I'm used to it now. Obviously I do feel that extra responsibility as a captain. I think all captains do. You always feel that added pressure. The important thing is how you respond to it and I believe that I've enjoyed my time as captain of England and I think that I've done quite well.'

The Real Madrid midfielder led the England side out in Geneva almost exactly five years after first being handed the captaincy by caretaker manager Peter Taylor for the friendly with Italy in Turin in November 2000. Although England lost 1–0, Becks impressed and he kept the job when Sven-Goran Eriksson took over. Beckham said, 'When I was given the captaincy, people were doubting. They thought I was the wrong person and some still do now. But it's five years on and I want to keep the job as long as I can. I was always hoping it wasn't just for the one game. I wanted to lead my country out more than that, and I have done.

'At the time, it was a great honour to be given the captaincy by Peter Taylor. It was a case of keeping hold of it, proving I could be a captain and a leader. It is one of the biggest honours in any player's career and now to be playing in my 50th match as captain is amazing for me. I want to be captain and play for as many years as possible. The best way of being in the history books would be to win the World Cup, but we have a lot of hard work to do before then. If we work hard and get the luck we need in a big competition, you never know.'

Eriksson quickly identified Beckham as the leading light of the new generation from which his team would be drawn and let him keep the armband. It was a shrewd decision: of the side that started in Turin only Rio Ferdinand joined Beckham in the starting XI for the friendly with Argentina, and only Kieron Dyer, Gary Neville and David James of the others still have a chance of making this year's World Cup squad.

But the bar will always be raised in terms of expectancy, not least for Beckham, whenever England face Argentina. He said, 'You don't prepare for a game like that differently because in World Cup finals you have to prepare for each game as if you're playing against an Argentina or a Brazil. You want to win every game, but obviously there is a different sort of atmosphere in these matches. When we were leading up to playing Argentina in Japan, people were talking about it for two or three weeks. Even when the draw was announced, people were talking about the two of us meeting. You always want to put yourself up against the best players and the best teams, and Argentina for me are one of the best teams in the world.'

The 30-year-old has had mixed experiences against Argentina to say the least, so it was remarkable that his landmark as captain should come against this particular country. Famously, he was sent off against them in the 1998 World Cup, then scored the penalty which beat them in the 2002 finals. 'Playing against Argentina is a very patriotic game for our country, our fans and the players, so it's a good one for us.'

Beckham endured a torrid time after his sending-off during France 98 and he was vilified on his return to Britain. However, he insisted his abiding memory remains his winning goal four years later. 'In '98 it was tough. I went through a tough time for maybe three years after that, but four years later I took the winning penalty. That is the memory I hold.'

The three years after the 1998 World Cup were the most difficult for him. 'Without a doubt it was the hardest time for me as a footballer but I had a manager who was right behind me. Before every game, Manchester United fans were incredible for me. Outside Manchester United, I had family and friends who stuck by me because it was three years of not just me getting it but my family getting it. That was the tough part.'

Things got to the point, according to Diego Simeone, where Becks even learned to swear in an Argentine dialect just to improve his method of insulting Simeone when they meet in Primera Liga games! Whatever anyone says, Beckham doesn't dislike all current Argentinean footballers. Beckham himself said former Real Madrid team-mate Esteban Cambiasso was 'a great person' and Diego Maradona is his idol. There's also the fact that Juan Sebastian Veron and he were good friends when they were at Manchester United together. 'I really don't know why they don't like me,' said Beckham. 'It's weird I have had so many problems with them.'

Yet, in 1998, Veron pointed to the tunnel to encourage referee Kim Milton Nielsen to send him off. Nice touch that. 'That episode made me a lot stronger and a lot harder person,' Beckham said. 'It was harder for my parents than anyone. I can handle things now.'

Nearly four years later, in April 2002, it was another Argentinean, Deportivo La Coruna's Aldo Duscher, who broke Beckham's foot with a tackle and sent the nation into a panic about the captain's metatarsal. Medical bulletins about the state of Beckham's injury dominated the news for the next six weeks and he went to the World Cup still not fully recovered.

Beckham's next red card after his dismissal against Argentina was against Mexican side Necaxa in the World Club Championship in Brazil in January 2000. The referee was Horacio Elizonda – from Argentina. The first time he was sent off for Real

Madrid, it was for a foul on Valencia's Argentina international Pablo Aimar. Then there was a nasty injury sustained at the hands of Murcia's Jose Luis Acciari.

'During my first season at Real Madrid,' Beckham said, 'every tackle, every booking, every problem, turned out to be connected with an Argentinean player, which was bizarre. I haven't got a problem with them. Maybe you should ask one of them what their problem seems to be with me. We want this game to be peaceful. That's what every player wants going into every match. We don't want these problems on or off the pitch.'

Changing subjects, the Real Madrid star also identified John Terry as a future England skipper. He added, 'John has the qualities to be a captain. At Chelsea, he proves he is a great captain and many players in his team come out and say he is a great captain. With a great manager like Jose Mourinho picking him as captain, he is definitely a leader in the team. He has got the kind of inspirational qualities an England skipper needs.'

For all Beckham's status as one of the world's top players, he has never lit up a major tournament. At the 2002 World Cup, Beckham was not properly fit after his encounter with Aldo Duscher and, in Euro 2004, he missed two penalties. He said, 'There have been the odd couple of games where I have been close to being at my best in tournaments. But there have been a lot of people out there who have documented the fact I haven't done as well in the World Cup as I could have done. I always want to put people right. Let's hope I can do that in this World Cup.'

Beckham believes England's depth of talent now gives them a great chance of ending 40 years of hurt. 'We have two of the best strikers in the world in Wayne Rooney and Michael Owen and we want them on fire. But we also have midfielders who can score goals which is good. Now we have qualified, it has relaxed the players. Even the atmosphere this week has been so much better than it was in the last couple of months when we met up.'

As well as a captain, Sven-Goran Eriksson recruited an ally in the man from east London and, whenever criticism of team or captain has flown, the one has been the other's most vocal supporter. Beckham believes Eriksson's faith helped him mature after his St Etienne humiliation. 'It definitely helped change me [as a person],' Beckham said. 'At the time, people were doubting I was the right person to be captain. It's the biggest honour I have ever been given in football. I want to keep it.'

Beckham's chances of beating Bryan Robson's record as captain – let alone Billy Wright and Bobby Moore – probably depend on his convincing Eriksson's successor that he remains first choice in midfield. The clamour for him to be replaced has been stilled for now by his form for Real Madrid and Sean Wright-Phillips's indifferent showings for Chelsea. He professes to be unfazed by the criticism.

'When a player reaches the age of 30 and there are younger people behind you waiting to get in the team, there are always going to be people saying you shouldn't be in the team. I accept it because that's the way football is these days, but I don't accept that I shouldn't be in the team. I want to be captain for as many years as possible.'

Beckham knows that, if he is ever to achieve the fulfilment he plainly craves, he needs a blameless World Cup. Despite so many shining contributions in qualifying, his tournament appearances so far have been mostly insipid.

In 1998 Diego Simeone intervened and, four years later, injury prevented him from playing to his potential. His evasion of a tackle in the build-up to Brazil's equaliser in the 2002 quarter-final ultimately proved just as telling as his penalty against Argentina earlier. He intends to make amends in Germany, with the ultimate aim of quieting dissenting voices by emulating Moore in lifting football's top trophy.

'The World Cup is the biggest football competition in the world. For me to go to a World Cup is an amazing occasion. It's every player's dream to win it,' he said. 'There's been the odd game [in the World Cup finals] where I've been close to my best. Let's hope I can do it in this one.'

Beckham insists England players have not been greedy over bonuses for the World Cup. The players were criticised for negotiating £225,000 each to win the tournament. Beckham, however, claims that figure is wide of the mark. He said, 'The truth is that we are earning less this World Cup than we were for the last tournament. I know for a fact that every one of the players would play for our country for nothing. There is money in football and we talk about bonuses every time a big competition comes around – and there is always criticism of the players when bonuses are agreed. But money isn't the motivation, not at all.

'When you are a 15-year-old watching the World Cup, you don't dream of playing in it because you can make loads of money. Players don't think like that; you want to be there to play on that stage. We don't go into a game thinking we can make money for winning. There is too much pride and passion in our team to even suggest that. The FA make money and the players always get bonuses, that is a fact. And if we do not succeed, then the money is not there.'

Beckham knows that, to reach the highest level, to become one of the all-time greats, he has to achieve things in the World Cup finals. The best players he has played against have done just that, as he said, 'Ronaldo and Romario. I think those two Brazilians are blessed with so much natural football skill it's incredible.'

As for the most influential midfield player, he said, 'Well, there are different types of midfielders. Firstly, you've got the likes of Roy Keane and Bryan Robson who are great ball-winners. They also get forward and motivate teams by the way they play. But then you've got players like my Real Madrid team-mate Zinedine Zidane, who can change a game in a split second. So these different types influence in different ways.'

Beckham admits playing for Real Madrid has turned out to be far harder than he thought. Real have not won a trophy since his £25m move from Old Trafford in the summer of 2003. Beckham said, 'When you join Real Madrid, you think games are easy. But they aren't. You get the odd games when everyone in your team is on top of their game and you go on and batter teams, but it doesn't happen as often as I thought it would.'

Beckham could have joined Barcelona, who also bid for him, but he opted for Real where he has vowed to end his playing career. 'When Barca go on and win, it's tough for the team and the whole city. But I've always said I want to win something for Real Madrid and England because it would be a huge lift for me. I think I'll end my career in Madrid – although I thought I would end it at Manchester United. I've got one more season and the club want to talk about a new contract, but we haven't sat down and discussed it yet. I've probably found a happy medium to my life in Madrid. The attention I get hasn't changed but I'm enjoying it. We're moving into a new house and my family life is good.'

But having only ever received a red card for Manchester United – at the World Club Championships in Brazil in January 2000 – Beckham has now been sent off four times in his Real Madrid career and twice for England.

Eriksson is adamant, however, that Beckham is the right man to lead England, despite the claims of players such as Chelsea captain John Terry. 'Maybe [Terry] is waiting, yes,' Eriksson said. 'But Beckham will be the captain. We have many players who could be captain and everyone wants to be captain, but I can't see any reason why I should change.'

| Name | Caps | As captain |
| --- | --- | --- |
| Billy Wright | 105 | 90 |
| Bobby Moore | 108 | 90 |
| Bryan Robson | 90 | 65 |
| David Beckham | 86 | 50 |
| Alan Shearer | 63 | 34 |

| Kevin Keegan | 63 | 31 |
| Emlyn Hughes | 62 | 23 |
| Johnny Haynes | 52 | 22 |
| David Platt | 62 | 19 |
| Gary Lineker | 80 | 18 |

## BECKHAM'S ARGY-BARGIES

JUNE 1998: Sent off for retaliatory kick at Diego Simeone in the World Cup finals last-16 clash with Argentina in St Etienne

JANUARY 2000: Argentine referee Horacio Elizondo gives Beckham the second red card of his career for a foul on Necaxa's Jose Milian in a World Cub Championship match in the Maracana Stadium

APRIL 2002: Fractures metatarsal bone in foot after foul by Deportivo La Coruna's Argentine defender Aldo Duscher. Beckham goes to the World Cup in Korea and Japan, but is nowhere near fully fit

JUNE 2002: Scores penalty winner against Argentina to avenge France 98 defeat in Sapporo, turning his back on a handshake from Simeone before taking the kick

DECEMBER 2003: Angry confrontation with Deportivo's Argentine Lionel Scaloni, who accuses Becks of making a crotch-grabbing gesture towards him at the final whistle. He refuses to shake the England captain's hand after he had been fouled – and then promises revenge when the pair next met in La Liga

JANUARY 2004: Beckham needs four stitches in his right ankle after a foul from Murcia's Argentine defender Jose Luis Acciari

JANUARY 2004: First red card in a Real Madrid shirt after fouling Valencia's Argentine Pablo Aimar

OCTOBER 2005: Deportivo's Argentinean midfield pair Scaloni and Duscher target Beckham in a Spanish league match – but the Real Madrid star refuses to rise to their bait

# SEVEN

**MICHAEL OWEN:**
ENGLAND'S GREATEST-EVER GOALSCORER

Michael Owen is on course to become England's greatest-ever goalscorer and, if he can top the scoring charts in Germany, then England can bring home the World Cup trophy. Throughout the world, Owen is perceived as a goalscorer who needs to deliver in the finals to become an all-time legend.

Argentina hardman Roberto Ayala admires Wayne Rooney as much as anyone, but fears Owen's goals more. After all, Owen was only 18 when he startled one of the biggest global footballing nations as he danced around Ayala on his way to scoring his wonder goal during France 98 to establish himself as a brilliant talent on the world stage.

But Valencia defender Ayala enthuses just as much over England's latest wonder kid 20-year-old Wayne Rooney, after branding him a 'remarkable and special player'. Ayala said, 'Owen and Rooney are very special. They are very important and probably the best partnership in the world. Rooney is a remarkable player. He is the best talent I have seen in a long time. He is not a typical English player – he is very special. He has great movement, vision and passing. He scores spectacular goals and has a temperament as well. All of the big players have a temper. You need that to be special. If you take it away, you take away the player.

'He can do special things at the World Cup. I saw him at Euro 2004 and he was so young and yet so talented that he was probably the best player in the tournament. England now have a player who can give them something special, something different and that will make them successful. England have a special player in Rooney. He is unpredictable. To win tournaments, you need big players. Brazil have many special players – Ronaldo, Ronaldinho and Robinho. Italy have Totti. That is what sets them apart and now England have another.'

Ayala warned that Owen must now win the trophy since his wonder goal against Argentina will not be enough on its own to make him a World Cup legend. 'Everyone remembers Owen for the goal he scored in France,' added Ayala. 'But he will not want to be remembered for that goal alone. To be successful for countries like England means winning the trophy.'

Owen himself is convinced that the current England team would beat both his previous World Cup sides and also believes that there is even more strength in depth in Sven-Goran Eriksson's camp than in the superstar-laden squad he left behind at Real Madrid when he signed for Newcastle United.

The 25-year-old is convinced that Eriksson's starting side is better than either the team Hoddle sent to France or the Swede took to the Far East in 2002. Owen said, 'If everyone plays to their maximum, this is the best team of the three. We've got such good players. The standard in training is unbelievable. With the players we've got here, if everyone is on song in any particular match, I wouldn't be fearful of anyone.

'When I went to my first tournament in 1998, we were full of real experience. For a lot of players, it was their last big tournament. In 2002 it was a very inexperienced team. This one is in the middle:

we've a bit of everything. Ability-wise, this is a fantastic team when it's playing and functioning in the right places. This group has the quality to be the best team I've ever played in. Of course, it's so difficult for everyone to play well on the same day. But that's what we're going to have to do to win the World Cup, so we've got to do it. We've shown that we can play well as a group, although not as often as we'd have liked. The important thing – for the manager, the players and everyone else – is to peak next June.'

Owen says he feels refreshed after quitting the biggest club in the world, Real Madrid, to return to the Premiership. The dressing room he left behind in Spain included David Beckham, Zinedine Zidane, Raul and the Brazilian quartet of Roberto Carlos, Ronaldo, Julio Baptista and Robinho. But Owen insisted, 'There's more quality in this England squad.'

Owen added, 'There are more quality players. At Madrid we had the big *Galactico* thing, where there were five or six world-beaters. In this England squad, we've got players in the same league as them. But at Madrid, while the rest of the lads were good, hard-working players, they're not a patch on the ones who are outside the team we've got here. And when you go down to the next batch of players outside the first team, what we've got is very strong as well.'

The game against Argentina in Geneva was one of just four warm-up games before Eriksson and his squad arrive in Germany, and the striker, fourth in the all-time England scoring list, agreed that messages must start being sent out. To back up his words, he later scored twice in the 3–2 win to bring his total to 35 goals in his 75 appearances. Owen said, 'This is an important game. We need to gauge how we're doing against one of the other favourites. Now we've qualified we need to gain confidence individually and collectively. When you win, there are so many spin-offs – you gain confidence, the whole country is happy and you get a better send-off going to the World Cup.

'It all tends to roll into one. And if you lose there are question marks here, there and everywhere. If we can, we will go and play in the English way. It's just that sometimes it's foolish to go and do something that would hinder our chances of winning a game. Argentina will back themselves to have a lot of the ball; they're not going to just defend. That's why we get good games when we play them or Germany or Brazil – you both fancy your chances and go for the win. I don't fear them or anybody.

'If you're mentally strong, as a team or individually, that's important. I do feel we sometimes get a bit indulgent and think we're the only ones who exist or can have disappointment, and that nobody can feel as low as us. How do Spain feel? Or Italy? All these teams. We're in that bracket and they must be saying the same things we are. I don't think it's right for us to think we've got a deficiency because we lost a penalty shoot-out or two. It's maybe heart-breaking for us. But it was heart-breaking for Spain to lose to their arch-rivals in Portugal.

'If we play any of the top teams, we can beat them. Whether it's Argentina or Brazil or anybody else, they might have some cracking players and some of the best attackers in the world. But we've got some of the best defenders. And, if we can nullify their attacking players, I'd always fancy us scoring a goal.'

Sadly, Owen required an operation on the broken bone in his right foot which he picked up against Tottenham in the 2–0 defeat at White Hart Lane on New Year's Eve. He broke his fifth metatarsal which ruled him out for 'several months'. Owen reacted philosophically: 'It's disappointing but everyone gets their fair share of injuries. If there's any consolation, I've got plenty of time before the World Cup.'

When asked if the injury would affect his World Cup, Owen replied, 'Not from what all the experts are telling me. There are no quick ways; it's two and a half months or three months, I don't know what it is, but it's the same for everyone. Loads of people have had it done – Rooney, Beckham, Gary Neville and Stevie Gerrard.'

Eriksson will monitor Owen's recovery. He told the FA website, 'Obviously, I'm very disappointed for Michael. It's very bad luck for him and for Newcastle United. Michael is a fantastic striker and a very important player for his club and for England. I hope he returns to fitness as soon as possible and I will follow his progress very closely.'

The then Newcastle United manager Graeme Souness said, 'Michael Owen has broken his fifth metatarsal in his right foot. He's had it X-rayed and he will obviously be out for several months now. It's a similar injury to David Beckham's. It's an almighty blow for us. Even when you're not playing particularly well, you feel that you can win games with Michael in your team. I can't tell you how big a miss he will be. It's an absolute disaster for him and for us.'

David Beckham recovered from his similar injury in 2002 and went on to play in the World Cup finals, although he was not fully fit and appeared to be less effective. Let's hope Michael Owen can do better in Germany.

# EIGHT

**WAYNE ROONEY:**

THE WORLD'S BEST YOUNG STAR

'Rooney has the same bullish look as Gazza when he came through. He runs at players in the same way. He has great control and a great shot with both feet and he scares defenders. He showed that in Euro 2004 and he'll do that in the Premiership and Champions League. To score a hat-trick on his debut is special.' **David Beckham**

'He loves the big stage and the sky is the limit for him, it really is. He's got everything going for him and is looking the complete player at 18 years of age. Is he as good as me? Now don't be silly! You go through all the greats at Manchester United and you've certainly got to put him in there.' **George Best**

'He's not the same type of finisher as Michael Owen or Ruud van Nistelrooy, but he is definitely the sort of player I would pay to watch. He is someone who plays with absolutely no fear and, when you have a striker like that, then there are no limits. English football is very fortunate to have such a great striker.' **Thierry Henry**

Wayne Rooney starts the World Cup finals as favourite to win the inaugural Gillette/FIFA Best Young Player award. Let's hope he does. If Wayne wins, England win because, if Rooney ends up the best young player – if not *the* best player full stop – in Germany, the nation will have a wonderful chance of bringing home the trophy.

England coach Sven-Goran Eriksson knows his best chance of glory in Germany lies with wonder boy Rooney. As he observed, 'Wayne Rooney is only 20 but has everything. Alex Ferguson said he was the best young talent he has ever seen and I agree with that. I have never seen anything like him at his age. He can defend, score, beat people. His vision is incredible and he is so strong. Wayne is a massive talent – and a good boy as well.'

Rooney has now overtaken David Beckham as the most talked-about footballer in the land. Whatever Rooney does, the kids copy – just like Becks. In the case of the England captain, it meant kids changing their hairstyles. As for Rooney, following his torrent of F-words on the pitch against Arsenal, teachers blamed a new tidal wave of swearing in classrooms on the Liverpool-born teenager. But Rooney is big news, and even more so now he's with the biggest club in the world, Manchester United.

The broken metatarsal that saw him limp out of England's European Championship quarter-final against Portugal is now accepted as the moment when Sven-Goran Eriksson's chances of lifting that trophy came to an abrupt end. Once again, in the World Cup finals, it will be Rooney to whom England look for inspiration to land football's biggest prize.

Real Madrid, Barcelona, Chelsea and Arsenal are still trailing in the slipstream of Manchester United in the Deloitte's Rich List. And Rooney is the richest kid in football.

His transfer is the biggest for a teenager – at £27m, he is the costliest forward in the country. He earns £5m a year in endorsements on top of his enormous £35,000-a-week salary and he's only just turned 20. Together with fiancee Colleen, he is rarely off the front pages of Britain's national newspapers.

Manchester United fans begged Sir Alex Ferguson to buy him and, in his first season, he scored some memorable goals. With long-range lobs, blistering volleys and a hat-trick on his Champions League debut against Fenerbahce, Rooney set Old Trafford alight with his goal skills and thrills.

Hero at Manchester United, hate figure at Everton, question marks may stand over his temperament, but he is backed by all the top professionals, from England coach Sven-Goran Eriksson to Pele. Legends such as George Best and Sir Bobby Charlton have praised him unstintingly, while everyone inside Fortress Old Trafford protects him against outsiders who try to bring him down. The kid from the tough streets of Merseyside has become the new Goal King of Manchester United.

AC Milan coach Carlo Ancelotti predicted Rooney could emulate the goalscoring feats of European Footballer of the Year Andriy Shevchenko. 'If Rooney is handled in the right way, then, like Shevchenko, we'll be talking about a truly great player in terms of world football. He will face problems along the way, but he undoubtedly has the talent to be one of the best. Already he is proving that. He has faced big games and come through them and will do again. He is playing very well but I still believe he can improve and become an even greater player.'

Gary Neville observed, 'Why not look at the positive things about him and say, "God, what an exciting player to watch." Look at [Eric] Cantona. We'll look back in 30 years and say, "I'm glad we had Eric, with his volatile temperament. That's what gave us all those experiences, those moments of magic." Not everyone can be like Gary Lineker and never get booked. That'd be all a bit boring, wouldn't it? People say, "Oh, he [Rooney] earns that much money. He should behave in a certain way." Why should he? Rugby players punch each other in the head and they're gentlemen. Football players don't do things half as bad, and they're thugs. Why?'

United fans derided him as 'Fat Boy' before he joined their ranks, but now he is a hero to them. Rooney said, 'I know when I go back to play Everton I will get the same stuff shouted at me. It happens. That's football. I just laugh at it. It's just the fans being football fans. I would do the same if I was still in the crowd.'

In fact, home fans chanted, 'Fat Boy, what's the score?' as United won 3–2 in his first encounter with them. He said, 'I remember the stick I got – I just laugh at it. It was the same with most grounds I played at. Since I've started playing football I've matured a lot, especially in the last 18 months.'

Rooney did not know what welcome to expect from United's supporters when he first arrived, but he quickly settled in. 'It was nice to see them outside Old Trafford waiting to see me after I'd signed, shouting my name and saying I'd made the right decision. Having the England lads like Scholesy and the Nevilles here has helped me settle in, too. I'm really looking forward to playing here, especially against the best players in Europe.'

He added, 'All I ever wanted to do was play football. That's all I was ever focused on. I was forever practising with my mates. It's not just natural ability. We used to play round the back of the house by some garages and use one as a goal. We'd all take a turn in goal and play until it was dark. That definitely helped me a lot.'

Immediately, he came under pressure to live up to another Old Trafford legend – Eric Cantona. And the comparisons with 'Le King' started even before he was given Cantona's coveted old coat peg in the dressing room. Rooney said, 'Cantona was a brilliant player. It's flattering to be compared to him because of what he achieved, but I've only been playing professionally for two years. I've got to prove who I am. There's going to be expectations, but I am confident that I can fulfil them. There's no reason why we can't win the European Cup with the squad we've got. Manchester United is a massive club and I hope I can stay here for the rest of my career.'

Rooney also revealed Everton tried to plunge him into Premiership action as a 15-year-old. He said, 'Walter Smith tried to put me on the bench against Arsenal when I was 15. My name was on the team-sheet but I think the FA stopped him. I was gutted as I'd told my friends and family.'

When Rooney was three weeks short of 18, Ferguson said, 'Everyone can see for themselves the potential in the boy. When Wayne gets over the adolescent development, nothing will stop people comparing him to the great players we have had here.'

'I'm speechless,' beamed Rio Ferdinand after seeing him play.

'Scary,' grinned Ryan Giggs.

'He's good. He's very good. In fact, for 18, he's unbelievable,' goalkeeper Roy Carroll (now with West Ham) said.

When he signed Rooney, Ferguson was upset that his mention of Cantona led some journalists to believe he was comparing the two as players. What he was talking about was Rooney's similar potential to influence. 'In terms of impact, he could be the same as Eric,' said Ferguson. 'There's no doubt about that.'

Rooney's impact at Old Trafford was immediate. 'It's amazing,' said former stalwart Paddy Crerand. 'United supporters had been down in the dumps after the team's start to the season. Now you go out into Manchester and they're wandering up to you saying, "We're going to win everything."'

Crerand, a United hero from the era of Bobby Charlton, Denis Law and George Best, continued, 'What's he got? What's he *not* got? He can head it and hit it with either foot. He's as brave as a lion. He's a very intelligent player. Some top footballers take six or seven years to understand the game properly. That kid understands it like it's natural to him. If there's anyone you could compare him to, it's Bobby [Charlton], because of the force of his shooting, but, really, Rooney's unique.

'No matter how talented he is, it's still a big thing for an 18-

year-old to walk out into that arena at Old Trafford and perform the very first time. Some people have said Fenerbahce made it easy, but the goals he scored didn't depend on anything the opposition did or didn't do. His second goal: how many kids do you see doing little dummies outside the box and smacking the ball into the net?'

It was the act, Crerand said, of a brilliant senior pro.

Much was made of Rooney's generosity in swapping shirts at full-time with Fenerbahce's Marco Aurelio, thus giving away a precious artefact. What seems to have eluded people is that Rooney changed his jersey at half-time: the one in which he started his first United game and scored his first goals was tucked safely inside his kitbag. It will be worth tens of thousands one day.

Sven-Goran Eriksson watches Manchester United too. 'I have never known such a clever player at such a young age,' Eriksson said. 'Roberto Baggio was similar, but Rooney is the more complete player because he's strong as well. It is difficult to see a weakness in his game.'

Eriksson played his part in launching Rooney's career, giving him his first England start in a qualifying match against Turkey when he was 17. 'It was not a difficult decision. After seeing him in training, it was fair that he should play. My only fear was when to tell him he was in the side. I didn't want to give him too much time to dwell on it, so I ended up telling him after lunch on the day of the match. He just shrugged and said, "Right." His confidence is incredible. He is wonderful to work with. It was purely his performances in training that persuaded me to use him against Turkey. You could just see he was ready to play.'

The immediate problem for Eriksson was who to play alongside Rooney. Michael Owen was conspicuously uninvolved at Real Madrid, whereas Jermain Defoe played every week for Tottenham and suggested in Poland that his time had arrived.

Eriksson considered axing Owen and linking up Defoe with

Rooney. But, as Owen said, he and Rooney link up well. 'Wayne's got more of a creative element to his game and I'd like to think I have more of a goalscoring element to mine. Each game is different and you have to dovetail in the best way you can. I don't think Wayne enjoys trying to get in behind defences as much as I do. His game is all about touch and feel and scoring from long distance, which is something I don't do half as much.'

The Real Madrid striker believed Rooney's Champions League hat-trick confirmed he was establishing himself as one of world football's great talents. 'The early signs are all there. He's still only 18 and, from what he's shown so far, he has been phenomenal. He could be England's Ronaldo or Zidane figure. We've already seen that he can win games on his own. He was fantastic the other night. It wasn't just his hat-trick; his game as a whole was very good too. It's all the more remarkable that he's been out so long. Playing great on your debut has been done by many people, but to play great on your debut after not kicking a ball for so long, that is very good. I know how hard it is to be out for weeks and then try to come back. That was what made it so impressive.'

Although he was quick to point out that other England strikers like Jermain Defoe and Alan Smith are also clearly in the frame, Owen makes no secret of the fact that he feels he and Rooney are ideal partners up front. 'He's also got that string to his bow where he can see a pass and he plays in that position where he can afford to be inventive, whereas I play further forward. But, if the roles are reversed and I take a ball to feet as happened in the Croatia game, then the end result is a goal, so it doesn't make any difference.'

Rooney's Premiership debut fell flat. There were no goals in front of a record Premiership crowd, and it was a massive anti-climax after his thrilling Champions League bow. Alan Smith rescued a point for Manchester United in a 1–1 draw against Middlesbrough. The Teessiders' boss Steve McClaren observed, 'Wayne Rooney is a superb player. He can score at any level he wants. To stop people like him and Ruud van Nistelrooy, you need to be organised, do everything correctly and have a bit of luck. We had all those things today.'

Carlos Alberto played alongside Pele for club and country and he is tipping Rooney to be just as special. The 1970 World Cup-winning captain, who coached Azerbaijan, England's Group Six opponents, admitted he is a big fan of the Manchester United youngster. And the biggest compliment he can pay is to say 18-year-old Rooney can star on the world stage just as Pele did when he was a kid in 1958. The Brazilian said, 'I saw Wayne play during Euro 2004. He is very good and we know he is going to cause us headaches. There have been other good players since Pele – like Ronaldo – but I know Rooney is special and has a great future. I like players who touch the ball, who try to score goals. You do not have to be Brazilian to be a good player. There is no such thing as English style or Brazilian style when you have the best players. I love watching Manchester United because of their style. Now they have added another very good player in Wayne, who has so much talent.'

Eriksson couldn't wait for Rooney to resume his international career. Rooney was assigned the role in the hole behind Defoe and Owen that is cut out for him. Before the game with Azerbaijan, the England manager said, 'He seems to be very happy. He always has a big smile on his face and is doing very well. You couldn't tell he'd been away from football for such a long time. I went to see him last week and he was incredible. If you are his opponent, it's not easy to play against him because he can do a bit of everything. In fact, he can do a *lot* of everything. His strength is that he can beat people and score goals; he can play up front or as the second striker or in the hole. He's intelligent enough to play in any position, all of them. The fact is that he was almost the top scorer in Euro 2004 and he didn't even play three and a half games. That says everything on that level. He's a goalscorer.'

Another goalscorer Ian Wright was stunned to learn he is one of

Rooney's heroes. 'It's great to hear Wayne is a fan of mine – I thought he would hate me for scoring against his team so often. I love watching Wayne play. I was at the Everton–Arsenal game where he first made an impact and, like everyone else, I was curious to see this 16-year-old kid who was on the bench for a Premiership match. But I only needed one look at him to see he was the real deal. His touch, his confidence and his goalscoring instinct were there for everyone to see right from the start. I think what he is doing in the game is just phenomenal. He was unbelievable at Euro 2004 and to go on and score a hat-trick on his Champions League debut – with the pressure he was under – was an awesome achievement. He has got the lot. His temperament is fantastic and he is going to be a massive star for the next decade. I'm just glad he's English.

'I was just an out-and-out goalscorer, a poacher if you like. But there is so much more to Wayne's game – he constantly brings other players into the game by the way he passes and lays the ball off. I suppose the one thing we have in common is that we are both fearless. I was always willing to go in where it hurts to get goals – and Wayne is exactly the same. Other than that, I can't say he has been influenced by me in an obvious way. But I'll gladly take the fact I'm one of his favourite players. That is a terrific compliment.'

Against Wales in the World Cup qualifier, Rooney looked superb in his new role behind Owen and Defoe, with the accolades pouring in even though he didn't score in the 2–0 victory that put England top of the group. Rooney enjoyed playing behind the front two, even though he will always consider himself a striker. Rooney admitted, 'It's not a role I ever imagined myself playing because I'm a striker and I like ducking and diving with my back to goal. But Paul Scholes was a big loss to England when he retired from international football in the summer, so I wasn't too surprised when it was first suggested I play in that position. To be honest, I was almost expecting to be asked to play there when the manager named five strikers in the squad. It's something new for me and a role I still have to get used to. But as a professional footballer you have to be good enough to play where you're told by the manager.'

Against Wales, Rooney was assisted by the frequency with which Owen and Defoe made penetrative runs. Rooney hit a post, had another effort cleared off the line and went close on a number of other occasions as he revelled in the freedom of the wide open spaces of Old Trafford. Owen revealed that Eriksson's entire game plan revolved around Rooney. 'It was all worked around Wayne. Me and Jermain were told to peg the Welsh defence as far back as possible to give Wayne the maximum space to use his ability. Playing with three up is not as simple as it looks. The manager doesn't just pick his best XI and say, "Go out and play." You have to think about different things when you change formations. But there were times against Wales when it worked a treat.'

Not even the assorted jibes and taunts of the visiting Welsh supporters could ruin Rooney's first Old Trafford international as a Manchester United player. The cocky teenager responded to chants of 'you fat b******' and 'you only score in a brothel' by waving a fist at his tormentors and pointing to the name on the back of his shirt. He declared with a laugh, 'I just wanted to let them know I'd heard what they were singing.'

Next up were Azerbaijan. England moved into pole position in their World Cup-qualifying group, having taken 10 points from their opening four games in the wake of their 1–0 win in Azerbaijan. Beckham may have been missing through suspension and injury, but stand-in captain Michael Owen led by example in heading home the 24th-minute winner in Baku. Rooney gave his all. One blot for Eriksson was the fact that Rooney, Ashley Cole and Nicky Butt all picked up bookings.

Eriksson revealed that the Old Trafford ace believes England will get the most out of Rooney by letting him continue to float rather than being tied to frontline duties. The England boss said, 'Wayne likes to play there. He told me that twice. Of course he has the ball a lot in that position, more than if he plays up front. Sometimes he can go away from markers and that gives him more time to pass the ball. It's normal in that position and I think he's doing very well. He wants to persevere with it. I think he's defending very well too. He was coming back to help the other three midfielders. And there were some excellent passes he gave in the game.'

Euro 2004 won Rooney many fans across the continent and his hat-trick for United in their 6–2 rout of Fenerbahce stimulated much interest. In football-mad Italy, his exploits were splashed across the front page of the top-selling sports daily *Gazzetta dello Sport*. Its headline roared: 'Rooney debut hat-trick – immediate phenomenon'. The report inside added, 'Hurricane Wayne was unleashed at Old Trafford. It was a work of art that outclassed all expectations. It was an out-of-this-world performance.' The paper's website referred to him as 'the baby phenomenon' who 'came up with three masterpieces'. Norwegian TV showed the game live and drooled over Rooney's display for a full half-hour after the game. His goals were shown from all angles and the pundits analysed his performance from start to finish. The newspaper *Adresseavisen* referred to him as 'the biggest talent ever in English football'. In Germany, the media focused on the astonishing praise from Fenerbahce's German coach Christoph Daum. The former Stuttgart manager said, 'That was an unbelievable debut and this is just the start. He could become the player of the century.' In France, the headline in the dominant *L'Equipe* sports paper shouted simply: 'Hip, Hip Rooney'. In Sweden, the *Aftonbladet* newspaper said, 'It was the King's goal show.'

Outside football, Rooney will struggle to match Beckham's fame because of the Real Madrid player's showbiz lifestyle which is always going to attract attention. But with United's popularity around the world – especially in Asia – Rooney has the potential to become a household name among sports fans across the globe.

Former superstar George Best, who sadly died last year, reacted to Rooney's debut, describing it as good as any he has ever seen. Best became a teenaged Old Trafford legend in the 1960s and went on to become one of the world's greatest players. He watched Rooney's stunning debut hat-trick and said, 'Wayne's just getting better and better. The lovely thing about him is his temperament – he loves the big stage and the sky is the limit for him, it really is. He's got everything going for him and is looking the complete player at 18 years of age. Is he as good as me? Now don't be silly! You go through all the greats at Manchester United and you've certainly got to put him in there. He can handle himself, has two good feet, is good in the air. He's got it all.'

Best also backed United manager Sir Alex Ferguson to keep Rooney on the straight and narrow. 'The fact that he's playing for Manchester United means he's going to get hounded 24 hours a day. But he's got the top man looking after him in Sir Alex.'

David Beckham was gobsmacked at the way his England team-mate destroyed Fenerbahce. 'Rooney has the same bullish look as Gazza when he came through. He runs at players in the same way. He has great control and a great shot with both feet and he scares defenders. He showed that in Euro 2004 and he'll do that in the Premiership and Champions League. To score a hat-trick on his debut is special.'

Rooney's third was a spectacular free-kick that Beckham would have been proud of. Becks joked that Rooney will have to score a few more before he lets him have a crack at set-pieces for England. 'I don't know about letting him take free-kicks for England though! He might get one or two – we'll have to wait and see.'

Thierry Henry underlined the potent force United have acquired. 'I always said he is an amazing player. He is the kind of player that any team would like to have. He has the sort of forward's instinct which you cannot buy and no coach can teach. You are born with it. Of course you also need good team-mates around you to give you the ball and help set up chances. And Rooney has those players at

*Top*: England fans show off a giant banner depicting Bobby Moore lifting the 1966 trophy.

*Bottom*: Wales captain Ryan Giggs looking despondent in the September 2005 qualifying match his side lost 1-0 to England.

Joe Cole in England's qualifying match against Austria on 8 October, 2005.

*Top*: Fans cheer England in the Austrian match.

*Bottom*: Frank Lampard scores a penalty for England against Austria at Old Trafford.

*Top*: Sven in characteristically ebullient mode at England's qualifying match against Poland on 12 October, 2005.

*Bottom*: Fans turn the stadium into a St George's flag.

*Top*: England and Poland players line up for the national anthems.

*Middle*: Rio Ferdinand takes a shot for England.

*Left*: Ref Kim Milton Nielson with Wayne Rooney, who he sent off the previous month in a Champions League game and who sent off Beckham in the 1998 World Cup finals.

That's one! Owen racks up the first goal against Poland.

Lampard scores against Poland and, *inset*, celebrates.

John Terry takes the captain's armband from Michael Owen.

Manchester United. But I like the sort of striker who will score all on his own if he wants to, and Rooney showed again the other night that he is capable of doing that. He can shoot from distance, get on the end of crosses, hit free-kicks – anything. He's not the same type of finisher as Michael Owen or Ruud van Nistelrooy but he is definitely the sort of player I would pay to watch. He is someone who plays with absolutely no fear and, when you have a striker like that, then there are no limits. English football is very fortunate to have such a great striker.'

Denis Law tipped Rooney to shatter his Old Trafford records. Law scored Manchester United's highest total for a season with 46 and also leads the field with 18 hat-tricks. Scot Law, still acclaimed as 'The King', said, 'Rooney can do the lot. He will eventually have all the United goalscoring records. I don't even see why he can't overtake my 46 in a season.'

Rooney was the first United player to score a hat-trick on his debut in 99 years, Charlie Sagar doing it to Bristol City in 1905. Even by Rooney's standards of defying all reasonable expectations, his first appearance for Manchester United will go down in the club's annals as the most impressive debut that Old Trafford has ever witnessed. He left the pitch to a standing ovation after a performance which incorporated vision, finesse and the embryonic signs of a partnership with van Nistelrooy. And when Rooney curled his free-kick into the top right-hand corner, even Eriksson, disregarding his usual decorum, jumped out of his seat.

It was during his summer expedition to Portugal with England that Rooney became hardened to the prospect of leaving Goodison Park. Already frustrated by dressing-room chatter over the next Champions League campaign, Rooney felt his outstanding performances in Sven-Goran Eriksson's side had ended any lingering doubts over his ability to compete with the very best. 'After Euro 2004, I knew I could play with the top players and in the big tournaments. The Champions League is the biggest club tournament in the world and it was frustrating not being able to play in it. I still regard Everton as a massive club. I've played for them for two years and have supported them all my life. If Everton had been in the Champions League, it would have been a different matter. But I wanted to further my career. It was time to move on and Manchester United is the right choice.'

Where would the prodigy play? 'Wayne is a total footballer who can play anywhere, though maybe I won't use him in the back four!' Ferguson insisted. 'Any midfield position, up front, or off the front. His best position would probably be just behind the striker, because his options are open there and he has the ability to beat men, which is very important in that role. He could also play with two other strikers. I'm just excited about the potential. We are talking about a fantastic player.'

Eriksson was convinced Manchester United were getting a genuine superstar. 'If Wayne plays like he did at Euro 2004, you would have to say he is world class. Absolutely the best. No manager in the world would say no to having him in their squad and I'm sure he'll have a fantastic career. He showed in Portugal what an absolutely fantastic talent he is – but he is still only 18 and I'm sure he will be much better in the future. I was asked what makes Wayne so good and I said it is the fact he is so very cold. I have never seen him nervous or worried about anything. I had Roberto Baggio at Fiorentina when he was 18 and he was always very confident. But Wayne is even more cool about his own skill. I realised that the first time he started a game in the European Championship qualifier at home to Turkey. I told him on the morning of the game he would be starting. Anyone else would have been scared. But not him – he just said, "OK." That was it. That is why I think he is a guy who will always keep his feet on the ground. But give him a ball and things will happen.'

Rooney was left out of England's opening World Cup qualifiers in Austria and Poland since he was still recovering from the broken bone in his foot suffered during the Euro 2004 defeat by Portugal in June. Eriksson admitted, 'I am sorry for Wayne and for England that he is not available because we don't have another Rooney.'

United's collection of stars were also in the grip of 'Roo Mania'. Paul Scholes could see the teen striker bagging a load of goals and becoming a legend at both international and club level. Scholes, who opted out of international football at the age of 29, said, 'To see a lad of his age doing what he can do is unbelievable. When he's fit again, he'll come back and score a lot of goals this season. He'll be a lot more confident after the way things went for him in Portugal. He's going to be a legend for England.'

The capture of Rooney may have used up virtually all of Fergie's budget for new players the following summer, but he was so determined to land the Everton striker he persuaded the Old Trafford board they had to act straight away or risk losing out.

United legend Paddy Crerand was delighted at the prospect of seeing Rooney in a red shirt. 'The first time I saw him, when he was 16, I thought, "This lad is going to be a star." His arrival means the competition for places now is going to be extreme. Alex Ferguson has a proven track record of bringing on young players. He guides them, he looks after them – and also takes no nonsense. Wayne could not be in better hands.'

Former United boss Wilf McGuinness believes United now have the best two youngsters in world football. McGuinness said, 'Ronaldo and Rooney are the two best teenagers playing at the moment. If they develop like we hope, then just look at the future. It's going to be great. Rooney did well at Euro 2004 playing against some of the best defenders. I think international football brings the best out of him. The higher the level of football, the better Wayne Rooney will perform – and I think he's come to a great club with a manager who's going to help him mature.'

Ferguson first saw Rooney in the flesh when the teenager gave centre-back David May the run-around in a reserve game. Then the boy wonder came on as a substitute to play a 19-minute cameo in a match at Old Trafford in October 2002 that is otherwise remembered for United scoring three goals in the last four minutes. 'He battered us,' Ferguson said, before adding in wonderment, 'At 16 years old! You don't forget things like that.'

Diego Maradona first tipped Rooney to follow in the footsteps of some of the game's greatest players after the European Championships. Maradona said, 'I like the look of Wayne Rooney; he has the talent to be a great footballer. I've seen footage of some of his games – no wonder defenders are scared to death of him. I like the fact he appears to play with no nerves or fear and it's rare to see a player of that age play with such confidence. It's unfair to put pressure on a player so young by making unnecessary comparisons with other players. I know how it used to annoy me when I was trying to make a name for myself in my own right without people pressurising me to live up to other great players. It's not footballers or coaches that do that. It's the media who want to build a player up and burden him with unrealistic expectations.'

Maradona can see a bit of himself in Rooney. Worrying! He has a similar build and he's strong, quick and not easily knocked of the ball. But his character comparison is far more interesting. 'I never felt fazed by games and the magnitude of those games. Naturally you get nervous when you're playing in the finals of the World Cup, but as an individual it all went over my head. Perhaps that's why I played with such confidence and maybe that's why this lad does as well. All I do know is he has immense talent. Some people would say that type of attitude borders of arrogance but I was never arrogant and he doesn't strike me as being that either.'

Maradona forecast that the next few years will be critical for Rooney's progress. 'I don't know Wayne Rooney, but he seems to be a fairly level-headed individual. You have to focus on your football and to a point ignore everything else. From 18 to your mid-20s, your talent should shine through. But football is littered with washed-up players who promised so much and delivered little.'

When the experts reflected on the European Championships, Gerard Houllier believed Rooney would have been the player of the tournament if he had not been injured. The former Liverpool boss, spokesman for UEFA's technical study group, named Greece skipper Theo Zagorakis as man of the finals. But Rooney, Sol Campbell, Ashley Cole and Frank Lampard were in a UEFA All-Star squad. Rooney also finished as the second-leading scorer with four goals. Houllier said, 'Rooney was amazing and the way he was going he would have been the player of the tournament. He had great games against France, Switzerland and Croatia and scored four fantastic goals. It's a shame he picked up his injury but he has been a revelation to many people.'

Rooney was the fans' favourite England debutant ever. Rooney won the hearts and minds of the England supporters. Fans believe he made the biggest impact of any English player at a major tournament in the modern game and voted accordingly. Over 25,000 Three Lions supporters responded to the survey commissioned by England sponsor Nationwide and it was Rooney – with almost 49 per cent – who they believed outshone the contribution of any other England player at a European Championship or World Cup. Paul Gascoigne's impact at Italia 90 came second with 20 per cent, while Gary Lineker and Michael Owen came in third and fourth respectively.

One in five English supporters also believe Rooney can inspire England to go on to win the 2006 World Cup in Germany. Over 26,000 fans responded to another survey, commissioned by Nationwide, asking the question: 'Based on England's performance at Euro 2004, how will they fare at the 2006 World Cup in Germany?'

Nearly 18 per cent believed the Three Lions will lift the trophy, while 12 per cent did not think England would even qualify. Once again, however, the majority of England supporters said that their country will reach the quarter-finals with a massive 30 per cent supporting this view.

Rooney, though, was circumspect about all the adulation. 'I am still only 18 and have scored a handful of goals for England. And I am certainly not calling myself Pele, that's for sure! It was flattering to hear people saying that but I don't go along with it, especially when you consider everything Pele did. I do not see myself as a national hero, whatever anyone has been saying and writing about me. I know who the main players are in the England set-up and I am not there with them just yet. Just look at players like Michael Owen. His record at international level is frightening.

'Obviously, I am delighted with how things have gone so far – apart from my broken foot – but my aim is to still be up there in five or 10 years. If you believe all the things written about you when you're doing well, you have to look at them when you are not having the same success. You only need one bad game and things change, and that can knock your confidence if you let it. It can all become too much if you let yourself get carried away by it.'

Rooney has no doubts the right man is in the hot seat to spearhead the campaign for glory at the 2006 World Cup. 'I think Sven is a great manager. I have worked with him for just over a year and, although he isn't as loud as some managers, he definitely gets his views across. And all the players respect the way he works. I heard his comments about me and for a top footballing man like him to say something like that was very flattering. When you lose any game, you can see just how disappointed Sven is – and he certainly was when we went out to Portugal on penalties. Maybe he doesn't show it that much but, if you know him as well as I do, you know he is hurting just as much as everyone else. He desperately wanted us to go out and win the whole thing – and we all believe that, if we'd won that quarter-final, we would have gone all the way. I have never seen Sven lose his temper, but he will certainly tell you if you have done something wrong, even though he won't shout at you. He doesn't throw things around the dressing room – he doesn't have to get angry. He is the England manager, so if he tells you to do something you listen and take it in. Before each game, he just told us to go out, do the best we could, enjoy it but try to win.

'When I first got into the squad, I didn't really say much to anyone at all. But these days I am probably one of the loudest. My relationship with Sven now is much closer than it was. I talk to him a lot and give my opinion back. I don't mean that I tell him I won't do things, I just feel more confident in saying what I think. At the hotel he doesn't join in the games with the rest of the squad, but people don't understand the amount of work he has to do as manager. It is a hard job but he is doing well.'

He also feels he links up well with Owen. 'Michael likes to play on the shoulder a lot more, while I like to drop in and that suited us. But Sven is very precise at spelling out the tactics, although at the same time he's not afraid to tell his players to play their normal game. We certainly don't like to be told, "Stay over there and don't move out of that place," because there is a lot more to the game. Sven realises that and we all appreciate his approach.'

Rooney's first tournament happened so suddenly. 'It first hit me that I would be going to Euro 2004 when all the players flew to Italy for a get-together six days before we went to Portugal. We did some hard training but it was really quite relaxed. Then we met up at Sopwell House to fly to Portugal with our wives and girlfriends. That's when everyone realised we were really going. We had been waiting, talking about it for such a long time and now it was finally here. There was a great buzz. During the week away in Italy, the squad got closer together than we had before. And we had various games that helped us all bond together, like little leagues on the computer and pool competitions. I'd rather not talk about my record – I'm more of a snooker player! But it all meant that, by the time we got there, we were closer than ever before and we were just waiting for the first game. It was more like a club set-up than an international one.

'The first game against France was very difficult. The heat was unbelievable and I have never experienced anything like it. I felt as though my head was going to explode and at half-time we all jumped into ice baths in the dressing room. It helps your legs recover but you don't have a lot of time. You get into the dressing room, strip off and jump in. We get out, start getting ready again and normally for the last five minutes coach Sven-Goran Eriksson gives us his team talk. The heat was intolerable but we did some training after the French game to get used to it. The Switzerland game kicked off nearly three hours earlier than the French game, and so it was even hotter – although it didn't feel as bad.'

France beat England 2–1 and Rooney recalled, 'During the match, Claude Makelele tried to wind me up. He was standing on my foot, standing on my heel and all that. It is sad a player of his talent needs to try to get someone booked or sent off. When people try things like that, it just makes me want to beat them more. Before the game, Sven-Goran Eriksson told us to do the best we could, enjoy it but try and get the victory. Losing was a major disappointment. Afterwards, you could see the lads were down but Gary Neville was great. He told us, "The French are meant to be the best in the world and we beat them over 90 minutes. It was just in the last three minutes they beat us."'

When England beat Switzerland 3–0 in the next game, Rooney made the rest of Europe sit up and take notice with a dream double. Gerrard completed the rout. After the shock of the French match, the result lifted the entire nation and put Rooney's name on everyone's lips. Rooney recalls, 'I scored my first goal of the tournament. It came after a good run from Stevie Gerrard, who gave it to David Beckham. Becks pinged it to Michael Owen and he just chipped it on my head from six yards. I couldn't miss. As it was against the run of play, it gave us a bit of relief. However, I have no idea where the cartwheel came from! It was just a reaction. I got my second after Darius Vassell had done really well to hold off a defender. He played me in; I had a touch and hit it as hard as I could. Luckily, it bounced off the post, hit keeper Jorg Stiel on the head and went in.'

England needed just a draw to progress to the quarter-finals, but produced a scintillating display to see off the Croatians 4–2. Once again Rooney was the star of the show. His 45th-minute strike gave England a half-time lead and his second made him the leading scorer in the tournament. Rooney recalled, 'Before this game, the Croatia manager Otto Baric was talking about the possibility of me getting sent off but, to be fair, I don't think any of the Croatian defenders got near me to try it. I got my third goal of the tournament in this match. Paul Scholes squared it for me and I just hit it as hard as I could. Goalkeeper Tomislav Butina got a hand to it, but I think the power took it past him. I thought it was in when I struck it; the ball swerved a bit, he did get something on it but it still went in. My second goal in that match was probably my favourite. Michael Owen played it straight into my path just inside their half and I ran on with only the keeper to beat. I looked up into the right-hand corner of the goal and their keeper dived a bit early, so I just rolled the ball in the other corner. I only decided where to put it as I ran towards Butina before celebrating with Scholesy.'

England's final game of the tournament against Portugal ended 2–2, with Portugal winning 6–5 on penalties. Skipper David Beckham and Darius Vassell missed their spot-kicks. Michael Owen had given England a dream start and England held out until Spurs striker Helder Postiga's late equaliser. Sol Campbell had a last-gasp goal controversially wiped out by Swiss ref Urs Meier to take the match into extra-time. Rui Costa's rasping 110th-minute shot put Portugal ahead, but Frank Lampard levelled five minutes from the end of extra-time to bring on the dreaded shoot-out.

Rooney recalled, 'When I went off after injuring my right foot, I knew my tournament was over but we were winning at the time so I still felt confident. Unfortunately, we couldn't hold on and they scored inside the last 10 minutes. They scored again in extra-time but we fought back to take it to penalties. We know anything can happen in a shoot-out and, unfortunately, we went out. I could only watch from the team hotel, I couldn't do anything about it.'

Rooney was taken to hospital, had his foot put in plaster and then he was taken back to the team hotel with Colleen. Rooney recalled, 'At the end of the night, I was at the hotel, waiting for the rest of the team to come back and was just devastated we were out of the competition. I was cut up because we knew, if we had gone through against Portugal, we had a real chance of winning the tournament. It is the lowest I've ever felt. I really felt for the lads out on the pitch because I knew I should have been out there with them. It was fortunate for me that Colleen was with me, because it meant there was someone to talk to and watch the rest of the game with. When the lads came back, there was a bit of food laid on for everyone, but that was the last thing on anyone's mind. It was really flat. I can't remember ever feeling so low after a football match. All of us just went to bed to try and bury the disappointment. We genuinely believed we could go on to win the tournament if we had beaten Portugal.'

Rooney saw flashes of the action on a tiny television in a Lisbon hospital – and was on the way back to the team hotel when he discovered the game was heading for extra-time. 'They had a little telly in the hospital and I kept getting little glimpses of the game. It was agony. Then, just as I was leaving, one of the Portuguese lads ran out to tell me it was 1–1. Then I started getting worried. I got back to the hotel for extra-time – and that's where I watched the rest of it with Colleen. It was so difficult to take, knowing I should have been there playing.'

Despite battling on for a few minutes after being injured, Rooney knew immediately the injury was serious. 'I was in real pain and tried to run it off but I couldn't. I knew straight away it was something pretty bad. I knew I had to come off. There wasn't instant pain. I didn't feel anything when I ran with my boot off; it was only when I put it back on and put a bit of weight on it. That really started to hurt and I knew I had to come off. I went in the dressing room and put some ice on it for five or ten minutes, then they took me to hospital and I got it X-rayed. They saw straight away there was a clear break. It wasn't that difficult for me at the time. We were 1–0 up and, although I was disappointed about my foot, the lads were in front. Unfortunately, it didn't stay that way.

'They told me it was the metatarsal, to be honest I don't know much about it. I just knew it was a bone on the outside of my foot and it was broken!'

Rooney's injury has drawn comparisons with Beckham, who also suffered a broken metatarsal before the 2002 World Cup. Beckham was quick to offer a few words of advice. 'David and Gary Neville have both had the same injury and they have both told me not to rush back. They have told me it will only make it worse if I rush, so the advice is to relax and come back when it is right. It is just coincidence that it is the same injury as David had; it isn't a jinx or anything. I had the same people looking after me as looked after him but they only really spent one day with me – and that was the day after I did it. Since I came home, my own people are looking after me.'

Twenty-four hours before Beckham's penalty shoot-out horror, he fluffed a spot-kick from exactly the same place. England's skipper blasted his effort high over the bar against Portugal, while Rooney had missed with his first attempt during a practice session. 'I just scuffed it, not like Becks. But, as I hit it, it just bobbled. I more or less kicked the floor. I couldn't believe it when it went all the way to penalties and exactly the same happened to David when he took his kick. Who knows. If I'd had to take one for real, I might have done the same as Becks!'

Rooney was one of Eriksson's five picks to take a penalty in the quarter-final. Rooney said, 'I was down to take a penalty. We went training in the stadium the day before and the players took four or five each. We noticed then that the penalty spot was a bit sandy. When you put your planting foot down, your foot almost sank into the ground. So we had known from the night before the game how hard it would be to take penalties, though that's not an excuse. It was the same for both teams. It was simply a dodgy penalty spot, even if top players should be able to cope. It was really hard to keep your feet. The spot was in such terrible condition it collapsed under you when you put any weight on your standing foot. It was always going to be even tougher than usual for whoever was taking one. But it was unbelievable when that miss happened to Becks. I knew what he must have been going through, having made such a hash of my own. I felt absolutely terrible for him.'

Rooney immediately started casting half an eye forward towards the 2006 World Cup. 'There are plenty of other good young players around at the moment, like Jermain Defoe, Ledley King and Glen Johnson and, if we can stay together, we must have a great chance. That has to be the ultimate ambition, to win the World Cup. That would be the same for any player in the world. You cannot get any better.'

Gary Lineker increased the pressure on Rooney by suggesting that he could be better than Bobby Charlton, whom Rooney did not get within a decade of seeing play live. His first big tournament memory is of seeing Paul Gascoigne score against Scotland in Euro 96, while for him 1966 might just as well have been 1066.

Rooney is already fighting hard to retain a sense of perspective, while all around him others are losing theirs. He said, 'Just to be spoken of in the same sentence as Bobby Charlton, that's a big thing for anyone. Bobby Charlton was a great player: he's been there and done it and I'm just at the beginning of my career, so I've got to go out and prove myself. I think you take the compliments and just say thank you, that's always welcome. Everyone who wants to give me compliments, that's fine, but I just want to concentrate on doing my own thing. If you're getting told these things at a very young age, it can cause problems because you can get a little big-headed.'

Rooney is also learning that, once you pull on an England shirt, there is no allowance made for age or inexperience, be it an on-field performance or that private party for his girlfriend. No gentle ride was forthcoming after his disappointing display against Japan which, as he pointed out, was his first game for almost a month, and at a time when it is open season on anyone weighing an ounce more than Posh, his beefy frame has all but led to accusations that he is that pariah of all pariahs, a bad role model.

The great thing, though, is that all he needs to do to make the critics eat their words is to play really well in the World Cup finals and he has the talent to do so. He has that talent in spades.

# NINE

## SVEN-GORAN ERIKSSON AND SIR ALF RAMSEY: A COMPARISON

### SVEN-GORAN ERIKSSON

Wayne Rooney insists that the England players want to win the World Cup for Sven-Goran Eriksson, for what will be the Swede's swansong as England manager. After the World Cup draw in Leipzig, Rooney expressed solidarity for the Eriksson, despite the fact that, after a wobbly period at the start of last season, the media suggested he had 'lost' the dressing room.

Rooney said, 'There is a feeling we should win it for Sven. He's a great manager. All the players like him and respect him. He respects us and, more importantly, he trusts us. He treats us as professionals. He believes we know what is best for ourselves. He has been so unlucky in the way we have gone out of tournaments in the past. Hopefully, this time we can win it and, if there is anyone who deserves that success, it is him.

'We have done pretty well out of the draw. We have avoided some really dangerous teams like Holland and the Czech Republic. England can win the group – I have no doubts about that. We don't fear anyone but we cannot be complacent. We know we have to be totally focused. My dream scenario would be to face Brazil in the final and, hopefully, score the winner. They are probably the best team in the world and, if we are going to win it, we will have to beat them.'

Sven-Goran Eriksson is positioned firmly in the public eye to a degree that Sir Alf Ramsey would have found incomprehensible. The modern media have mushroomed to the extent that they provide blanket coverage of football, but for those on the receiving end of front-page news about their private life such intrusion can be a daunting experience. Some survive it, while others wilt under the intense pressure. The first foreign coach to the England team has been, right to the end, able to absorb more than most: whether he privately feels the strain or not, publicly he rarely showed it until the newspaper sting which effectively brought forward the agenda of his future and pre-empted the end of his reign after the finals in Germany. There are, though, several similarities between Sir Alf and Sven.

Eriksson has gone to extreme lengths to bind himself to the team. When the FA was adamant that Rio Ferdinand would not be allowed to take part in the match with Turkey in Istanbul after the missed drugs test, the Swede, by his reticence, declined to ally himself with his employers. Loyalty to the squad was more important. In return, the players trust him, as well they might, considering that no star had ever been dropped by him until Ferdinand was left out against Austria in the penultimate qualifying tie.

Both the Swede and Sir Alf come across as lacking passion. The truth is that this is not the case with either of them. Sir Geoff Hurst recalls that, when he bumped into Sir Alf many years after the '66 triumph, there was still a dispassionate air about him. Yet Sir Geoff observed, 'He wasn't really cold because there was passion in his preparation, and he had great power over the players.'

Those who claim that the defeat by Brazil in the 2002 World Cup came from Eriksson's failure to galvanise the players at half-time must feel, four years on, that the players are even less likely to be inspired now. Let's hope they're wrong!

Does he have a ruthless side? He seems almost embarrassed by the question. 'Well, if you talk to my friends, they would say sometimes: not very often, but sometimes. But, if you are angry, you can get that message to a player, or players, by talking to them. It's not necessary that you shout at them.'

Nevertheless, in his dealings with the media, Eriksson has resorted to Big Brother tactics, making sure his press conferences are filmed after being misrepresented in so many interviews.

Asked for one word to describe his management style, he came up with 'democratic', meaning he leaves a lot down to the players themselves. One example of senior players ignoring the customary chain of command in football came to light with the disclosure that, during the qualifying stages for the World Cup, Beckham and Lampard decided between themselves who was to take England penalties.

But Eriksson has no intention of altering his coaching style. 'I am like I am and, if inspiring players is standing on the touchline and shouting, I will not do that because I am not that kind of character. Inspiration, you always have that. Going to a World Cup, if you do not have inspiration then you should not be there. If I have to tell players something about behaviour or about tactics, I do it and I prefer to explain it: the reason why we must change and the reason why we must do things. That is my way of being a leader.'

In fact, he prefers Beckham to be his on-field leader rather than the more aggressive Terry. 'Beckham will be captain in Germany,' he stated. 'I cannot see any reason why we would change that. He is doing a great job and he will be important for us in Germany, so I will not change that.'

Eriksson describes his current squad as 'much stronger' than in 2002, and plans to keep his changes to a minimum in the final warm-up games, as he explained: 'Probably we are going to start with the best team – the team we hope to start with in the World Cup – but during the matches you have to change players because otherwise you come into the World Cup with players who have not been playing for one month, so there will be some changes for those three friendly games.'

Eriksson may be erring on the side of optimism when he says 10 of the best 50 players in the world are English, but what is certain is that four members of his England squad were on FIFA's 30-strong shortlist for World Player of the Year. Steven Gerrard almost single-handedly drove Liverpool to the most unexpected of European Cup successes; Frank Lampard was outstanding in Chelsea's unstoppable march to the Premiership title; Wayne Rooney would get into any team anywhere. And then there is David Beckham. He has returned to form with Real Madrid this season and is now looking assured on the right. Eriksson is not a confrontational manager and he never likes to chip away at a player's confidence. Taking the captaincy from Beckham, as some have advocated, would have a devastating impact on his confidence; it would have far greater ramifications even than dropping brilliant striker Jimmy Greaves in 1966 when Alf Ramsey made a purely footballing decision, choosing Hurst ahead of the recognised first choice goal-scorer.

While not going as far as to claim Eriksson will lead England to World Cup glory for the first time in 40 years, FA chairman Geoff Thompson is confident that the present team can emulate the recent feats of England rugby players and cricketers by mounting a serious challenge at the summit of their chosen sport. England travel to Germany with high expectations of improving on disappointing performances in recent World Cup finals, which saw them return after the second round in France in 1998 and the quarter-finals four years ago.

Thompson said, 'We do have an opportunity now in the World Cup and it would be a marvellous achievement for the whole of the country if we won. When we won the Rugby World Cup and the Ashes, we have seen what a difference a national team makes to the country.

I remember us winning the World Cup in 1966 and to do that again in my period of office would be fantastic and almost unbelievable.'

The 1–0 win over Austria, followed by Holland's result later that evening, ensured that England would proceed to the World Cup. 'The atmosphere was excellent at dinner,' Eriksson reported, when asked how his players had reacted to news they had qualified. 'We've qualified for the World Cup and I am convinced we will get good results.' Eriksson wants the critics to appreciate his side. 'Famous teams, extremely good teams, are struggling and may have to go into the play-offs,' he pointed out, thinking of France and Spain.

His command of international events, however, was brought into question when he went on to state wrongly that the European champions Greece had already been eliminated. (That came later!) 'This is a better team than it was in Portugal or Japan and at [Euro 2004] we went out for almost nothing,' he said, with reference to the penalty shoot-out defeat by the hosts, Portugal.

The manager has something to prove. Eriksson insists England are on the road to World Cup glory despite those dismal defeats in Copenhagen and Belfast. 'I always want to entertain,' said Eriksson. 'I was sure we'd qualify for the finals. We've done that. We will have a very good World Cup – that is my conviction. Whether you believe me is another question. I said a long, long speech to the players last week – much longer than usual. The message got through and they went out and did a very good job against Austria. I was extremely happy when I left Old Trafford on Saturday. Qualifying for the World Cup is not a small thing. It's why every England manager does the job. We have done excellently to qualify one game early.'

His answer to his media detractors was clear: 'My dream is the same as your dream – to win a big tournament, the World Cup. We've not done that yet, but we have gone close twice. We have an extremely good team. We haven't shown that this season, but this team, with not too many injuries, is a better team than the one in Portugal and a better team than in Japan. And in Japan and Portugal we went out in the quarter-finals because of almost nothing. That is one of the reasons I am convinced we can win. In eight months the big party starts again.'

When the FA swooped for him late in 2000, his Lazio side were reigning champions of Serie A, but until then he had been in danger of the sack.

Eriksson came in as an antidote to Kevin Keegan, who resigned confessing that he could not quite think what to do when England were losing to Germany at Wembley. Michael Owen was confused at Euro 2000 when Keegan wanted him to play as the target man, while Alan Shearer hared after too many through-balls. The man in charge before Keegan, Glenn Hoddle, had famously upset several players, including Beckham.

When Eriksson started work in January 2001, the FA could be confident that there would be no more such idiosyncrasies, or so they thought. The team have disappointed in the finals of the major tournaments, but his results in the qualifiers are a record to be proud of, with the exception of that night in Belfast.

However, given his own assessment that he has a highly impressive generation of footballers at his command, defeats in the quarter-finals of the World Cup and European Championship are unsatisfactory. Yet, he was a hero when England delivered a 5–1 rout in Munich. In a lethal expression of his counter-attacking style, the team even outdid the Germans in efficiency as they lorded it in every department that day.

Keegan, Hoddle, Terry Venables and Graham Taylor were all gone in three years or less. Before that, Bobby Robson survived for eight years and departed at his own behest after the 1990 World Cup, but managers were treated very differently back then. Robson stayed in place despite losing all three games at Euro 88 and that is the kind of record that would command the axe today.

And so we head off to the Finals with expectations high, despite all the trials and tribulations. Eriksson knows Rooney will be his ace card. 'Wayne is an extraordinary player, one of the best I have ever coached. He's only 20 yet he already has 23 caps for England, which is incredible. I don't think even Pele had that many for Brazil at 20. Rooney can be a big star at the 2006 World Cup. At Euro 2004, he played fantastically well but then got injured against Portugal. People are always asking that a person should be perfect. Wayne is a genius as a player – he has everything – but he also has a temperament. When you are a big star, everything you do, every mistake you make, will be criticised. I don't think that's fair – you can't be perfect.'

England's base is 25 minutes' drive from the German spa town of Baden-Baden, a town made famous by its 19th-century visitors – among them Queen Victoria, Bismarck, Turgenev and Dostoyevsky. They will have the use of FC Buhl's pitch as their official training ground. The team will stay in the 'fantastic' Buhlerhohe hotel, a secluded five-star resort in the Black Forest Mountains, with sweeping views of the Rhine valley, emphasising the five-star luxury of this generation compared to far more modest accommodation back in 1966. Victoria Beckham might be staying in the Dorint, another hotel in Baden-Baden.

'I'm delighted with the hotel. It's so important we have the right base camp, as this will be the players' home and set the atmosphere as we prepare for our games,' Eriksson said. 'We've already identified a training ground five minutes from the hotel which we will use every day and it is a good travelling distance to the venues we have been drawn to play in during the group phase.'

Eriksson added, 'Hopefully this hotel will be the launch pad for us to achieve success in Germany.'

Once a home for retired Prussian officers, the hotel is isolated enough to offer the England players complete privacy. It also has a luxury spa, a Michelin-starred restaurant and a couple of original Van Dycks hanging in the wood-panelled bar. A large German imperial eagle looms over the courtyard.

David Beckham and co will not be the first celebrity guests.

Germany's post-war Chancellor, Konrad Adenauer, used to visit for holidays, and Boris Becker and Germany's goalkeeper Oliver Kahn got married there. 'It's marvellous,' said Herr Striebel, the mayor of Buhl, the neighbouring town to Baden-Baden. A former defender in Germany's amateur league, he is a big fan of the English game. 'You have some of the world's greatest footballers. Beckham is the *non plus ultra* on the field. There's Owen. And you have Rooney, who is always good for a goal.'

But would they beat Germany? 'England is always an unpleasant opponent,' Striebel said without hesitation.

Eriksson's laidback manner has alienated some fans and provoked antagonism in certain sectors of the media, but he is relishing the challenge of leading England into the finals, where they will face Paraguay, Trinidad & Tobago and Sweden in what looks like a relatively straightforward group.

Speaking in the January edition of *FIFA* magazine, Eriksson revealed he dreams of going on an open-top bus ride through London just like England's rugby players did after they won the World Cup in 2003. 'I think we can win it. For people here, winning the 2006 World Cup is a big, big dream. The fans have dreamed about it for nearly 40 years and a lot of people now think we have a chance of winning. It will be very difficult, but all our players saw what happened when England won the Rugby World Cup. The team went to Trafalgar Square in London and hundreds of thousands of people came to cheer them. This country will go mad – beautifully mad – if we win the World Cup. We have a team of players with the right experience – and that's why I think we have a chance to win.'

Just as Eriksson is convinced his England team is better than the one he inherited from Kevin Keegan five years ago, so the 57-year-old Swede believes he too has improved since his first game in charge – a 3–0 win over Spain at Villa Park. 'We are much better today [than in 2001],' Eriksson told TheFA.com. 'We are technically better, we have the right age – many of them have played the World

Cup before – and the confidence is much higher. I have much more experience of international football today too. I know what is going to happen in a tournament and I know how to prepare much better than before 2002. And, now, here we are knocking on the door of the World Cup, which is fantastic. The players know we can beat anyone and we don't need to be afraid of anyone.'

But off-the-field problems were never too far away. In an unguarded moment, Eriksson told an undercover reporter – posing as a rich Arab – he would quit as England coach if they won the World Cup, and suggested he would be prepared to become manager of Aston Villa as part of a hypothetical takeover. It was the end for him. Days after stressing the importance of creating the right 'ambience' when he took over, the Swede indiscreetly told the reporter his opinions of Beckham, Ferdinand, Rooney and Owen.

It remains to be seen what effect the revelations will have on his players in the run-up to the World Cup. 'He is lazy sometimes,' Eriksson said of Manchester United centre-back Ferdinand and then, referring to Ferdinand's United team-mate Rooney, he talked of the player having a 'temper' and 'coming from a poor family'. Eriksson added that skipper Beckham was 'a bit frustrated' at Real Madrid and that he would be able to phone the England captain to persuade him to return to English football with Villa.

Eriksson also made reference to Michael Owen, who joined Newcastle in a £17m transfer from Real Madrid after a deal could not be struck with his former club Liverpool. According to the *News of the World* report, Eriksson said, 'I talked to Michael Owen and said, "You are happy?" He [Owen] said, "Not really with the club, but economically I never earned that money in my life." So they paid the salary more than Real Madrid did. He [Owen] said, "They gave me a house, they gave me a car, it's incredible." They had to do it because in any other way he wouldn't have gone there.'

Still told *Sky Sports News*, 'They're the kind of things that would be said in conversations up and down the country in what you would think is a confidential manner. They are not damaging. He has not said that any player is not good or cannot be trusted.'

The meeting with the 'Fake Sheik' took place in Dubai after Eriksson was approached for a possible consultancy role in a football academy project. Still told FA officials of the approach, adding, 'I wrote to [FA director of development] Trevor Brooking saying we had an approach and we don't know much about it, we'd like to listen to what they're saying. [I said] But it's a consultancy; if it in any way encroaches on his contract with the FA then of course we will tell you. We got a reply from Brian Barwick saying, "No problem, just keep us informed with what it is and, if any decision Sven takes would impact on his contract, then we would want to be the first to know." So it was done properly and correctly from the beginning.'

Despite the revelations, Still insisted Eriksson is 'totally committed' to England's World Cup bid. 'Sven is totally committed to doing the very best for England at the World Cup and it would be a scandal and a disaster if entrapment of this kind did anything to destabilise that situation.'

However, Still admitted he felt embarrassed at being fooled into believing the meeting in Dubai was genuine. 'It seemed completely innocuous,' Still added. 'It seemed to be just one of the many offers Sven gets to do this, that or the other, 99.9 per cent of which he has nothing to do with.'

Although the takeover of Villa was hypothetical, the club distanced itself from Eriksson's comments. A club spokesman said, 'It was a hypothetical conversation between two independent parties and, as such, nothing to do with Aston Villa.'

The FA issued a statement insisting that Eriksson continues to enjoy the full support of the organisation. 'This follows conversations between FA chief executive Brian Barwick and Sven, and subsequent conversations involving Brian with FA chairman Geoff Thompson, International Committee chairman Noel White and senior FA figures.' Eriksson said, 'I have spoken with the players concerned today and I have been very pleased with their reaction and am confident my relationship with them has not been damaged in any way.'

But in the end it was announced that Eriksson will step down as England head coach after the World Cup. The announcement followed a day of intense negotiation between the Swede and FA chief executive Brian Barwick and both set of advisors. The FA confirmed it on 23 January. A compensation deal was hammered out between Eriksson and Barwick, with the Swede agreeing a one-year pay off if he failed to find a new job in that first year, as the FA would pay him the shortfall in his deal for the first two years in his new post.

Eriksson took legal action and described the Sunday newspaper story as a 'scandal' and suggested it was difficult for the national team manager to concentrate on his job in England. 'I'm not allowed to speak about that because it's a legal action but "scandal", that's what I think about it,' he said. 'I think it could only happen in this country, that's for sure.'

He dismissed the idea that the controversy would be detrimental to England's World Cup campaign. 'If you talk about myself, my coaches, the players, the players couldn't care less about it. I spoke to many of the players and they don't care.'

Michael Owen appealed for Eriksson to be shown total support, saying, 'It shouldn't affect us, but it'll affect us if we don't stop talking about it, and everyone just gets behind the team and everyone else for the World Cup. We don't want to use that as an excuse if we don't do well, so we'd prefer to just concentrate on the football side."

Owen believes there could even be a certain advantage in the current situation, with England having known before previous major tournaments that their manager would be leaving. 'I think at Euro 96 when I think the country knew that Terry Venables was going to leave, and then again the World Cup in 1990 with Bobby Robson. On both occasions they got to the semi-finals. If that's anything to go by then hopefully we can go another step.'

## SIR ALF RAMSEY, MANAGER OF ENGLAND FROM 1963 TO 1974

Sir Bobby Charlton is best placed to compare the teams created by Sir Alf and the one Sven-Goran Eriksson will be taking to the finals in Germany.

As a Manchester United director, he has seen David Beckham develop into the England captain, watched Wayne Rooney take the step up from Everton to Old Trafford, and observed Rio Ferdinand's defensive qualities at close quarters.

Yet, for all the individual talent available to Eriksson, Sir Bobby is concerned that he has yet to convince us that he has an outstanding 'team'. Sir Bobby believes this is England's best chance for 40 years to win the World Cup and the missing ingredient is a team blend. If Eriksson can find the magic formula, England can bring home the trophy.

Sir Bobby argues, 'If you are comparing 1966 with 2006 then we have to start with the 1966 "team", and by that I mean that we were totally a team. That developed three years before we won the World Cup, to such an extent that we considered ourselves unbeatable and we were virtually unbeatable right up to the finals. We knew what we were doing together and we worked together as a team. Anybody made a mistake they were chastised. Nobody was better than anybody else; nobody was treated as being better than anybody else.'

Sir Bobby is not in the business of criticising managers or other club's players, so what goes unsaid says it all. Clearly, Eriksson has yet to discover that togetherness with his England players, and there has been plenty of adverse criticism about certain players receiving special treatment, such as the prioritising of the captain and the sense of security David Beckham possesses in terms of team selection, irrespective of how much the Real Madrid star may deny such suggestions.

The other contentious issue on the agenda is one of tactics and formation, and again Sir Bobby concentrated on Sir Alf's strengths when he recalled, 'We played 4-3-3 which was quite easy to understand and, once he implemented it, he didn't really change it once it started to become a winning formula, and that happened pretty much as soon as he introduced it.

'One of his first matches was a defeat by France, and it was quite heavy, but as soon as we went on a tour of Czechoslovakia and Switzerland and we bloomed and blossomed as players, so did the system. England didn't have a good reputation for travelling well and winning games at that time, but we came back from that tour with three wins and we knew from that time that the world was our oyster.

'Everything slotted into place, but the first time the system and our team was acknowledged by the media came when we beat Spain in Madrid – by then it was so obvious what was happening. The Spanish full-backs stayed in their normal positions, but you could see they were looking across their back line at each other wondering what to do without any wingers to mark. But, even though they had no one to mark, they stayed exactly where they had been programmed to position themselves, while we played straight through the middle.'

Sir Bobby can see few similarities between Eriksson and Sir Alf as he explained, 'We didn't have a quiet boss, by any means. We all knew our responsibilities and we also knew we were answerable to the boss if we didn't do our jobs. I don't see that in Sven. He has a different approach; his way of dealing with it is a quiet way, unlike Alf.

'We were also lot of big names in our time but Alf had us all in line and got us to gel together as a team and a unit. Most importantly, he got us to perform consistently and that is still lacking in the present England team.'

Sir Bobby is concerned that England can raise their game against the top sides but can also be mediocre against the not-so-good ones. His concern is that it is sometimes impossible to switch on the good form when you need it. He added, 'I am sure England have a chance, a good chance, perhaps their best chance in 40 years, but I would like to see a bit more consistency instead of the form being up and down depending on who we are playing. Every game has to be a big game and winning is a good habit.

'The problem with England is that, if they lose they are judged, and every time they win they are judged completely differently. There is even a lack of consistency in the way England are assessed!'

Ramsey employed a man-marker in midfielder Norbert 'Nobby' Stiles, who performed similarly to Claude Makelele, protecting the defence and allowing his three truly world-class players – Banks, Charlton and Moore – greater freedom to express themselves. There were arguably better teams than England in the 1966 finals – Hungary, the Soviet Union, West Germany and Argentina – but few were as well organised and prepared. The hosts secured a remarkably simple path to the final.

England avoided their main rivals in the group stage but then faced a formidable Argentina team, who had qualified with the West Germans in the quarter-finals. Man for man, Argentina were superior to Ramsey's squad, and they had in their captain, Antonio Rattin, the finest midfielder in the world at that time. How to sweep away this obstacle? With 10 minutes left in the first half, a German referee sent Rattin off for 'violence of the tongue', even though the referee spoke no Spanish; by this criterion Wayne Rooney would already have been banned for several lifetimes. The 10-man Argentina team struggled on, only to succumb 1–0. In a match played the same day, an English referee sent off two Uruguayans in their match against West Germany, handing the Germans an easy victory. Coincidence? Then, there was the controversy over the final, when England scored a third 'goal' in extra-time against Germany, but video evidence has never established conclusively whether it was a goal and more often suggests that the strike should have been disallowed.

Sir Alf liked a hardman in his teams and the successor to Stiles in the England team was Norman Hunter, nicknamed 'Bites yer legs'. He will always be remembered for the error that cost Sir Alf Ramsey his job, the mistake that allowed the Poles to beat England, although goalkeeper Jan Tomaszewski had as much, if not more, to do with it.

Norman rates Sir Alf as one of the best the game has seen. And he compares Eriksson favourably to the 1966 World Cup hero. Even before the qualifier with the Poles, which England won to top the group, Hunter said, 'Despite losing to Northern Ireland, England have a great record under Eriksson. I remember that the knives were out for Alf, just like they have been for Sven, which seems to go with the job. One bad mistake and you're a goner. There are quite a few similarities between the two. They don't always come across as very demonstrative in public and appear quite reserved, although I remember Alf being very passionate about football. But his attention to detail was immaculate and I think it's the same with Sven.

'The other thing that strikes me is that they both have the respect of their players. You never hear anyone who played under Alf in the England squad complain about him. And that's the same with the present England players and Eriksson. He's got the loyalty of the squad. That's so important. I wanted to play as much for the manager as for England. I think the current England players probably feel the same about Sven. Also, Alf had a nucleus of six or seven players that he picked every time. Then he put people in around them. And that's what Sven does too.

'I personally think he's a good manager. I think he'll do all right. I wouldn't knock Sven. Just look at his record. Overall it's very, very good. That's all you can look at – the qualifying situation. It's not as gloomy as people make out. I think this team can do well in Germany. I'm not saying they're going to win it but they've got players with genuine quality. OK, there have been some poor results, against Denmark and Northern Ireland. But everybody seems to forget that in my day England didn't play well in every international. I remember going to Malta and only beating them 1–0. If it hadn't been for Gordon Banks we would have lost – and against a team like that it would have been unheard of.'

Hunter would have got a lot more caps if it hadn't been for the imperious form of the great Bobby Moore. He said, 'I still played in quite a few games – but I'm never given a chance to forget about Poland 32 years ago! Every fourth year, when we try to qualify for the World Cup, we always seem to draw bloody Poland. And there's me on telly missing the ball on the halfway line, Barry Davies commentating and them scoring.'

On 17 October 1973, at Wembley, Poland took the lead in the 55th minute in a rare breakaway raid. Hunter, the most feared tackler in English football, mistimed a 50-50 challenge with Robert Gadocha on the touchline and the ball went to Domarski, who shot under Peter Shilton. Clarke equalised from the spot but the draw meant England failed to qualify for the 1974 World Cup.

Hunter said, 'I should have had that tackle. I should have put their fella and the ball into the Royal Box. And then Shilts should have thrown his cap on it. But these things happen; you don't make mistakes on purpose. I've never played in a more one-sided game in my life than that one. I've sat through that match again on video and it's unbelievable how we didn't win it 6–1 or more. I sat and watched that game from the halfway line. I was hardly involved. If we'd have qualified, Alf wouldn't have gone. He was changing the team. He was giving new people like me, Paul Madeley, Clarkey, Channon, Chivers and Tony Currie a chance. Great players. I still think the approach was right – all-out attack.'

If Sven wants to emulate the great Sir Alf and lift the World Cup, his players are going to have to perform brilliantly where it counts, out on the pitch. That way, this generation will also have great memories to last a lifetime.

# TEN

**GUIDE TO THE WORLD CUP FINALISTS:**

THE GOOD, THE BAD AND THE UGLY

## 194 TEAMS, 847 GAMES AND 2,464 GOALS

As is always the case with the four-yearly FIFA World Cup preliminary competition, the world's biggest football tournament has once again served up a treasure trove for statistics lovers. While there was no increase in the number of teams that entered the 2002 qualifiers (194) – and that figure can barely increase significantly given the number of FIFA member associations – the number of matches required to determine the 31 teams that would join hosts Germany in the final competition rose by almost 10 per cent, with some 847 games played across the six geographical zones. Over 18 million spectators – approximately 22,000 per match – attended matches and celebrated a total of 2,464 goals (averaging 2.91 per game).

When Brazil tore apart Argentina in last summer's Confederations Cup final in Germany, they firmly established themselves as favourites for the World Cup. The current side – boasting such glittering attacking luminaries as Kaka, Adriano, Julio Baptista,

Ronaldo, World Player of the Year Ronaldinho and the 'new Pele', Robinho – has to be rated as one of the best ever, even by Brazilian standards. But can they hope to eclipse the great team from the 1970 World Cup?

Pele – Edson Arantes do Nascimento – thinks it is impossible to compare the two. 'Six months before the World Cup, I think Brazil had the best team,' said the legendary, three-time World Cup winner. 'To compare with 1970 is a little complicated because before 1970 some newspapers used to compare the team from 1958, which was special, with the team from 1970. My point of view is that in 1958 we had more individual players than in 1970 – Didi, Zagalo, Santos, Garrincha. What we had in 1970, as well as good players, was time to prepare. I remember back then, because we didn't have too many exhibition games, we played together, with the qualifiers and the preparation, for one whole year. Then the side became a real team.'

With the heavy demands on players today, Pele fears that the current Brazil side can never hope to replicate this sense of togetherness. '[Carlos Alberto] Parreira doesn't have one year to practise with the players. They have good players who play for different teams. Individually they are very good, no doubt – two great players in each position. But maybe as a team it is complicated. It is difficult to compare with 1970. They were more unified – Tostao, Jarzinho, Gerson, Rivelino.'

The burden of being pre-tournament favourites is, however, unwelcome in Pele's eyes. 'Every national team that goes to the World Cup as favourites has problems,' he cautioned. 'The last time it was France and Argentina – they didn't qualify; in 1982 Brazil was the best team in Spain – they didn't win; Holland was twice, in Germany and Argentina, the best team – they didn't win. I warn against being favourites. But Brazil has a good team, no doubt.'

The successful Brazil side of 1958 were the only non-European team to win on the continent – in Sweden. But since most of the

Brazilian squad are now based with European teams, the task seems easier this time, though 'it is not only an advantage for Brazil as a lot of nations have most of their players playing for big clubs in Europe now.'

'It was my first World Cup and I was 17 years old,' reminisced Pele of the 1958 tournament. 'To be with the team was like a dream for me. It was my first time travelling in Europe. The Brazil team trained near the Swedish team and the England team, and France was close as well. I looked around and saw that only Brazil had black players. I thought, "Why don't the other teams have black players?" I was surprised.'

That has since changed and, aside from his immeasurable contribution to the playing side of the game, Pele also takes great pleasure in having represented black players during a time of social change. 'Now I travel with Brazil and FIFA and see that every team has black players, all over the world. The social situation has changed. It makes me feel proud to be part of that. Football brings everyone together. Football is the biggest family in the world: FIFA has more affiliates than the UN. I feel proud, also, to be part of this social contribution.'

Pele's reputation was built on a sense of fair play as much as for his wonderful array of skills, but he feels some of this spirit is being lost in the modern game.

'The way young players play the game and treat each other has changed a little bit,' he said, 'because there is too much money involved. This is a danger for the future of football. I make a joke about some players – they sign with Real Madrid in Spain and kiss the shirt and say, "I love you Real Madrid." Tomorrow they go to Manchester United, kiss that shirt saying, "I love you Manchester United." It makes me laugh.'

# THE 2006 WORLD CUP FINALISTS

## ANGOLA
Federation: Africa
World ranking: 62
Coach: Luis Oliveira Goncalves
Player to watch: Fabrice 'Akwa' Maieco (Qatar Sports Club)
Road to finals: Winners of Group Four ahead of Nigeria on the head-to-head rule
World Cup record: First-time qualifiers

## ARGENTINA
Federation: Conmebol
World ranking: 4
Coach: Jose Pekerman
Player to watch: Juan Roman Riquelme (Villarreal, Spain)
Road to finals: Runners-up in group
World Cup record: 1930, 1934, 1958, 1962, 1966, 1974, 1978, 1982, 1986, 1990, 1994, 1998, 2002
Tournament best: Winners in 1978, 1986; Runners-up in 1930, 1990

## AUSTRALIA
Federation: Oceania
World ranking: 49
Coach: Guus Hiddink
Player to watch: Marco Bresciano (Parma, Italy)
Road to finals: Winners of Oceania; Winners of Oceania/CONMEBOL play-off against Uruguay
World Cup record: 1974
Tournament best: Group Stage in 1974

## BRAZIL

Federation: CONMEBOL

World ranking: 1

Coach: Carlos Alberto Parreira

Player to watch: Ronaldinho (Barcelona, Spain)

Road to finals: Winners of group

World Cup record: 1930, 1934, 1938, 1950, 1954, 1958, 1962, 1966, 1970, 1974, 1978, 1982, 1986, 1990, 1994, 1998, 2002

Tournament best: Winners in 1958, 1962, 1970, 1994, 2002; Runners-up in 1950, 1998

## COSTA RICA

Federation: CONCACAF

World ranking: 21

Coach: Alexandre Guimaraes

Player to watch: Paulo Wanchope (Al-Garafah, Qatar)

Road to finals: Third in group

World Cup record: 1990, 2002

Tournament best: Round of 16 in 1990

## CROATIA

Federation: UEFA

World ranking: 20

Coach: Zlatko Kranjcar

Player to watch: Dario Srna (Shakhtar Donetsk, Ukraine)

Road to finals: Winners of Group Eight ahead of Sweden on the head-to-head rule

World Cup record: 1998, 2002

Tournament best: Third place in 1998

## CZECH REPUBLIC

Federation: UEFA

World ranking: 2

Coach: Karel Bruckner

Player to watch: Pavel Nedved (Juventus, Italy)

Road to finals: Runners-up in Group One; Winners of play-off against Norway

World Cup record: First-time qualifiers*

*Czechoslovakia reached the finals in 1934, 1938, 1954, 1958, 1962, 1970, 1982, 1990. They were runners-up in 1934, 1962

## ECUADOR

Federation: CONMEBOL

World ranking: 37

Coach: Luis Fernando Suarez

Player to watch: Christian Lara (El Nacional, Ecuador)

Road to finals: Third in group

World Cup record: 2002

Tournament best: Group stage in 2002

## ENGLAND

Federation: UEFA

World ranking: 9

Coach: Sven-Goran Eriksson

Player to watch: Wayne Rooney (Manchester United, England)

Road to finals: Winners of Group Six

World Cup record: 1950, 1954, 1958, 1962, 1966, 1970, 1982, 1986, 1990, 1998, 2002

Tournament best: Winners in 1966

## FRANCE

Federation: UEFA

World ranking: 5

Coach: Raymond Domenech

Player to watch: Florent Malouda (Lyon, France)

Road to finals: Winners of Group Four

World Cup record: 1930, 1934, 1938, 1954, 1958, 1966, 1978, 1982, 1986, 1998, 2002
Tournament best: Winners in 1998

## GERMANY

Federation: UEFA
World ranking: 16
Coach: Jurgen Klinsmann
Player to watch: Bastian Schweinsteiger (Bayern Munich, Germany)
Road to finals: Qualified as hosts
World Cup record: 1934, 1938, 1994, 1998, 2002*
Tournament best: Runners-up in 2002*
*Outside of unification, Germany played separately as East and West between 1949 and 1990 and were represented at the World Cup in 1954, 1958, 1962, 1966, 1970, 1974, 1978, 1982, 1986, 1990. West Germany won the World Cup in 1954, 1974, 1990; and were runners-up in 1966, 1982, 1986. East Germany qualified only once in 1974, reaching the second group stage.

## GHANA

Federation: Africa
World ranking: 50
Coach: Ratomir Dujkovic
Player to watch: Sulley Ali Muntari (Udinese, Italy)
Road to finals: Winners of Group Two
World Cup record: First-time qualifiers

## IRAN

Federation: Asia
World ranking: 19
Coach: Branko Ivankovic

Player to watch: Ali Daei (Saba Battery, Iran)
Road to finals: Runners-up in Group Two
World Cup record: 1978, 1998
Tournament best: Group stage in 1978, 1998

## ITALY

Federation: UEFA
World ranking: 12
Coach: Marcello Lippi
Player to watch: Luca Toni (Fiorentina, Italy)
Road to finals: Winners of Group Five
World Cup record: 1934, 1938, 1950, 1954, 1962, 1966, 1970, 1974, 1978, 1982, 1986, 1990, 1994, 1998, 2002
Tournament best: Winners in 1934, 1938, 1982; Runners-up in 1970, 1994

## IVORY COAST

Federation: Africa
World ranking: 41
Coach: Henri Michel
Player to watch: Didier Drogba (Chelsea, England)
Road to finals: Winners of Group Three
World Cup record: First-time qualifiers

## JAPAN

Federation: Asia
World ranking: 15
Coach: Zico
Player to watch: Naohiro Takahara (Hamburg, Germany)
Road to finals: Winners of Group Two
World Cup record: 1998, 2002
Tournament best: Round of 16 in 2002

## MEXICO

Federation: CONCACAF

World ranking: 7

Coach: Ricardo Lavolpe

Player to watch: Jose Fonseca (Cruz Azul, Mexico)

Road to finals: Runners-up in group

World Cup record: 1930, 1950, 1954, 1958, 1962, 1966, 1970, 1978, 1986, 1994, 1998, 2002

Tournament best: Quarter-finals in 1970, 1986

## NETHERLANDS

Federation: UEFA

World ranking: 3

Coach: Marco van Basten

Player to watch: Rafael van der Vaart (Hamburg, Germany)

Road to finals: Winners of Group One

World Cup record: 1934, 1938, 1974, 1978, 1990, 1994, 1998

Tournament best: Runners-up in 1974, 1978

## PARAGUAY

Federation: CONMEBOL

World ranking: 30

Coach: Anibal Ruiz

Player to watch: Nelson Haedo Valdez (Werder Bremen, Germany)

Road to finals: Fourth in group

World Cup record: 1930, 1950, 1958, 1986, 1998, 2002

Tournament best: Round of 16 in 1998, 2002

## POLAND

Federation: UEFA

World ranking: 23

Coach: Pawel Janas

Player to watch: Maciej Zurawski (Celtic, Scotland)

Road to finals: Runners-up in Group Six; Second-best runners-up

World Cup record: 1938, 1974, 1978, 1982, 1986, 2002

Tournament best: Third place in 1974, 1982

## PORTUGAL

Federation: UEFA

World ranking: 10

Coach: Luiz Felipe Scolari

Player to watch: Cristiano Ronaldo (Manchester United, England)

Road to finals: Winners of Group Three

World Cup record: 1966, 1986, 2002

Tournament best: Third place in 1966

## SAUDI ARABIA

Federation: Asia

World ranking: 32

Coach: Marcos Cesar Paqueta

Player to watch: Hamad Al Montashari (Al Ittihad, Saudi Arabia)

Road to finals: Winners of Group One

World Cup record: 1994, 1998, 2002

Tournament best: Round of 16 in 1994

## SERBIA & MONTENEGRO

Federation: UEFA

World ranking: 47

Coach: Ilija Petkovic

Player to watch: Dejan Stankovic (Inter Milan, Italy)

Road to finals: Winners of Group Seven

World Cup record: First-time qualifiers*

*Yugoslavia reached the finals in 1930, 1950, 1954, 1958, 1962, 1974, 1982, 1990, 1998. They reached the semi-finals in 1930, 1954 (fourth).

## SOUTH KOREA

Federation: Asia
World ranking: 29
Coach: Dick Advocaat
Player to watch: Park Ji-Sung (Manchester United, England)
Road to finals: Runners-up in Group One
World Cup record: 1954, 1986, 1990, 1994, 1998, 2002
Tournament best: Fourth place in 2002

## SPAIN

Federation: UEFA
World ranking: 6
Coach: Luis Aragones
Player to watch: Fernando Torres (Atletico Madrid, Spain)
Road to finals: Runners-up in Group Seven; Winners of play-off against Slovakia
World Cup record: 1934, 1950, 1962, 1966, 1978, 1982, 1986, 1990, 1994, 1998, 2002
Tournament best: Fourth place in 1950

## SWEDEN

Federation: UEFA
World ranking: 14
Coach: Lars Lagerback
Player to watch: Zlatan Ibrahimovic (Juventus, Italy)
Road to finals: Runners-up in Group Eight; Best runners-up
World Cup record: 1934, 1938, 1950, 1958, 1970, 1974, 1978, 1990, 1994, 2002
Tournament best: Runners-up in 1958

## SWITZERLAND

Federation: UEFA
World ranking: 36
Coach: Kobi Kuhn
Player to watch: Alexander Frei (Stade Rennais, France)
Road to finals: Runners-up in Group Four; Winners of play-off against Turkey
World Cup record: 1934, 1938, 1950, 1954, 1962, 1966, 1994
Tournament best: Quarter-finals in 1934, 1938, 1954

## TOGO

Federation: Africa
World ranking: 56
Coach: Stephen Keshi
Player to watch: Emmanuel Adebayor (Arsenal, England)
Road to finals: Winners of Group One
World Cup record: First-time qualifiers

## TRINIDAD & TOBAGO

Federation: CONCACAF
World ranking: 51
Coach: Leo Beenhakker
Player to watch: Chris Birchall (Port Vale, England)
Road to finals: Fourth in CONCACAF group; Winners of CONCACAF/Asia play-off against Bahrain
World Cup record: First-time qualifiers

## TUNISIA

Federation: Africa
World ranking: 28
Coach: Roger Lemerre
Player to watch: Francileudo dos Santos Silva (Toulouse, France)

Road to finals: Winners of Group Five
World Cup record: 1978, 1998, 2002
Tournament best: Group stage in 1978, 1998, 2002

## UKRAINE

Federation: UEFA
World ranking: 40
Coach: Oleh Blokhin
Player to watch: Andriy Shevchenko (AC Milan, Italy)
Road to finals: Winners of Group Two
World Cup record: First-time qualifiers

## UNITED STATES

Federation: CONCACAF
World ranking: 8
Coach: Bruce Arena
Player to watch: Landon Donovan (Los Angeles Galaxy,
United States)
Road to finals: Winners of group
World Cup record: 1930, 1934, 1950, 1990, 1994, 1998, 2002
Tournament best: Semi-finals in 1930

* World rankings as of 1.1.06

## A–Z OF TEAMS LINING UP WITH ENGLAND IN THE FINALS

### ANGOLA

A bunch of little-known players who primarily earn their living in their own domestic league took Angola to the finals. A goal 10 minutes from time by striker and captain Fabrice Akwa against Rwanda was enough to put the Black Panthers through at the expense of the millionaire stars of Nigeria, whose 5–1 thrashing of Zimbabwe in Lagos was not enough. Angola finished top thanks to their superior record against Nigeria, with whom they finished level on points. The fact that they have managed to win Group Four at the expense of the Super Eagles is all the more remarkable considering their squad contains hardly any players known outside their own country.

Akwa plies his trade in Qatar and midfielder Edson plays for Pacos Ferreira in Portugal, but the majority of the squad play at home in the Angolan league. 'Great! Great! fantastic! I hope we try to do a good job in the World Cup,' said an ecstatic Akwa after the Rwanda game. 'This is a great thing for a country like Angola. We will start to prepare ourselves for the finals in Germany.'

Angola have built on a decent youth team, but horrific civil unrest has defined their people's life for most of the last 30 years, with an estimated million lives lost between independence from Portugal in 1975 and the ceasefire in 2002. They have a longstanding football culture, and most Portuguese national teams of the last 20 years have benefited from players with Angolan roots. Four years ago, they had a good enough set of teenagers to reach the last 16 of the world Under-21 championships. This time, group opponents Nigeria did the required, thrashing Zimbabwe. In turn, Angola, who needed three points, then did the unprecedented: they won in Rwanda, which nobody else in their group had done. Now they have a new national hero: Fabrice Akwa who scored the goal that took them to Germany.

Akwa has done time in the Portuguese league, and was employed for a while at Benfica. Though the *Palancas Negras* draw a number of their players from European clubs, they will arrive in Germany distinctly short of household names. One, though, to note is Pedro Mantorras, the Benfica striker who not so long ago was celebrated as among the finest young strikers in the world.

## ARGENTINA

Argentina are second only to Brazil in the betting for the World Cup and blessed with a frightening array of talent, which is why their defeat at the hands of England in Geneva gave fresh hope to Sven-Goran Eriksson's team. It was a major blow for Argentina to go ahead twice only to lose 3–2, but it might also prove to be a wake-up call as they are deeply concerned that the dismal experience of 2002 in the Far East must not be repeated.

Jose Pekerman's team were the first major side to qualify with a breathtaking 3–1 victory over Brazil in Buenos Aires in June. But in a confidence-sapping run, they lost their final three away games and with them first place in the group. The defeat by England was just as debilitating.

It increased anxieties that arriving at the best line-up was still some distance away. Even before the defeat by England, former World Cup-winning coaches Cesar Luis Menotti and Carlos Bilardo found themselves in rare agreement that Pekerman should name 10 or 12 players who would definitely be on the plane to Germany. 'Now there's great uncertainty, nobody knows who is a first choice and that leads everybody to voice opinions,' said Menotti. He was alluding to the discord between veterans such as Roberto Ayala and Chelsea's Hernan Crespo, and the younger generation. 'Something's up: things aren't going well,' said Bilardo. 'Something's going on between the players.'

Absent again from the squad that faced England in a friendly in Geneva was Juan Sebastian Veron. The midfielder's reputation may have suffered from his spells at Manchester United and Chelsea, but the man known as *La Brujita* (The Little Witch) still casts a spell in Argentina. Not, though, over Pekerman, who has ignored the Inter midfielder's claims since he took over as national coach after Marcelo Bielsa's surprise resignation barely a month after winning gold in the 2004 Olympics.

Pekerman came with an outstanding record at youth level, having coached Argentina's Under-20 side to three world titles and two South American championships. He promoted a number of players who had 'grown up' in his teams. Veron's role as captain went to the

Villarreal full-back Juan Pablo Sorin, a veteran of the 2002 World Cup side, and his position as midfield linchpin went to Juan Roman Riquelme, the Barcelona playmaker currently on long-term loan to Villarreal, who put on a virtuoso performance against England. Before that, Bilardo had called for Veron's restoration to the squad, as had the player himself: 'If I were Pekerman, I would pick me.'

The signs, though, are not good for him. Veron's former team-mate Crespo, however, started and scored in Geneva despite his lack of playing time for Chelsea. But another striker, Carlos Tevez, is on top form; the 21-year-old hit a superb hat-trick as Corinthians thrashed the Brazilian champions Santos 7–1.

Argentina's last World Cup final was in 1990 and they have noticeably failed to punch their weight since their successes of 1978 and 1986. The national psyche is split between two major events: Sir Alf Ramsey calling them 'animals' in the 1966 tournament and, two decades later, when Diego Maradona teased, tormented and dumped England out of the 1986 World Cup. Maradona's continuing importance to their psyche is reflected in a recent offer made by Argentine FA president Julio Grondona. Likening himself to a groom awaiting his bride, Grondona explained that the offer made to the football legend was an open one. 'He has the possibility of working in the coaching set-up. Everything depends on him.'

On the field, the quest for a new Maradona has been frustrating. Crespo is proven at club level, but the departure of Gabriel Batistuta has left a void at international level. Goals and natural goalscorers remain in short supply, which partly explains the recall of Inter Milan's Julio Cruz from the international wilderness.

Lionel Messi, 18, such a success at Barcelona, and Juan Roman Riquelme are exceptional. The Villarreal midfielder is Argentina's fulcrum, directing play and fizzing in shots. Riquelme is rediscovering the form at Villarreal that guided Boca to successive Libertadores Cup titles.

While the likes of Valencia's Roberto Ayala and Inter Milan's Javier

Zanetti will be part of the European legion, two of the better younger talents have chosen an alternative trail – in Brazilian club football. There are high hopes for Javier Mascherano, a midfielder, who earlier this year moved from River Plate to Corinthians where he linked up with compatriot Tevez. Despite injury, Mascherano is believed by many experts to be potentially the best young midfielder in the world.

But, until Messi, Independiente's 17-year-old Sergio Aguero or another hopeful stakes a sustained claim to the mystical No.10 shirt, serious doubts about their strikers remain. At 18, Messi is already a star at Barcelona and the latest to be hailed as his nation's football saviour and one of the world's most exciting teenagers.

He led his country to victory at the world Under-20 championship in Holland last July. He was the outstanding player in Argentina's success at a tournament where they have a strong tradition and where their star attacking player is almost inevitably celebrated as the new Maradona. It happened to Pablo Aimar after the 1997 tournament, to Javier Saviola in 2001, and now to Messi.

Maradona tends to anoint his successors quite freely and he had Messi on his chat show on Argentinean TV shortly after the youth championship, gleefully encouraging the public to see a bit of himself in the youngster. They are both short with a preference for the left foot and they also share a connection with Barcelona, where Maradona played and partied in the 1980s. Barca youth-team coach Guillermo Hoyos, a contemporary of Maradona in Argentinean junior teams, said, 'He has that same low centre of gravity. He can take on two or three people and, when you think he's going to lose balance, somehow keeps his feet and beats the goalkeeper. I'd only ever seen Diego do that, until I saw Leo. He's got artistry and magic.'

## AUSTRALIA

Australia beat Uruguay on penalties at Sydney's Telstra Stadium to reach the World Cup finals for the first time in 32 years. The

Socceroos, having lost the first leg of their play-off 1–0 in Montevideo, pulled level with Mark Bresciano's first-half goal and the match went to a penalty shoot-out. John Aloisi clinched victory with their fourth spot-kick.

After a wait of 32 years since their only appearance at football's biggest tournament, Australia will be in Germany after holding on in front of 82,698 fans. Among the crowd was Hollywood actor John Travolta, who celebrated with the Socceroos in the changing room after the dramatic finale.

Australia coach Guus Hiddink, who is also in charge of Dutch side PSV Eindhoven, now has the opportunity to enhance his World Cup pedigree after taking joint hosts South Korea to the semi-finals in 2002. Hiddink certainly has the players to make an impact at next year's tournament, with the enterprise of Merseyside duo Tim Cahill and Harry Kewell giving Australia possibilities going forward. 'Now the focus will be on going to the World Cup and not making up the numbers, but putting in some great performances and hopefully even progressing,' goalkeeper Mark Schwarzer said after the Uruguay game. 'We want to achieve great things – we've got the team to do it and the manager to do it. Everyone is pulling in the right direction.'

Hiddink, 59, took over from Frank Farina last summer and achieved instant success, although those familiar with his record will not be surprised. Seldom in charge of wealthy teams, he has won five league titles, four domestic cups and one European Cup, with PSV Eindhoven in 1988. In 2004–05, his defensive-minded PSV team won a league and cup double and reached the Champions League semi-finals, although his South Korea team was based on all-out attack. His club career has also included spells – some extremely short – with Fenerbahce, Valencia, Real Madrid and Real Betis.

Football is Australia's most popular sport, with more people playing the game than Australian Rules football, rugby league, rugby union or even cricket, and the country was united in support of the Socceroos, who had suffered the heartbreak of losing play-offs for the past two tournaments. Mark Viduka, the Australia captain, had called for a sea of green and gold to help them overcome the 1–0 deficit from the first leg, and a passionate crowd in the Telstra Stadium, with thousands more watching on giant screens around the country, were not to be disappointed.

### BRAZIL (HOLDERS)

Sven-Goran Eriksson's right-hand man and master scout, Tord Grip, believes England can win the tournament providing they can beat Brazil. 'The tournament may be in Europe, but I see the Brazilians as the test of quality that the rest will have to overcome if they are to be crowned best in the world. Most of their strengths are in attacking areas. In Adriano, I believe they have the best striker in Europe at the moment. When I watched them play, he was in devastating form. They didn't miss the absent Ronaldo. And, alongside Adriano, they have Robinho, Kaka, Ze Roberto and the wonderful Ronaldinho. In terms of attacking options and invention, they must be the best in the world.

'When you assess their key men, there are so many in attacking areas it can be frightening. Brazil play a diamond formation and it's a very exciting system. They try and thread passes through you. The width is provided by their fast-raiding full-backs, Roberto Carlos and their new exciting discovery Cicinho. Cicinho is ready to succeed Cafu at right-back. He looks a great prospect. Cafu's 35 now and a real veteran but his athleticism is still outstanding. He does a vital job. Coach Carlos Parreira does worry about their defence and does a lot of work on defending. They play a back four with Lucio and Roque Junior as their centre-backs. Leeds fans, who remember Roque Junior's unhappy loan spell there, will be surprised that he's still a regular for Brazil.

'You can see why Parreira is so keen to improve his team's defending as a unit. But at the other end he knows he has players who can always conjure up goals. As I said, knock out Brazil and there's every chance you'll win the World Cup.'

Brazil coach Carlos Alberto Parreira does not want to hear the word 'magic' again in the run-up to the World Cup. After the world champions completed the qualifiers with a 3–0 win over Venezuela, Parreira said he would keep his ultra-attacking line-up with four out of Robinho, Ronaldo, Ronaldinho, Kaka and Adriano. But he said he would not be calling it the 'Magic Quartet', the name favoured by the Brazilian media. 'The word magic is not part of our vocabulary,' Parreira told reporters after the game in Belem. 'We're not getting involved in this sort of talk. I want to hear words like efficiency, productivity, winning well, sweat, perspiration and talent.'

Brazil, who finished top of the 10-nation South American group with 34 points, ahead of Argentina on goal difference, will arrive in Germany as hot favourites, their usual pre-World Cup position. It is hardly surprising: as well as reigning world champions, they are holders of the Copa America and the Confederations Cup, while Brazilian club Sao Paulo are holders of the South American Libertadores Cup as well as being FIFA Club World Champions after victory over Liverpool in Japan.

Months ahead of the finals, Parreira had virtually settled on his line-up. It is likely to be the one which started that final qualifying game: Dida; Cafu, Juan, Lucio, Roberto Carlos; Emerson, Ze Roberto, Kaka, Ronaldinho; Adriano, Ronaldo. For the time being, Real Madrid's Robinho will have to sit on the bench along with other great players, who would walk into any other national team.

'Other teams have problems deciding who will be picked; we have problems deciding who will be left out,' said Parreira. 'Some very good players will miss out because we can only take 23.'

Parreira's final choice for Germany would be based on an assessment of Brazil's 18-match qualifying campaign, which lasted all of two years and one month and began when Rivaldo was still a regular and Kaka a mere hopeful. 'For me, the qualifiers were great, I claimed my place in the team,' said Kaka.

Among the players on the fringe of the final 23 are Fenerbahce midfielder Alex, who was recalled for the final two matches against Bolivia and Venezuela after nine months out of the squad. Others uncertainties include midfielders Gilberto Silva and Renato, Real Madrid's Julio Baptista, plus Gustavo Nery and Gilberto, the two candidates to be Roberto Carlos's understudy.

The prospect of the first Brazilian triumph in Europe since 1958 is fuelled by the genius and finishing power of Ronaldinho, Robinho and Ronaldo. Robinho is sure to emerge as the tournament unfolds. It was another Three Rs who triumphed in Yokohama in 2002: then the Brazil coach, Luiz Felipe Scolari, profited from the brilliance of Ronaldinho, Ronaldo's revived scoring instinct and the last knockings of Rivaldo as a major performer.

In 2006, the Brazilians, yet again, promise to light up the world, just as they did in Sweden 48 years ago when they unleashed a miracle of precocity in the 17-year-old Pele, and in 1970 when Pele, again, Tostao, Gerson and Carlos Alberto defined all the beauty, and the majesty, of football.

In the year of England's triumph in 1966, Brazil were kicked cruelly out of the tournament by Portugal and Hungary, but, while England look for the symmetry of 1966 to 2006, the Brazilians will be looking back to Sweden. 'In our team's history,' said Parreira, 'to go to a World Cup as favourites means we don't win it.'

But Brazil's talented individuals will not be concerned about the superstition that South Americans find it harder to win World Cups in Europe. The 2006 Brazilians are seasoned Europeans, carrying a smart collection of Bundesliga titles, Italian *scudetti*, Spanish La Ligas and Champions League medals. They also have stability: eight of the team were together in South Korea and Japan; three played at France 98. 'We're a united group, who all know each other very well,' said Ronaldinho.

Brazil's antique full-backs – Roberto Carlos and Cafu are a combined 67 years old – are still galloping forward; every other team will try to exploit the spaces these two thoroughbreds leave behind them. There are uncertainties in defence. At centre-half, Bayern's Lucio requires an established partner. Roque Junior, the Leverkusen defender, captained his country against Bolivia, with most of the first XI rested. Against Venezuela he was replaced by Juan.

In front of the back four, Juventus's Emerson remains a fulcrum, as he should have been at the last finals, but he injured a shoulder playing goalkeeper in a kickabout before the first fixture. Next to Emerson, Parreira has asked Ze Roberto, another Bayern man, to adapt his game from outside-left to central midfield, noting that Ze Roberto is currently closer to a regular place with Brazil than with his club.

Beyond the first XI, the next four or five places in Parreira's World Cup finals party will go to the likes of Lyon's Juninho Pernambucano, Madrid's Robinho, Arsenal's Gilberto Silva and, if he returns to form after a long injury, Barcelona's Edmilson.

Parreira could select a further three just from Barca, or another four from Lyon if he wanted. At most, he will select only one or two still employed within Brazil.

At the World Cup finals, there might be enough talent to make yet another Brazilian XI, assembled from players whose Brazilian passports have been traded for others to embark on an international career.

Portugal? Coached by Brazil's Luis Felipe Scolari, their prospects are partly defined by Deco, born on the other side of the Atlantic, and now a naturalised Portuguese. Spain? A poised Brazilian midfielder Marcos Senna, Spanish-qualified by residence, is offering himself to a grateful Spain coach, Luis Aragones. Japan's Brazilian coach Zico will make Alessandro Santos (Alex), born in Sao Paolo, one of the first names in his squad. Clayton, another Brazilian, will play his third World Cup tournament for Tunisia.

Mexico have already capped Zinha, a Brazilian working in their league, and may be tempted to grant a place to the teenager Giovani dos Santos, whose father is from Brazil. Germany's centre-forward Kevin Kuranyi was born in Rio de Janeiro.

Ailton, Dede and Leandro, three Brazilians operating in the Bundesliga, were offered seven-figure sums to make themselves available to Qatar, whose government would give them instant citizenship in time for their World Cup qualifiers. None had any connection with the country. FIFA blocked the plan, though they were too late to bolt their door on the four Brazilians who acquired Togolese passports suddenly in 2003 and were selected by Togo's then coach, the Brazilian Antonio Dumas, to represent the country. Only two of them, Alessandro Faria and Jefferson de Souza, took part early on in Togo's remarkable qualifying run. They still have their Togolese passports in case they are needed.

## COSTA RICA

Having qualified alongside the United States and Mexico for their second successive finals, Costa Rica have established themselves as the third-strongest team in North and Central America and their style of play makes them perhaps the most popular from the region for the neutral.

A wonderfully adventurous approach helped to light up the last World Cup finals as they outplayed Turkey, who went on to reach the semi-finals, in a 1–1 draw and were involved in arguably the tournament's most entertaining game, a 5–2 defeat by Brazil.

Costa Rica's attacking strategy was evident again when they built a two-goal lead against France before going down 3–2 in a World Cup warm-up game. Perhaps their tactics reflect the heritage of Alexandre Guimaraes, who has returned as coach having led the team in 2002. He was born in Brazil and moved to Costa Rica at the age of 11.

Most of the team are based in their own country, but Paulo

Wanchope and Winston Parks, the two senior strikers, play in Qatar and Russia respectively. Paulo Wanchope became Costa Rica's all-time leading scorer last month with his 43rd goal in 67 appearances. The long-legged striker rejected a career in basketball before turning out for Derby County, West Ham United and Manchester City and is still baffling defenders in Qatar with his ability to keep the ball when it seems he does not have it under control, and vice versa. He has said that he will retire after the finals. Another attacking option is the podgy Ronald Gomez, whose expertise from free-kicks has helped him to win more than 100 caps.

Costa Rica use a 3-5-2 system with a defensive line that includes Luis Marin, who made his 117th appearance against France. Coach Alexandre Guimaraes is synonymous with Costa Rica and the World Cup. He was the midfield creator when they reached round two in 1990, beating Scotland along the way, and he was the coach in their only other finals appearance three years ago. In the latest qualifying campaign, the team seemed to have little chance of making the finals after their opening games, so Guimaraes was recalled to his former post and success followed.

Interesting fact: Costa Rica beat China at the 2002 World Cup finals, despite the Chinese population being at least 300 times larger than their own.

## CROATIA

Croatia may not be among the favourites, but they have at least established themselves as a member of the elite. Since being admitted to international competitions by UEFA and FIFA, Croatia have qualified for five out of six major tournaments, and the one time they failed to do so, for the Euro 2000 finals, they missed out by a single goal. What makes the Croats proud is this amazing qualifying record: in all World Cup- or Euro-qualifying games since 1994, Croatia have suffered no more than five defeats and, in World Cup qualifiers alone, just one – in September 1997 in

Copenhagen. Besides, the Croats have yet to be beaten in a competitive game at home.

In the qualifiers for the forthcoming World Cup finals, Croatia finished top of a very competitive Group Eight, ahead of Sweden, Hungary, Bulgaria, Iceland and Malta. Sven-Goran Eriksson's assistant Tord Grip said, 'They are my dark horses. They have a very experienced team packed with big powerful players like Igor Tudor and the Kovac brothers. They remind me of the way Greece played in winning the last European Championship. They use a 3-5-2 system and are happy to play on the counter-attack. Up front they have Rangers' big striker Dado Prso. They really are a handful at set-pieces because their aerial power is so great. Their lack of discipline has let them down in the past. If they show some self-control, they're my tip as outsiders.'

Midfielder Niko Kranjcar is the only domestic based player in the starting XI. He was promoted from the Under-20s by his father – the manager. Coach Zlatko Kranjcar, appointed in July 2004, has been praised for putting every player in his natural position, renouncing the experimentation so dear to his predecessor Otto Baric.

The defence is the team's strongest component, a guarantee that Croatia will never be thrashed (unless Brazil proves different in the opening game of Group F in Berlin). The midfield has been the sore spot since the retirement of the famous trio Prosinecki–Boban–Asanovic. Young Niko Kranjcar is technical, talented and packs a potent shot, but lacks speed and running capacity. His namesake Kovac has precisely the opposite virtues and defects. Jerko Leko was expected to be the Croatian Ballack of sorts, but has sadly disappointed over the past two years. Stopper Igor Tudor has been recycled and is currently used as a defensive midfielder with satisfactory results. The flanks are well covered by the indefatigable Srna on the right and Babic on the left. Their attack is interesting and potentially prolific, but has recently been dented by injuries. Ivica Olic, considered Alen Boksic's successor, is recovering from a cruciate ligament surgery and Prso's wobbling knees present a perennial threat to his fitness. Still, the cocktail, including the naturalised Brazilian Eduardo da Silva and Club Brugge's Bosko Balaban, could be made to work.

## THE CZECH REPUBLIC

Tomas Rosicky ensured that the Czech Republic gained safe passage to the finals with the goal in Prague that gave his team a 1–0 win over Norway in their play-off second leg and a 2–0 win on aggregate. The Czechs, who had not qualified since becoming an independent nation after their last appearance as Czechoslovakia in Italy in 1990, needed only a draw after winning the first leg in Oslo.

Rosicky gave them insurance in the 35th minute, however, driving a low shot into the corner of the net after Milan Baros's effort from just inside the penalty area had deflected off John Arne Riise. 'This is the peak of my career,' Karel Bruckner, the Czech Republic coach, said moments before his players picked him up and carried him on to the pitch to the delight of the crowd. 'We showed our character tonight. I'm proud of how they played.'

The team, Euro 2004 semi-finalists – which included Vladimir Smicer and, playing with the captain's armband on for the first time in more than 16 months, Pavel Nedved, their outstanding midfield player – never cracked. Norway were denied as Petr Cech made several fine saves to record his second successive clean sheet.

Tempers flared near full-time when Riise fouled Zdenek Grygera as they challenged for a header. Riise appeared to come off worse, lying prone on the ground for several minutes and receiving a yellow card from Graham Poll, the English referee.

Borussia Dortmund target man Jan Koller reports that all signs are right that he will be ready for World Cup duty with the Czech Republic. The 32-year-old suffered a serious knee injury in October, but is making yeoman's progress in rehab. 'My recovery is going strictly according to plan,' he told German tabloid *Sport*. 'The doctors must first of all say that my health is 100 per cent, but I believe that at the end of May I will be fit to play in the World Cup.'

The Czech Republic made the play-offs via a tough group that contained the Netherlands and Romania. Thanks to the attacking prowess that brought them 35 goals (the highest tally in European qualifying), only the Czech Republic were able to keep the Dutch in their sights.

## ECUADOR

Aston Villa defender Ulises de la Cruz, Felix Borja, Paul Ambrossi and former Southampton and Crystal Palace striker Agustin Delgado were particularly impressive when Ecuador qualified after a goalless draw with Uruguay. Coach Luis Fernando Suarez said, 'I thank all my players who, thanks to good results, have made the people of Ecuador happy again. I have some friends who have managed in a World Cup like Francisco Maturana and Hernan Dario Gomez in Colombia or Argentinean coaches Carlos Bilardo and Marcelo Bielsa. I'll talk to them to know their experiences.'

Ranked 37th in the world as they were at the start of the last World Cup finals, Ecuador play neat, skilful counter-attacking football, catching other teams on the break, but they probably don't have enough in their locker to trouble the bigger teams.

Ecuador were in for a shock when they drew hosts Germany in Group A. Some famous German names already see the group stage as a formality. Coach Jurgen Klinsmann was certainly not daunted after seeing his side drawn against Poland and Ecuador as well as their opening-day opponents, Costa Rica. He said, 'We are very satisfied. This is a group we can win. It could have been more difficult. The ball has been passed to us – all we have to do is score. Ecuador are a strong team and Poland will be a difficult match but we will be full of enthusiasm.'

German legend Gunter Netzer added, 'There is no excuse if they do not make it to the next round.' Former international Stefan

Effenberg agreed. 'We should end the group stage with nine points,' he predicted, while German tennis hero Boris Becker said, 'There are definitely harder groups than ours.'

Goalkeeper Oliver Kahn was asked what he knew about Costa Rica and Ecuador. 'Not much, almost nothing. Both of these teams' ways of playing are virtually unknown in Germany. We didn't have a chance to watch their qualification. We don't get as much information about them as we do about Argentina or Brazil, for instance. We still have time to enquire, to learn what kind of soccer they play, what their strengths and weaknesses are. There's no doubt that we'll know everything we need to know in time for the World Cup. We'll know them both inside and out.'

But are Ecuador capable of beating Germany? 'Anything's possible in the World Cup finals.'

## FRANCE

On 12 July 1998, *Les Bleus* ignited all of France when they took Brazil apart in a sensational 3–0 World Cup final victory on home soil. A million euphoric Frenchmen and women sung and danced all night long on the Champs Elysees. The superbly talented Zinedine Zidane crowned a glittering tournament performance with two goals against the South Americans in the final.

France, founder members of FIFA, have competed in 11 FIFA World Cup finals, but the 1998 achievement eclipses all else. Dazzling performances from players like Zidane, Youri Djorkaeff and Fabien Barthez enraptured the footballing world. Under coach Aime Jacquet, the home team were simply unbeatable.

Sixty years earlier in 1938, France had hosted another World Cup. On that occasion the host team were less fortunate, going out in the quarter-final to eventual champions Italy. Twenty years later, in Sweden in 1958, Just Fontaine set a finals record with 13 goals – a record that remains unbroken to this day. Two years after winning the 1998 World Cup, France continued their sensational run by triumphing in the 2000 UEFA European Championships. They defeated Italy 2–1 in the final with an extra-time golden goal by David Trezeguet in Rotterdam.

France duly travelled to the 2002 finals in the Far East as both world and European champions but, in the ensuing debacle, *Les Bleus* failed to score a single goal and finished bottom of their first-round group. Beaten 1–0 by first-time participants Senegal in the opening match, they drew 0–0 with Uruguay and lost 2–0 to Denmark before returning home. Two years later at Euro 2004, it was pretty much a case of same problems, same punishment. Beaten in the quarter-finals by Greece, the French were now forced to admit that their golden period was over.

Put in charge of a France team in the throes of transition, coach Raymond Domenech has come in as a new coach and is trying to find his best players and fit them into the best team pattern. They've come through a difficult period, and a difficult qualifying group, to scrape into the finals. Most people remember France as kings of 1998, but that team has been broken up. They have persuaded Zinedine Zidane, Lilian Thuram and Claude Makelele to return to international football, but there are also a lot of emerging players who are not proven at the very top level. There is no doubt about the talent of many of them – for example, William Gallas, Patrick Vieira, Trezeguet, Djibril Cisse and Gregory Coupet – but whether they can gel in the finals is another matter.

Their match-winner is Arsenal's Thierry Henry. He won their vital game in Dublin with a brilliant goal. They're going to need Thierry at his best if they're to make an impact in Germany. France, though, are good enough to be potential quarter-finalists.

Real Madrid magician Zinedine Zidane has let it be known that he could retire from the game after appearing in Germany. The playmaker believes *Les Bleus* have every reason to hold out hope for the tournament in Germany, after veterans such as he and Thuram returned to the national side in autumn. 'I'm certain that we have a team capable of achieving something great,' declared Zidane. 'Our players belong to the best European clubs. We still miss a little something to do well. We will have to work to have it again.'

## GERMANY (HOSTS)

Germany's problems are illustrated by the fact that they have not beaten a leading nation since the last-ever game played at Wembley six years ago. Having witnessed the attacking quality of Brazil during the Confederations Cup, the power of Ronaldo, the pace of Adriano and the creativity of Ronaldinho, not to mention Kaka, Jurgen Klinsmann said that the current world champions will be the team to beat.

Germany ran the eventual winners close, going down 3–2 in the semi-finals after drawing 1–1 in a friendly, and Klinsmann thinks that Carlos Alberto Parreira's side are beatable. 'Brazil are rightly favourites as they're an outstanding team with outstanding individuals,' he said. 'You can beat Brazil but you need to have a very, very good day. There is endless talent behind those outstanding individuals and an absolutely outstanding coach. But in football anything is possible and, if you get the right day and your players are on top of their abilities, you have a chance to beat them.'

Klinsmann feels that Germany will start the tournament among the second group of leading nations, including England. 'We have a lot of respect for England but we would see ourselves on the same level and both among the favourites,' he said. 'We had a really great experience at the Confederations Cup, but we had defensive problems with young players coming in.'

There is one thing Klinsmann would like to steal from England. 'The team spirit,' he answered, 'getting a team to really stick together. That was something I learned by playing in England, especially in the environment of so much passion in the stadiums.'

Tord Grip refuses to write off the hosts, despite the enormous scepticism in their own country. The England coach's right-hand man observed, 'Jurgen Klinsmann has done a very good job as coach. Given all the years in which they have man-marked and used a sweeper system, Jurgen has switched to a British defensive system with an orthodox back four including Chelsea's Robert Huth at centre-back. They tend to play a diamond system and Michael Ballack is excellent operating just behind their strikers. Klinsmann is bringing through some bright young talents like Schalke's Kevin Kuranyi, who has scored 14 goals in 27 internationals. Home advantage will be a great help to them. They already know where they're going to stay and play. They reached the final last time. The team has changed since then and I see them as semi-finalists this time.'

Klinsmann's appointment as coach, before he had turned 40, swept away the Rudi Voller era which ended at the European Championship with the failure to reach the knock-out stages. The award of hosting rights removed the need to qualify, providing much needed breathing space and the new coach has taken advantage by experimenting.

But Klinsmann's appointment created huge controversy because he is plotting World Cup victory on home soil from 6,000 miles away close to Huntington Beach on the Californian coast. Klinsmann lives near Los Angeles for the sake of his Californian wife, his two young children and his own preferred lifestyle. He commutes twice a month via an 11-hour flight. He acknowledges that persuading Germany's traditional football federation that managing from the other side of the globe could be viable took a long time. 'But you have to look at the bigger picture. Commuting is not a problem for me and, if some on the federation were sceptical, it helps me a lot to look at things from a distance. I can focus on priorities and not get lost in daily football, which eats you up.'

In his first managerial role, Klinsmann has one of the most moderate squads the country has produced. In a team meeting at the start of his reign, his players agreed on a footballing philosophy that could have been taken from his time at Tottenham, with the emphasis on speed, style and attack. Just as they were under Osvaldo Ardiles at Spurs, the results have been mixed, with an impressive third-place finish in last summer's Confederations Cup overlooked after defeats by Turkey and Slovakia.

Now, Klinsmann is a partner in an American marketing company. He founded and funded Agapedia, his own charity to help kids. But he is equally concerned about his charitable defence, with no sign so far of a successor to Jurgen Kohler and Stefan Reuter. When Germany lost 2–0 to Slovakia, their back line was humiliated in the first half, none more so than Per Mertesacker, the 21-year-old, who suffers taunts about his great height as regularly as Peter Crouch. One alternative is Robert Huth, also 21, but the Chelsea player was heavily criticised for his performance against Australia in the Confederations Cup. Thomas Hitzlsperger, who left Aston Villa for VfB Stuttgart, filled in at left-back against Slovakia, but looked out of his depth in a team that shipped 20 goals in ten matches. At least, Germany scored 27 in that same period, so they should be entertaining.

In Michael Ballack, their leading talent, they have a player who can score from midfield, while Bastian Schweinsteiger, his colleague in Bayern Munich's midfield, and Lukas Podolski, the Cologne striker, are two young players who have proved themselves at international level. Jens Lehmann and Oliver Kahn alternate in goal. Lehmann, No.2 to Kahn in the past four leading tournaments, does not get on with his rival.

Klinsmann's Germany, with attacking full-backs, a diamond midfield and two strikers, ensures plenty of goals at both ends. While their free scoring was obviously welcome, until recently they were conceding an average of 2.5 goals per game. Oliver Kahn complained, 'This can't carry on. We have to keep a clean sheet, so opponents have some respect for us again. We have to mix Jurgen's power tactic with a strong defence.'

This is now the most important tournament on German soil

since 1974, when the Franz Beckenbauer generation won the World Cup. Klinsmann feels this is an appropriate time for change. 'This World Cup has a huge importance to our nation, because, first of all, it gives this young, reunited country the chance to show a new face. There's so much energy, so many questions. We're in a transition period and people don't know which direction Germany will go. The World Cup gives us the opportunity to show all those different faces.'

## GHANA

Ghana's historic journey to their first finals began with a comfortable qualifying victory over Somalia, a 7–0 aggregate success that sent the Black Stars into the group stage. There they were drawn with 2010 World Cup hosts South Africa in Group Two and, after opening their campaign with a 1–0 defeat in Burkina Faso, they signalled their intent by beating South Africa 3–0 in Kumasi on 20 June 2004, a famous victory secured by goals from Sulley Ali Muntari and captain Stephen Appiah (2). They topped the group for the first time in September 2004 after beating Cape Verde Islands 2–0, again in Kumasi – now considered their lucky ground – but their momentum faltered after the sudden departure of coach Mariano Barreto, who quit to take over at Portuguese club Maritimo.

Sam Arday held the reins for a short time before the Serbian Ratomir Dujkovic took over in late 2004. His reign began with a draw against Congo DR but, after scraping a 2–1 home win against Burkina Faso on 5 June 2005, the Black Stars were back on track. A memorable 2–0 success in South Africa a fortnight later restored them to the top of the group. A place in Germany was now within reach and they held their nerve to beat Uganda before stamping their ticket in style with a 4–0 victory over Cape Verde in Praia.

For Ghana, a place on world football's greatest stage is long overdue. They have won four African Cup of Nations titles – in 1963, 1965, 1978 and 1982 – and twice captured the FIFA Under-17 World

Championship. Moreover, they have produced some of Africa's most talented footballers down the years – men like Osei Koffi, Abdulrazak Karim, Ben Acheampong, Afriye and George Al Hassan, in addition to 1990s stars Abedi Pele and Anthony Yeboah.

Ironically, their success comes at a time when they do not have as many big names but instead a youthful team with a disciplined approach fostered by coach Dujkovic, who offered an early taste of his no-nonsense approach by excluding former captain Samuel Kuffour from the squad. The shining lights in this Black Stars team are captain Appiah and Chelsea hardman Michael Essien – the most expensive player in the history of African football – who, together with Udinese's skilful Muntari, give Ghana a formidable-looking midfield. Up front, Asamoah Gyan and Dutch-based Matthew Amoah, back after almost two years in the international wilderness, ensure their team-mates' efforts are rewarded with goals.

## IRAN

Their world ranking is unrealistically high and they are not expected to navigate past group opponents Portugal, Mexico and Angola. Yet, many Iranians believe this is the strongest team in their history. Ali Daei, the 36-year-old barrel-chested striker is the world-record international goalscorer with 107. He was also the leading Asian scorer in qualifying with nine goals. He remains a prolific goalscorer and, while he didn't quite make the grade with Bayern Munich, five of his present Iran team-mates are playing in the country that will host the finals. Two are midfield regulars for the Bundesliga's top two teams: Ali Karimi having excelled as a playmaker since joining Bayern last summer and Mehdi Mahdavikia who has helped to inspire SV Hamburg.

Karimi, the Asian Player of the Year for 2004, has been dubbed the 'Persian Maradona'. Indulged for so long with Al-Ahli in Dubai, the Wizard of Tehran has learned the work ethic in Germany. The move to the German champions has made him a better player and

*Top*: Joe Cole takes on Poland's Marcin Baszcynski.

*Bottom*: John Terry and Rio Ferdinand acknowledge the crowd's appreciation.

*Top*: Eriksson celebrates with Ray Clemence following England's win over Poland.

*Bottom*: England in training.

*Top*: Young, Lampard and Terry line up to play Argentina in the friendly of 12 November, 2005.

*Bottom*: Beckham lines up a corner.

Rooney triumphant as he brings England level with Argentina in the first half.

Beckham shows the pride, passion and belief when taking on Argentina.

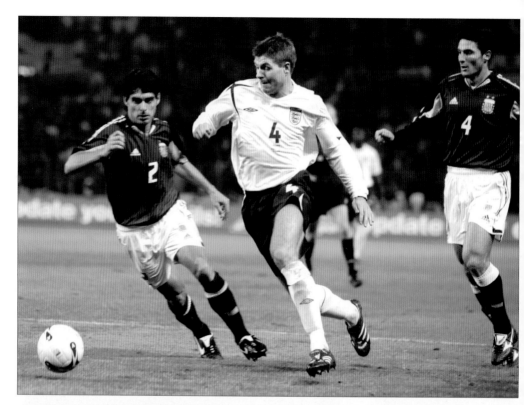

*Top*: The rampaging Gerrard flanked by Argentina's Roberto Ayala and Javier Zanetti

*Bottom*: Lampard tracks Argentina's Javier Saviola.

A young England supporter daydreams of victory.

Beckham shows his sheer delight as he celebrates with Rooney and Owen.

he is now trusted to deputise for Michael Ballack in the playmaking role when the great man is unavailable. At 27, he is the fulcrum of the Iran side.

Vahid Hashemian plays up front for Hannover 96, and he has been influential for his country since ending a self-imposed international exile of three years. Iran can also call on Moharram Navidkia of Vfl Bochum and Fereydoon Zandi of 1FC Kaiserslautern.

Constant pressure means that Croat manager Branko Ivankovic's bags are always packed and ready to go, but a comfortable World Cup qualification has won him great popularity plus a stay of execution.

The tournament's most eccentric goalkeeper could be Ebrahim Mirzapour, who likes punching so much he accidentally knocked Yahya Golmohammadi, his team-mate, to the ground with a blow to the head when coming for a cross against Japan. Iran have never played England, but Karim Bagheri managed an 18-minute career at Charlton Athletic six years ago.

The highest attendance in any qualifier in any region was 110,000 for the match between Iran and Japan in Tehran. As role models to their large population, Iran's players are banned from having curly hair, growing strange-looking beards and wearing ponytails, necklaces, earrings, rings or tight clothes.

## ITALY

Striker Luca Toni caught the attention of that great Dutchman Marco van Basten. The Holland coach, who was the most technically gifted goalscorer of his generation, was prompted to pay rare tribute after watching Toni take apart his young Dutch side in Amsterdam. 'Toni has everything you could want in a striker,' van Basten said. 'He's got speed, strength, is good in the air and is very clever.'

Since a £7m summer move to Fiorentina, he has found that 'everything I touch turns to goals'. With Italy coach Marcello Lippi a big fan, expect Toni, a muscular heir to Christian Vieri, to lead the line for his country in Germany.

Another striker with whom he has drawn inevitable comparison is Fiorentina legend Gabriel Batistuta, who has been lavish in his praise. Toni is not quite of that class, but he has that knack of timing and moves his 6ft 3in frame with deceptive grace. However, could he be Italy's answer to kebab-loving Gazza? 'I just can't stop eating,' he has admitted. 'When I go back home I simply can't resist the *gnocchi* and *tigelle*. But it hasn't stopped me playing well so far.'

Tord Grip said of Italy, 'They will be among the favourites. They're still proud of their tradition as great defenders. They're very solid at the back with Nesta and Cannavaro. With Buffon injured, they have had problems in goal, but I'm sure they'll solve that by next summer. Christian Vieri is not a regular in the Milan side at the moment [he has since moved to Monaco], but he can have a big impact at the finals. Milan's Alberto Gilardino is also a great talent – a definite star of the future.'

After returning home early from the 2002 World Cup and Euro 2004, Italy started showing signs of improvement under Marcello Lippi with a 3–1 win in Amsterdam as part of the World Cup build-up. 'It was important to have personality against Holland, but now we have to stay with our feet on the ground,' Alessandro Del Piero, the forward, said. 'It was just a friendly match and the future is more important, not this result.'

Italy boss Marcello Lippi says he has high hopes for the team's chances in Germany. 'We hope it might be our year, Italy's year,' he told *Corriere dello Sport*. 'We have a big hope – we are all convinced this team has big technical and moral qualities; we are convinced that in all matches these qualities will be put on the pitch.'

The manager didn't concern himself much with the stern test to be provided by Group E opponents, the Czech Republic, Ghana and the United States. 'The draw has been useful to know who we will have to meet,' said Lippi. 'Now me and my assistants will try to know better our opponents. I have a big faith in these guys.'

## THE IVORY COAST

Didier Drogba was shunted on to the back of an open-top army vehicle as the Ivory Coast, a country split in half by civil war, celebrated qualification for the World Cup. In the economic capital Abidjan, the scenes after they beat Sudan were of pure joy.

'You need to tell the world we are coming,' shouted coach Henri Michel, inviting everyone to drink a round of 'Drogbas', the one-litre beer named after the Chelsea striker. Street parties took place throughout this divided country, including in the rebel-held North. 'After this victory, we don't need to negotiate any more,' said one caller to national radio. 'Ivory Coast is unified. I know that God is smiling down on us!'

In Cameroon's capital Yaounde, reactions were somewhat different after the Indomitable Lions missed an injury-time penalty that would have put them through to the World Cup finals for the sixth time. Pierre Wome hit a post and the rebound went wide as they drew 1–1 at home to Egypt in Group Three. The Ivory Coast thus qualified at the expense of Cameroon.

Besides Drogba, the Ivorians have striking support in Aruna Dindane, a midfield anchored by the admired Didier Zokora and a defence built around Arsenal's Kolo Toure. Many of the Ivorian team grew up together at the country's leading football academy and moved en masse to Europe. The Ivorians have an old hand managing them too. Henri Michel, a Frenchman, will be handling his fourth different World Cup squad, having previously been in charge of France, Cameroon and Morocco.

## JAPAN

Despite some inconsistent performances, Japan ultimately showed their class as Asian champions when becoming the first team to book their passage to the finals. For good measure, they won that remaining game too, at home to Iran, to finish top of their section with 15 points from a possible 18.

Germany will be Japan's third successive finals. Since the inception of the professional J-League in 1993, they have progressed steadily and won consecutive Asian titles in 2000 and 2004. On the world stage, they missed out on USA 94 through a dramatic last-minute Iraqi equaliser in Doha, before finally making their finals debut at France 98. Eliminated in the first round there, they reached the second round on home soil in 2002 after Frenchman Philippe Troussier had led them to memorable victories over Russia and Tunisia.

After replacing Troussier in 2002, Zico guided an under-strength Japan side to the AFC Asian Cup in 2004, beating hosts China 3–1 in the final. Although some below-par performances subsequently prompted criticism of the Brazilian, Japan's qualification for Germany and their encouraging displays at the 2005 FIFA Confederations Cup has restored confidence in the national team. Japan have arguably Asia's most formidable midfield line-up in the Europe-based trio of Hidetoshi Nakata (Bolton), Shunsuke Nakamura (Celtic) and Shinji Ono (Feyenoord), and Kashima Antlers' set-piece specialist Mitsuo Ogasawara. Two-time Asian Player of the Year Nakata is arguably the best footballer Japan have ever produced, but Nakamura is now considered the player to pull the strings. By comparison with their midfield options, Japan have limited power in attack, although Gamba Osaka marksman Oguro emerged in 2005 to score some vital goals in qualifying and at the Confederations Cup.

After the finals, Japan boss Zico has declared his interest in finding a job in Europe, saying that his line of work would be too stressful back home in Brazil. 'After the World Cup, my time with the Japanese national team draws to an end,' he said. 'If I continue to coach, which I probably will, I see my future in Europe. In Brazil people are too concerned with the week-to-week results,' admitted the former *Selecao* star. 'I wouldn't even consider working at [former club] Flamengo.'

Japan have been drawn in a World Cup group with Brazil, as well as Australia and Croatia. Japan ace Hidetoshi Nakata claims that the side fear no one in the ever-tightening world of international football – not even group rivals Brazil. 'After eight years defending the Japanese team, I've learned a lot. One thing I can tell you is that the age of a football match being decided solely on the name and reputation of a nation has long gone. That was a point that I thought was well demonstrated during the 2002 World Cup. Many favourites were eliminated in the group stage, and there were also many surprises during the qualifying stage,' noted Nakata. 'Nowadays, things are getting much more even, and we don't fear any nation.'

## MEXICO

No team scored more goals than Mexico in the qualifying phase. This startling statistic is perhaps best highlighted by the fact that *El Tricolor*'s 67-goal haul was almost twice the figure by the Czech Republic. This feat was made possible by a combination of coach Ricardo Lavolpe's attacking style and the goalscoring prowess of strikers Jaime Lozano, Francisco Fonseca and, most impressively, Jared Borgetti. The Mexico No.9, known to his legions of fans as *El Zorro del Desierto* [The Desert Fox] was the top scorer across the world in qualifying. His total of 14 goals exceeded that of Brazil's Ronaldo, who scored 10, as well as Portugal's Pauleta and Togo's Emmanuel Adebayor, both of whom finished with 11. His closest rival was Trinidad & Tobago striker Stern John, who reached 12 goals thanks to his brace against Mexico.

Borgetti was one of the stars of the FIFA Confederations Cup in Germany in 2005, scoring three goals and subsequently earning a move to English Premiership side Bolton Wanderers. He then followed up his exploits in Germany with a double against Guatemala at the CONCACAF Gold Cup to become Mexico's all-time leading scorer.

By the autumn, Borgetti was back on the score sheet for Mexico with a vital strike in the 2–0 qualifying win over Costa Rica at the Azteca. That triumph moved *El Tri* to the brink of a place at the finals and gave the player the outright lead in the race to be top scorer in the preliminaries. To the relief of his superstitious fans, his tally of 13 then became 14 with a penalty against Panama two games later.

After Mexico were drawn in the seemingly easy Group D with Portugal, Iran and Angola, Mexico boss Ricardo Lavolpe showed his support for unused Bolton striker Borgetti who played a total of only 116 minutes in the first half of the season, and announced that he needed playing time to prepare for the World Cup. 'I am aware about Borgetti's situation in England and I must say that I am worried because he is one of the most important players of the Mexican national team,' said Lavolpe. 'He scored 14 goals for Mexico in the qualifiers and we need him to keep in that rhythm for the World Cup. If his English team is not going to use him, they could give him a loan deal to any Mexican team, who would welcome him with open arms,' asserted the coach.

## THE NETHERLANDS

Marco van Basten enjoyed a distinguished playing career. Yet, the three-time European Footballer of the Year never finished in a winning team against Italy, where he also enjoys legendary status, so his 16-match unbeaten run as Holland coach inevitably came to a crashing end against Italy in a World Cup warm-up game. On their first visit to the Amsterdam ArenA since that epic penalty shoot-out in the semi-finals of Euro 2000, the *Azzurri* won 3–1.

Van Basten had been trying to calm expectations that he will repeat his European Championship triumph on his return to Germany – banners linking 1988 to 2006 adorned the ArenA – so the defeat could prove a useful sedative. Holland's injury-hit team, including four players from the Under-21s, were outplayed by Italy in a classic counter-attacking display. But with Mark van Bommel and Wesley Sneijder to return in midfield along with the formidable attacking trio of Ruud van Nistelrooy, Arjen Robben and Robin van Persie, Holland should present a different proposition in the World Cup, although the area van Basten really needs to strengthen is the centre of his defence. On his full debut, centre-back Ron Vlaar had a nightmare, heading into his own net to give Italy a 2–1 lead and then being muscled off the ball by Luca Toni as the imposing centre-forward made the game safe.

In his first senior coaching job, van Basten has swung the axe, ending the international careers of Edgar Davids, Clarence Seedorf and Patrick Kluivert, though he could do with granting a pardon to Jaap Stam. The AC Milan defender retired from international football after Euro 2004, but on this evidence it would be worth trying to change his mind.

On 8 September 2004 when the Dutch secured a comfortable 2–0 win over major rivals the Czech Republic, it gave rise to renewed optimism. Moreover, van Basten now began to rejuvenate the Dutch squad. In came youngsters such as Dirk Kuyt and Hedwiges Maduro, alongside the maturing talents of Arjen Robben, Wesley Sneijder and Rafael van der Vaart. Everything soon clicked into place as the *Oranje* marched relentlessly on towards qualification.

After the brief hiccup of a draw in FYR Macedonia following their win over the Czechs, the Dutch notched up eight consecutive wins, setting a furious pace in anticipation of their penultimate qualifier in Prague. During the Leipzig draw, the Netherlands joined Argentina, Serbia & Montenegro and Ivory Coast in Group C, much to midfielder Phillip Cocu's disappointment. 'We couldn't have had a much harder draw,' he said. 'Argentina are favourites, Ivory Coast are the strongest African team and Serbia & Montenegro are not easy to beat.'

Van Basten remains Holland's greatest asset, though his coaching skills have by no means been kept secret. With AC Milan keen to appoint their former striker as Carlo Ancelotti's successor, the summer of 2006 may represent his team's best chance of glory.

## PARAGUAY

England have faced Paraguay twice before. In the 1986 finals, in Mexico City, a Gary Lineker brace and another from Peter Beardsley secured a 3–0 second-round victory. At Anfield in April 2002, England beat the Paraguayans 4–0 with Michael Owen, the captain, scoring his 15th goal in his 34th international.

Terry Butcher recalled England's 1986 clash with Paraguay in the Mexico World Cup and warned, 'Don't imagine that Paraguay will be some lightweight South American team, tip-tapping around with a little bloke who takes great free-kicks. They'll be well organised and powerful and, given memories of the 1986 finals in Mexico, can also be brutal. I'll never forget the game we had against them in the Aztec Stadium. We beat them 3–0. But it was a real battle. They surprised us by their approach. They wanted a real rough house. Gary Lineker was battered about all over the place and was carried off. It was a very physical game. Their game plan was to intimidate us – which was a surprise – but we stood firm and coped with it. The three-goal victory may look comfortable but it wasn't. Roque Santa Cruz is their main man now. He's a big powerful centre-forward who's had some injury problems but has done well at Bayern Munich. They also have a veteran striker in Jose Cardoza who's 34. He scored seven goals in their qualifying games and only Brazil's Ronaldo got more in the South American section.

'Opening games in World Cups are always nervous affairs, but it's essential we get off to a strong start. If we get three points from the first game and then beat Trinidad & Tobago, we should be looking at cruising through. I can't stress enough how important it is for us to beat the South Americans in our opening game in Frankfurt on 10 June. We'll gain confidence, grab the initiative in Group B and have the springboard to go on and win the World Cup.'

At France 98, it took a golden goal from Laurent Blanc to deny Paraguay, while four years later Germany's Oliver Neuville did the damage with two minutes left.

The *Albirroja* are out to make up for their previous disappointments, but their qualification was confirmed only on 8 October, in Maracaibo, Venezuela, with a 1–0 win. Despite suffering a heavy 4–1 defeat against Peru in their opening game, Anibal Ruiz's side soon bounced back and proved their worth with a series of impressive wins, both in Asuncion and away from home. Fans voiced their frustration during the 1–0 home defeat by Colombia in their final qualifier. A total of 28 points was two fewer than in their previous campaign, but enough to see them repeat their fourth-placed finish of 2001 – behind Brazil, Argentina and Ecuador. The final standings showed eight wins, four draws and six defeats, with 23 goals for and the same against. The highlights included a 1–0 victory over Argentina in September – their first qualifying win over their South American rivals.

After reaching three of the first six World Cups, Paraguay went into decline and missed out on six consecutive final tournaments. When they finally emerged at Mexico 86, Julio Cesar Romero and Roberto Cabanas steered the team successfully through the group stages, only to suffer that 3–0 defeat to England.

At France 98, they were captained by the outrageously talented goalkeeper Jose Luis Chilavert, who led the side to goalless draws against Bulgaria and Spain and victory over Nigeria. In the second round, Laurent Blanc's goal ended their unlikely dream. Four years later, in Korea and Japan, Chilavert was no longer at the peak of his powers, but the team once again exceeded expectations. A draw with South Africa, a loss to Spain and a win over Slovenia earned them a date with Germany in the second round. The charismatic goalkeeper and his veteran defence put on another brave display but again fell just short.

Their coach is the Uruguayan Anibal Mano Ruiz, one of only three coaches to survive the entire South American qualifying campaign. He took temporary charge from Italian Cesare Maldini after the previous finals, and was given the job on a permanent basis in April 2003.

In goal, Justo Villar is proving himself more than capable of following Chilavert, while Carlos Gamarra leads the back line with aplomb. Midfielders Julio Dos Santos and Edgar Barreto, part of the side that finished runners-up at the 2004 Olympics in Athens, have earned their place in the starting XI on the back of a series of energetic displays. Paraguay begin their campaign against England in Frankfurt on 10 June, and they hope to be around for a while. 'God willing, I won't be coming back from Europe until 9 July,' said Ruiz, a week before the draw in Leipzig.

Hopes are based on Paraguayan football's traditional strengths – solid defence, hard work and excellent team spirit – but they now have the firepower in star striker Roque Santa Cruz, who faces a struggle to be fit in time after suffering knee ligament damage while playing for Bayern Munich. Standing 6ft 1in, he's pacey and has a stunning eye for goal. Even without him, Paraguay have attacking options. Veteran Jose Cardozo is still a danger and Werder Bremen's Nelson Haedo Valdez has been a key addition.

Before the draw, Gerry Armstrong, Northern Ireland assistant manager, observed, 'Other teams had better watch out for Paraguay. They're very organised, solid and work hard for each other.'

## POLAND

Sir Alf Ramsey's England faced Poland at home 34 years ago, requiring victory to top a qualifying group for the World Cup finals in Germany. But there the parallels end. Ramsey's men drew 1–1, defied famously by the reflexes of Jan Tomaszewski, the Polish goalkeeper, and it cost the manager his job. This time England are going to Germany and Eriksson will be in charge.

Though England have since gained revenge by reaching two World Cup finals (1990 and 1998) at Poland's expense, the mere mention of Tomaszewski evokes bitter memories and warnings of future mishaps. Poles still cherish the goalkeeper, who retains a high profile in his home country, working as a television pundit. His heroics at Wembley on 17 October 1973 will never be forgotten. Faced with 35 attempts on goal, he kept out every one except for an Allan Clarke penalty.

Being the 'next Tomaszewski' is the ambition that sustains all Polish goalkeepers. Jerzy Dudek has been called clownish for some of his more mercurial moments with Liverpool. 'The clown? I don't mind being portrayed as the clown if I can perform against England like Tomaszewski did at Wembley,' Dudek said.

Competing against Dudek is Artur Boruc, the Legia Warsaw keeper who is currently on a one-year loan at Celtic, but being tracked by Premiership clubs including Arsenal. Dudek, with 51 caps, has been his country's No.1 since 1999, but through injury missed out on the Old Trafford night when the Poles were beaten 2–1 by a Michael Owen poacher's goal and a Frank Lampard volley which ousted Poland from the top of the group. Boruc was on the receiving end of the Owen–Lampard strikes.

Since Janas took over, Poland have won seven of their eight competitive games on the road. 'It suits our game to play away because it gives us more space. Our strikers thrive on it,' Dudek said.

The strikers he was talking about are Maciej Zurawski and Tomas Frankowski, an experienced pair who appear to have hit their prime simultaneously. Zurawski is Boruc's team-mate at Celtic and the poster boy of the Polish game. Frankowski, 31, was only called into the squad after Poland's first game with England. Boruc has six goals from six qualifiers, Zurawski seven from eight. In reserve is Tottenham's Grzegorz Rasiak.

## PORTUGAL

If their performance in qualifying is anything to go by then Portugal must rank as credible contenders. Luiz Felipe Scolari's side won nine of their 12 matches, finishing seven points clear of their closest rivals Slovakia, and scoring more goals than any other team in Europe. If the statistic of 35 goals scored and just five conceded was impressive, then so too was the contribution of striker Pauleta whose 11 goals not only put him at the top of the continental scorers' chart but also took him past the legendary Eusebio's record of 41 for his country. Ironically, Portugal's toughest matches came against the minnows of Liechtenstein. They surrendered a two-goal lead in an embarrassing 2–2 draw in Vaduz in October 2004 and 12 months later needed an 85th-minute strike from Nuno Gomes to secure a 2–1 win in Aveiro.

Germany will be the fourth finals in their history and Portuguese fans are still waiting for their side to match the exploits of Eusebio and co on their debut appearance in 1966, where they reached the semi-finals. The emergence in the early 1990s of a golden generation of players led by Luis Figo and Rui Costa raised hopes and in 2000 Portugal were European Championship semi-finalists. After a disappointing first-round exit at Korea/Japan 2002, Brazil's World Cup-winning coach Luiz Felipe Scolari took the reins and led the *Selecao* to the final of the 2004 European Championship on home soil. Although they lost out to Greece, they showed no after-effects in World Cup qualifying and Scolari's experience with Brazil is bound to benefit his charges in Germany.

The talismanic Figo is back in the squad, returning 12 months after withdrawing from international football in July 2004, but arguably a greater threat to opponents these days comes from the quick feet of another winger, Cristiano Ronaldo. Midfielder Deco is another player with plenty of tricks while in attack Pauleta's record speaks for itself. Portugal also have quality in a defence led by the excellent Ricardo Carvalho.

Some of the greatest Portuguese players have come from their former African colonies. Eusebio hailed from Mozambique. Ahead of Euro 2004, national coach 'Big Phil' Scolari, himself Brazilian, took it a step further, ushering in his naturalised compatriot Deco. Now the Portuguese have the exciting 22-year-old Benfica right-back Nelson. His performances have prompted coach Ronald

Koeman to herald him a 'great player who could become one of the best in the world'. Nelson is from the Cape Verde islands. He has not played for the Cape Verde national team and has received his Portuguese citizenship, freeing him to represent Scolari's side. Nelson's ability to go past players and whip in an incisive cross has been drawing interest from Europe's top clubs. AC Milan have been tracking him as a potential replacement for Cafu, but Benfica insist any club will have to pay the £18m trigger clause in his contract to sign him.

Felipe Scolari was Brazil's coach when they won the 2002 World Cup. He said, 'Portugal's credentials were demonstrated at Euro 2004 when we played England. It was a very even match. A new meeting between the two presents a daunting prospect and it is hard to say England are better than Portugal. In the game back in 2004, we were losing until the 83rd minute before coming back, taking the lead, then letting the English draw level again. So, there is a very strong balance between the two.

'At Euro 2004 we only lost to Greece and luckily they will not be in Germany. In the World Cup qualifying, we reached a new standard. Today, we are at the same level as any other great European nations – England, the Netherlands, Italy, Germany – but we still do not have a similar record. So, this winning habit is what we have to aim for. During qualifying we were already matching them. We finished top of our group, were not beaten and were the leading goalscorers of all the European teams. Now we have to concentrate on reaching a World Cup final. We have the chance and let's seize it.'

## SAUDI ARABIA

Under Argentinean coach Gabriel Calderon, Saudi Arabia qualified comfortably for their fourth consecutive finals, impressively undefeated through 12 qualifiers. They booked their ticket to Germany with a 3–0 home success against Uzbekistan and ended their campaign in style as Mohamed Al Anbar's goal secured a 1–0 win in Seoul.

Saudi Arabia have been Asian champions three times, in 1984, 1988 and 1996. Previously, the royal family had forbidden football in the kingdom until 1951, but those continental crowns encouraged the country's authorities to introduce full professionalism and this paid off with a first World Cup finals appearance at USA 94. The Saudis made a favourable impression on their tournament debut by beating Morocco and Belgium to advance to the second round where they lost to Sweden. After that memorable start, however, their subsequent appearances at France 98 and Korea/Japan 2002 have yielded one draw and five defeats from six matches.

The squad blends youth and experience, notably in the attacking duo of the 34-year-old Al Jaber and Yasser Al Qahtani, a decade younger but already his country's most expensive player following his $10m transfer to Al Hilal. Calderon recalled Al Jaber more than two years after his last international appearance in the 8–0 humbling by Germany in Korea/Japan, and the veteran showed why he is such a revered figure in Saudi football with three goals in the final qualifying round. Saudi Arabia had a forgettable campaign at the 2002 World Cup, but now they produced a run of brilliant displays to finish above the much-fancied Korea Republic. Indeed they beat the 2002 World Cup semi-finalists both home and away to confirm their renaissance.

Brazilian Marcos Cesar Paqueta was appointed the new coach of Saudi Arabia before Christmas. Paqueta, who coached Saudi club Al Hilal, replaced Argentine Gabriel Calderon following the team's poor showing at the West Asian Games. The Saudi Football Federation had warned Calderon that his job was under threat and, after finishing fourth in the West Asia tournament, decided to dispense with his services.

## SERBIA & MONTENEGRO

The Serbian player best known to English football is Mateja Kezman, whose goal at the Red Star Stadium secured a 1–0 victory over Bosnia-Herzegovina and guaranteed their place in the finals. Bought by Jose Mourinho from PSV Eindhoven with a reputation as a goalscorer based on his success in the Netherlands – 105 goals in 122 starts – he scored only seven goals for Chelsea and there were few protests when he left Stamford Bridge to join Atletico Madrid. Now, having earned Serbia a place on the big stage in Germany, he will have a chance to change UK fans' minds.

The 'surprise' was an appearance after the win over Bosnia in front of thousands of supporters in the city's Republic Square, where a stage had been set up in anticipation of victory. In scenes not witnessed in Belgrade since Red Star's penalty shoot-out victory over Marseille in the 1991 European Cup final, the party went on into the early hours. As the players were presented, Kezman got the biggest cheer.

Manchester United's Nemanja Vidic is a tough defender in every sense. In Germany, he will have to mark Ruud van Nistelrooy, Hernan Crespo and Didier Drogba, but you wouldn't bet against him coming out on top against all of them.

At 24 years old, Vidic has established himself in the Serb defence, a hardman stopper who is powerful in the air. Ilija Petkovic's side conceded just one goal in qualifying, the lowest total in the European qualifying section, and finished above Spain in their qualifying group.

Coach Petkovic said, 'I have emphasised many times that the most important thing is that we are in Germany. My first impression is that our group is the hardest, but we had the hardest group in qualification as well. I was optimistic then, and I am optimistic now. We are a small country, we are poor and we are in transition, but in the qualifiers we fought with big countries like Spain and Belgium. We fought with our hearts, with knowledge and with a desire to prove people wrong. We are not afraid of anything or anyone.'

## SOUTH KOREA

The milestone achievements of Korea Republic in 2002 are still a fond memory for many football fans in Asia and, as Germany draws closer, it is understandable that expectations will consequently be higher than ever for the continent's four finalists. Coach Jo Bonfrere was an early victim of these pressures when he found himself out of a job shortly after guiding the South Koreans to Germany. Dutchman Dick Advocaat took over.

Manchester United's recruitment of Park Ji-Sung is the highest profile of all the transfers from Asia, after he had enhanced his reputation with his national team and then PSV Eindhoven as a lively, resourceful wide-midfield player not afraid of hard work. He began his professional career seven years ago in Japan with the Purple Sanga club and established himself early on in the South Korean Olympic team. He had 30 full caps to his name – scoring the equaliser in a 1–1 friendly draw against England – by the time the World Cup came round, and he revelled in the extraordinary outpouring of enthusiasm that accompanied Guus Hiddink's team all the way to a semi-final against Germany in the World Cup finals 2002.

Park's goal beat Portugal to achieve the major target of a place in the knock-out stage, whereupon the Koreans eliminated Italy, then Spain, in penalty shoot-outs before a 1–0 defeat by the Germans. 'I didn't expect that we would do so well. I was really nervous taking a penalty against Spain. Then, against Germany, I think all our players were tired, because we had played so much,' he said.

'This time, in the World Cup draw, we are quite pleased to play Togo, France and Switzerland and have an opportunity to get through to the second round.'

## SPAIN

Spaniards were almost unheard of in the Premiership until the past couple of years. Now Liverpool have Jose Manuel Reina, Luis Garcia, Xabi Alonso and Fernando Morientes, all likely to be in the World Cup squad. They should be joined by Asier Del Horno of Chelsea and Jose Reyes of Arsenal, while Reyes's club colleague Cesc Fabregas is a good bet for inclusion too.

The European Championship triumph of 1964 is Spain's only major international trophy. Spain have qualified for 14 of the past 15 leading tournaments; they reached at least the second round in all but one of the past six World Cups. Spain's best finish in a World Cup finals came in Brazil in 1950, when they lost in the semi-finals, but, victory in 1964 aside, their supporters have had little else to cheer over the last 50 years. They are in the top-ten favourites this time, but the absences of Xavi (probably) and Raul (possibly) through injury would hit hard. Michel Salgado is the hardman of their defence and was once on the wanted list of Chelsea.

Iker Casillas has been Spain's goalkeeper since Santiago Canizares dropped an aftershave bottle on his foot before the 2002 World Cup to give his younger rival the role in the finals. There have been internal squabbles, notably Vicente on Carles Puyol after the Spain team-mates grabbed each other's throat during training: 'I'm not going to lie, there are players I have a better relationship with.'

Coach Luis Aragones navigated his side through the play-offs against Slovakia. He has reasoned that his team are still 'nowhere near' as good as they need to be. But, if the *Furia Roja* perform in Germany as well as they managed in the play-off games, international football's perennial underachievers might pose a threat. After all, Spain's progress to their eighth successive finals – and 12th in all – was rubber-stamped by a magnificent 5–1 victory in Madrid in the first-leg play-off.

Since replacing Inaki Saez, Aragones had not experienced defeat in 18 games as Spain convincingly went through the plays-offs. 'It was our duty to qualify and I'm very happy we've done that, but Spain have always been expected to do well and have often fallen below those expectations, so it would be foolish to say too much,' he said.

Perhaps ominously, Spain's headquarters for the finals will be the Sportschule Kaiserau in Kamen, near Dortmund, the base used by West Germany when they won the World Cup in 1974 and 1990.

## SWEDEN

Sven-Goran Eriksson's home nation can emerge as the surprise package. In some of their qualifying games, they were outstanding. They're a workmanlike side blessed with a little bit of flair that lifts them on to another level.

Zlatan Ibrahimovic, their lanky striker, is a big threat. His size alone causes defenders problems but he can put himself about and also produce a clever twist and turn to create an opening. Their other strong point is their defending. They defend as a unit. They're not a star-studded team – just solid, determined and well organised.

England's recent record against Sweden is poor. Alf Ramsey was the last England manager to record a victory over the Scandinavians back in 1968. The past 37 years have brought 11 meetings and not one English triumph, with their opening encounter at the 2002 World Cup offering the first indication that Eriksson's team did not have the stamina to sustain performances beyond half-time. Sol Campbell gave England the lead only for midfielder Niclas Alexandersson to equalise, and Sweden may pose the sternest test in Group B. Freddie Ljungberg, Anders Svensson, Tobias Linderoth and Henrik Larsson are familiar names to be faced in Cologne. Their last encounter was a friendly in Gothenburg last year in which England – despite a fine display by Jermain Defoe – put in a curiously lethargic performance and lost 1–0.

In all the euphoria that accompanied England's victory over Argentina at the last World Cup finals, it was quietly forgotten that

Sweden topped that group, overcoming Nigeria 2–1. To rejoicing in both nations, Anders Svensson's goal ensured Argentina's elimination in the group stages. Senegal, however, proved a pitfall in the second round. Euro 2004 provided another memorable moment: the elimination of Italy with a 2–2 draw against Denmark. What followed proved rather an anti-climax, as Sweden became one of the very few nations to have lost a penalty shoot-out to the Dutch in the second round.

Their campaign was founded on a first-class defence, which conceded just four times in qualifying. A side that is greater than the sum of its parts also won eight of their 10 matches and averaged three goals a game.

Sweden's success has been built on the managerial partnership between Lars Lagerback and Tommy Soderberg, who had been together as coaches since 1997. This union was dissolved after Euro 2004, when Soderberg left the senior side to take over coaching of the Under-21 team. Much English attention will centre on Ljungberg, although the Arsenal midfielder is not the force he once was. This will be his fourth major tournament and, at the age of 28, it might be his last.

Henrik Larsson, prolific ex-Celtic striker and currently at Barcelona, leads the attack. This will be Larsson's fifth major tournament. Larsson contributed five goals in eight games to Sweden's qualification campaign, where they finished just behind Croatia but avoided a play-off by being among the better second-placed finishers across the European groups. And, in a group including Bulgaria, Hungary, Iceland and Malta, Sweden were prolific.

Ibrahimovic scored eight times during the campaign and Ljungberg contributed seven to a team that scored an average of three goals a game. Lagerback, who has coached the senior team since 1997, said, 'In Sweden we've never had anything like these two. They are at the same level as Michael Owen and Wayne Rooney.'

Lagerback may take as many as 12 players with a history of

working in the British game to Germany. The line-up for Sweden's final qualifier, a 3–1 win over Iceland, featured a whole troupe of Premiership old boys: Teddy Lucic, late of Leeds United, and Erik Edman, once of Tottenham, were in the defence alongside the Sweden captain, Aston Villa's Olof Mellberg. Ex-Evertonians Tobias Linderoth and Niclas Alexandersson contributed in midfield, as did Svensson, the one-time Southampton player, and Marcus Allback, the former Villa striker, partnered Larsson up front.

The real danger for England lies in the figure of Ibrahimovic, who at 23 has the temperament, the youth and the looks to be one of the great stars of next summer. Bought from Ajax at a cost of £13m, he certainly has not been short of awards, having been voted Juventus's player of the season, as his goals sent the *Scudetto* to Turin.

For his part, Lagerback is relishing the clash with England. 'We can stop Rooney. We know we can beat England, that's for sure. The first thought in my mind was: "Wow, England again – this is almost like a parody." Now it feels OK. We have a tremendous statistic against them and it's a very long time ago since we lost against England. It's a close race between Paraguay, England and Sweden. We know the last match against England will be a tough one, but we know we can beat them. I know that Sweden can go all the way. On a good day we can beat every country in the world.'

## SWITZERLAND

After failing to qualify for France 98 and Korea/Japan 2002, Switzerland made amends for missing out on the previous two finals by claiming a place in neighbouring Germany. The away-goal rule was the decisive factor in their success as Kobi Kuhn's side edged through by a wafer-thin margin in a heart-stopping play-off against Turkey.

Despite falling 4–2 in their second leg in Istanbul, they advanced by virtue of their 2–0 victory in Berne four days earlier. The tournament in Germany will be the first World Cup appearance since

1994 for the Swiss who are due to host the 2008 UEFA European Championship jointly with Austria.

Switzerland made it to the round of 16 on their last finals appearance at USA 1994, but fell 3–0 against Spain. The current youthful and ambitious crop will hope to achieve at least as much in their country's eighth finals outing, and some observers believe they have the potential to emerge as the surprise package of the tournament.

Before the play-off second-leg defeat by Turkey, the Swiss had gone a full year and 14 straight games without defeat, evidence of the growing strength of a team that includes players who attracted rave reviews at various age levels. Their line-up in the play-offs featured Tranquillo Barnetta and Philippe Senderos, both of whom claimed UEFA European Under-17 Championship honours in 2002. Kuhn's men remained undefeated throughout their qualifying campaign in European Group Four, amassing 18 points from ten fixtures. The highlights of a solid campaign included two draws against France and an identical result against Ireland, although, in the tightest of all the European sections, the Swiss were left sweating right to the end before edging out Israel for second place.

The team marshalled by skipper Johann Vogel features a healthy blend of youth and experience. Veteran keeper Pascal Zuberbuhler barks out commands at the back, while Hamburg midfielder Raphael Wicky stamps his authority on the midfield. Starlets such as Arsenal stopper Senderos and Bayer Leverkusen's Barnetta unquestionably belong in the international game, while Alexander Frei from French first-division outfit Stade Rennes has at times shown a killer instinct in front of goal.

## TOGO

In Group One, leaders Togo had a rollercoaster of a ride in Brazzaville. They ended up 3–2 winners against Congo, but twice the Hawks had to come from behind before they were able to secure victory. Togo finished in their group ahead of Senegal, World Cup quarter-finalists in 2002, a towering achievement for a nation of barely 5.5m people, and due in large part to their towering sliver of a striker Emmanuel Adebayor, the 21-year-old ex-Monaco striker who moved to Arsenal during the transfer window. He described the away win over Congo as 'the match of my life'. Twice Congo led and, with Senegal beating Mali easily, Togo required their two comebacks. Eventually they won 3–2.

There will be no nation at the World Cup as reliant upon one player as Togo are upon 'Shedi' Adebayor, the main reason the small West African nation are going to Germany at all. He finished as the top scorer in the African qualifying zone with 11 in 10 games – scoring over 50 per cent of his team's goals as they pipped Senegal to qualification.

Despite standing a daunting 6ft 3in, he is incredibly swift, a lanky player whose strength and speed make him hard to mark. His physique marks him out as the type of player who will flourish in the Premiership. Before his transfer to Highbury, he turned down a £6m move to West Ham in the summer after a contract wrangle with Monaco. He was spotted by Metz as a 15-year-old playing for a Togo youth side at a tournament in Sweden and quickly established himself as one of the most promising forwards in French football. He was given his first full cap aged just 18 and was involved in the 2002 African Cup of Nations. A nickname is *de rigueur* for every African national XI, so we're hearing some new ones with all the debutants for 2006. Togo are the Sparrowhawks.

## TRINIDAD & TOBAGO

Trinidad & Tobago's veteran Dutch coach Leo Beenhakker warned England that his side will not be Group B makeweights.

Beenhakker, who guided the tiny Caribbean islands to their first World Cup finals via a two-legged play-off against Bahrain, was delighted to be drawn against England, Sweden and Paraguay and believes his team are capable of springing a few surprises. 'We were the last team to qualify,' he said. 'We came through the back door and we want to leave the tournament through the front door. We are going to enjoy it. We are not just here to participate and we won't be using the Olympic ideal of just taking part. We will prepare ourselves very well. Nobody needs to remind me that there is a difference in quality between England and Trinidad & Tobago. But that does not mean that we will be going to Germany as tourists. Definitely not.'

Beenhakker, 63, a former Holland coach who has managed Feyenoord and Ajax and took Real Madrid to three Spanish titles, said he has already taken Sven-Goran Eriksson's scalp. 'I played against him in the Champions League when I was coach of Feyenoord and he was in Rome with Lazio. I beat him in Rome. Nobody expected us to beat Mexico [in qualifying], and we did. We showed that it is about football, not mathematics.'

Trinidad & Tobago versus England at Nuremberg's Franken-stadion on 15 June is a fantasy for the likes of Falkirk playmaker Russell Latapy and Dwight Yorke, now with Sydney United. Beenhakker said, 'When we arrived in Trinidad, there were 20 very good individuals, but nothing resembling a football team. Forty years I have been in this job, and what you try to do is teach them to take control of the game.'

Latapy, though 37 and now in the backwoods of Scottish football, was recalled. Latapy is known as 'The Little Magician', while Yorke, the captain of the Warriors, is perhaps best known for his liaisons with page three models, such as Jordan, in his days with Manchester United. Supremo Jack Warner has also been scrutinising the small print in FIFA eligibility laws to see what might happen should he recruit Jlloyd Samuel and Bobby Zamora from Aston Villa and West Ham respectively.

Trinidad are only the fourth Caribbean nation to make it to the greatest show on earth – Cuba and Haiti have also qualified in the past. The islands have only 1.07 million inhabitants, and are the smallest nation – by population – to reach the biggest stage in world football. 'Words can't describe what I'm feeling right now,' Yorke said. 'To take this team to the finals – and as skipper – is something I'm so proud of. To achieve this is enormous. We needed our Warrior spirit and that's exactly what we showed.'

The 'Reggae Boyz' of Jamaica were eliminated after the first round, but Yorke plans to make the most of this opportunity. 'I've been with the national team since I was 16 and I'm finally going to a World Cup. I went to the Under-20 World Cup finals in Portugal in 1990, but this is something else. I've had a good career, winning medals with United, but this just tops it off. This is the icing on the cake. We are only a tiny country and to achieve this is enormous for all our people and everyone in the Caribbean. It can inspire all the young children and they will see us as heroes.'

The 'Reggae Boyz' brought spice to the World Cup finals in France in 1998; now, it is their Caribbean cousins, the 'Soca Warriors', who will boogie on down in Germany.

## TUNISIA

Tunisia secured a place at their fourth World Cup finals after they came from behind twice to draw 2–2 with North African rivals Morocco. The reigning African champions needed only a point to secure first place in Group Five, but the Moroccans took an early lead to stun the 60,000 crowd in the Rades Stadium. Only three minutes had elapsed when Hatem Trabelsi's pass was intercepted by Houssine Kharja who crossed the ball to Bordeaux striker Marouane Chamakh and he made no mistake from close range.

Thirteen minutes later, the hosts were awarded a penalty after captain Riadh Bouazizi was fouled in the penalty box by Youssef Safri and Brazil-born defender Jose Clayton scored from the spot to restore parity. Just before half-time, defender Talal El Karkouri restored the Moroccans' lead, but the Carthage Eagles had the last word when the same player failed to clear a cross off the line and nudged the ball into his own net.

Coach Roger Lemerre said afterwards, 'It was a very tough and tense game. The four goals were scored from mistakes, which proves that the players from both sides were under so much pressure. I have to confess that I never imagined this dramatic scenario for the game and most of the time I had no idea where the game was going.'

Lemerre named two uncapped players in his squad for the defence of the African Nations Cup in Egypt, defender Issam Merdassi and striker Amine Eltaif. The Tunisian media speculated that Lemerre would use inexperienced players for the tournament to save his seasoned internationals for the World Cup finals.

In 1978, Tunisia became the first African country to win a game at the finals when they beat Mexico 3–1 in their very first group match. A 1–0 defeat against Poland in the next match and a goalless draw against defending champions Germany were not good enough to see the North Africans through to the next round, but the victory over Mexico secured the Carthage Eagles a place in the history books.

Since then, Tunisia have appeared at two more finals, but they are still awaiting their second victory. In 1998, Tunisia lost to England and Colombia and drew with Romania, and, four years later, they lost to Russia and Japan and held Belgium to a draw. As one of the five African countries who played at Korea/Japan 2002, Tunisia did not have to play in the preliminary African qualifying rounds for the 2006 finals. And, under Lemerre, they more than lived up to their billing as favourites to reach Germany. They entered the qualifying competition high on confidence having won the CAF African Cup of Nations on home soil in February 2004. In the final, Lemerre's men beat Morocco 2–1 to lift the trophy in front of 60,000 delirious fans at the Rades Stadium.

As fate would have it, they encountered old foes Morocco again in their qualifying group, and once more the Eagles showed that they ruled the regional roost by coming out on top, even if both matches between the North African rivals finished level. Overall, the Tunisians enjoyed a fairly comfortable passage to Germany. Defeated just once – 2–1 by Guinea – Lemerre's team recorded six wins and three draws. What is more, courtesy of their contribution to a scintillating FIFA Confederations Cup in Germany in 2005, they showed they will be a force to be reckoned with this summer.

With top-class performers such as Ziad Jaziri, Santos, Adel Chadli, Radhi Jaidi and captain Hatem Trabelsi within their ranks, the Carthage Eagles have raised expectations, all the more so as young striker Haykel Guemamdia is gradually establishing himself among the finest strikers in Africa. Adding to their one win at a World Cup looks well within their capabilities and the ambitious Tunisians certainly will not want to stop there.

## UKRAINE

Denmark, Greece, Turkey and Ukraine was another tough-looking qualifying group, but Ukraine quickly asserted their superiority over the other sides.

Ukraine qualified with ease from Group Two, a section which had looked anything but straightforward. An impressive 1–1 draw away to Denmark in their opening match boded well and, on 17 November 2004, Oleh Blokhin's side went top of the group for the first time, having taken three wins and two draws from their first five matches. They were never to relinquish top spot and became the first European country after hosts Germany to book their finals place – the first in their history – after securing a 1–1 draw in Georgia on 3 September. The one blemish on their record, a 1–0 reverse at home to Turkey, came only after qualification had been assured.

Able to call on talents such as Alexandr Shovkovski, Andrey Rusol,

Andrey Voronin, Andriy Vorobey and, of course, Andriy Shevchencko, and with Blokhin, winner of the 1975 Golden Ball, at the helm, the time had clearly come for Ukraine to qualify for a World Cup finals. However, qualification alone will not sate their hunger and they will depart for Germany harbouring ambitions of achieving something memorable. Ukraine should not be underrated.

## THE UNITED STATES

Playing so often against Central American and Caribbean opposition means the US, like Mexico, benefit from a deceptively high FIFA ranking (eighth, above England and Italy).

But here they are for their fifth successive World Cup finals, with more and more players attuned to European football. Kyle Martino and Taylor Twellman scored their first international goals to give the US a 2–0 victory over Panama to finish top of the CONCACAF World Cup-qualifying group. The US, who had already qualified and fielded a reserve team, finished level with Mexico on 22 points, but took first place on their head-to-head record. They also won the CONCACAF Gold Cup. Voluble coach Bruce Arena led them to a quarter-final in 2002 – losing 1–0 to Germany – and they will hope to come through the first group.

The US are supposedly the eighth-best team in the world, yet few would expect them to fare better next summer than Spain, Portugal, England and Italy, all of whom are inferior in FIFA's eyes. Scoffing at the lack of passion for football in the US, Mexico coach Ricardo Lavolpe said after the World Cup defeat for his team in Ohio that the US had it easy because they played under no pressure from the country's inhabitants. 'My sister, my aunt and my grandmother could play on their team,' he said.

There are many players from the English leagues in the squad. Carlos Bocanegra, the defender, and Brian McBride, the forward, are both at Fulham. Eddie Lewis, the former Fulham left winger, is now at Leeds United. Claudio Reyna of Manchester City is captain.

And Jonathan Spector, the 19-year-old defender, is on loan at Charlton Athletic from Manchester United.

Interestingly, seven current Premiership clubs have fielded an American goalkeeper since 1995: Manchester United (Tim Howard and Paul Rachubka), Liverpool (Brad Friedel), Blackburn (Friedel), Tottenham (Kasey Keller), Charlton (Mike Ammann), Fulham (Marcus Hahnemann) and Bolton (Jurgen Sommer). No.3 keeper Marcus Hahnemann currently plays for Reading in the Championship.

Player to watch? DaMarcus Beasley. Fleet of foot and powerful, the left winger is a footballing Jonah Lomu.

# ELEVEN

**WORLD CUP STARS FROM THE PREMIERSHIP:**
AIMING FOR GLORY

The Barclays Premiership will effectively showcase the tournament between now and the summer. 2006 promises to be the most exotic, cosmopolitan competition in football history. Trinidad & Tobago (population 1.1 million) could face Japan (127.1 million); Angola (life expectancy at birth: 36.96 years) will be alongside France (79.28 years); and Iran (national motto: 'Independence, Freedom, Islamic Republic') will be in the same tournament as the United States ('In God We Trust'). The teams include Australia and Trinidad & Tobago, who will each have around a dozen players from the English and Scottish leagues in their squad. Yet it is the elite English league that will be most heavily represented in Germany, where up to 80 players who have made their 'home' in the Premiership will be sparring with each other. Here are some of them, plus some players from the lower leagues:

## THIERRY HENRY

Dennis Bergkamp paid Henry the ultimate compliment after saying the Frenchman is the 'complete and perfect' striker who does not have any weaknesses. Bergkamp already rates 28-year-old Henry as one of the greats of football history – with the potential to get even better. 'People talk of players from 20 or 30 years ago as being great players, but now people have the privilege of seeing Thierry and he's breaking record after record,' said Bergkamp. 'Years from now, people will realise that he is a very special player. I understand coming from my mouth that must mean something because I've played with a lot of good players but Thierry is very special. Statistically he's the best and that's for sure. For me, he is the most complete player. Even with great players, there is always something you can say, like he didn't do this or he didn't do that. I still have to find a weakness with Thierry. If you say he's not a really good header – well, the goals he makes with his head are tremendous. Maybe he does not put himself in that position but he can do it and there's no weakness there. He's the perfect player.'

## SHAKA HISLOP

Trinidad & Tobago will be many people's second-favourite team in England where several players are based, including West Ham's goalkeeper Shaka Hislop. 'I'd like to think that's the case,' says the veteran keeper. 'Now it's going to be a celebration of our football. We'll bring something new. I don't mean just football-wise; we Trinnies will bring our culture to Germany and maybe make it that much more colourful.' Born in Hackney in London's East End but raised in Trinidad, the genial Hislop arrived back in England via a football scholarship at university in the USA, where he studied for a degree in mechanical engineering, and established his goalkeeping credentials as a cult figure at Reading. He moved to Newcastle, West Ham and Portsmouth before returning to Upton Park in the summer. 'Now we've finally qualified, it's about enjoying the experience and putting the region's football on the map. We've progressed immensely over the past few months under Leo Beenhakker. We feel now that we can be a test for anyone.'

## CRISTIANO RONALDO

Master of the multiple stepover, Ronaldo is tipped as the young player most likely to contest the first Best Young Player of the tournament with Wayne Rooney. Yet, Manchester United suffered a rollercoaster season and the winger was caught on camera sticking his middle finger up at the home supporters following his club's 2–1 Champions League exit in Lisbon. Ronaldo, 20, issued a public apology. But Portugal coach Luiz Felipe Scolari insisted, 'Ronaldo was wrong with his gesture to the Benfica fans – but people do make mistakes. He is a young guy with a lot in front of him. But he needs to mature a little more, which is normal. I will speak to him and I am sure his team-mates will as well. He is going to pay the price for his inexperience at times. But he has apologised through the media and that shows he knows he made a mistake. That was the best thing to do after what happened in Lisbon.'

United boss Sir Alex Ferguson adopted a softly-softly approach to coax Ronaldo back to top form. Fergie said, 'Cristiano's confidence has been a bit down. The boy has had a turbulent time and a lot has happened to him over the past few months. You could not foresee his father dying. You never know how people will react to something like that, but it is normal for a young player to have a reaction.

'What we are trying to do now is ease him back into it and get his confidence back. You could see some of the confidence returning when he came on at Villa recently. That was great to see because he is a wonderful talent.'

## GABRIEL HEINZE

Gabriel Heinze was told not to give up on his World Cup dream by Argentina team-mate Diego Simeone. The combative Manchester United full-back ruptured his cruciate knee ligaments in the Champions League draw with Villarreal and was written off for the remainder of the campaign by Sir Alex Ferguson. Even if Ferguson's assessment proves to be inaccurate, the 27-year-old knows, once he gets over his injury, he will only have weeks to gain match fitness before the finals. 'All my national team-mates have phoned me,' he said. 'I spent many years in the national side and there was one phone call in particular that really helped me, when Simeone rang. He told me he had exactly the same kind of injury as I do before the 2002 World Cup. He told me not to pay attention to the comments that I may not return to play in the national team and that I may not even return to play. So I no longer ask myself when I am going to return to play and try not to get too anxious about things. I know that, if I did, it wouldn't be good for me.'

After getting through the tough first month of his recovery programme, Heinze progressed to cycle work and passed on some inside information on the likes of Wayne Rooney and Frank Lampard to Argentina coach Jose Pekerman ahead of the friendly in Geneva. How will his side do in the finals? 'Argentina have a chance of success but they need to make some changes – so of course do England,' he said. 'The match in Switzerland was an excellent game, but the result could easily have been different. Both teams have a chance of winning alongside Germany, Italy and, of course, Brazil.'

## ARJEN ROBBEN

Marco van Basten, the coach of the Dutch national team, was concerned at the number of injuries being picked up by Chelsea's Arjen Robben. He also suggested that the 21-year-old is regarded as Holland's most dangerous player and vital to their World Cup hopes. Although there are doubts at Chelsea about his form, and perhaps also ongoing questions over his psychological state, van Basten has already made it clear that, no matter what happens with his club, Robben will be a starter for his country in Germany.

Since his move from PSV Eindhoven to Stamford Bridge for £12m, he has suffered a broken ankle – which ruled him out for three months – and a broken bone in his foot which led to a six-week absence, as well as hamstring problems and a calf injury. He only made 29 appearances for Chelsea in the 2004–05 season.

The first part of 2005–06 was equally frustrating because of three separate hamstring problems. 'People have written that I'm injury-prone but I don't think so,' said Robben. 'If you look back at last season, it was kicks that you can't do anything about. This season it was the same problem that came back three times.

'I just hope it's all over now. I feel very strong again and hope to continue that way. It's just very difficult when you play, then stop again and don't get a rhythm going. It's a mental thing as well, and I think I'm mentally very strong. You have to fight and work hard to come back and I've been working my bollocks off.'

## ROBIN VAN PERSIE

Arsene Wenger has a formidable record for spotting, then developing, exceptional talent. Many at Highbury think the next in line is a 22-year-old Dutchman who arrived at Arsenal with a reputation for being difficult. He has since been rewarded with a three-year contract extension to keep him at Arsenal until 2011. The deal more than doubles van Persie's wage to £35,000 a week. The Dutch youngster was dubbed 'The Cobra' by Arsene Wenger after his deadly strike against Blackburn this season which brought his tally to seven goals in seven games.

Wenger considered a move for Michael Owen when he became available at Real Madrid in the summer. But the Frenchman reckoned that splashing £16m on the England star would have stopped van Persie from blossoming into one of the Premiership's top stars. Wenger confessed, 'I was tempted to sign Michael Owen but I knew I had van Persie, I had Reyes and I had Quincy – all players who can come out and score goals. At some stage you have to make room for your young players or they never play. If I had brought in Michael Owen, van Persie would not be playing.'

Van Persie joined Arsenal for £2.75m from Feyenoord in the

summer of 2004 but struggled to become a first-team regular in his first season and then faced rape allegations in the summer in his homeland. Suddenly life on and off the field is shaping up better. 'I am extremely pleased with my life over here,' he said. 'We have found the ideal house and with my new contract I don't have to worry about anything but football. That is exactly what I want – to focus only on training and playing matches and to become an even better player.'

Van Persie must follow the example of Highbury legend and compatriot Dennis Bergkamp, says his manager. 'He has the class to be as good as Dennis but there is a long way to go,' said the Arsenal boss.

## FREDDIE LJUNGBERG

Arsenal midfielder Freddie Ljungberg is confident the Swedes can get through from Group B. He believes it will be a special occasion when the countries go head to head but insists they have no reason to fear England – whom they have not lost to since 1968.

He said, 'I am not unhappy with the draw. If we are on top of our game, we will go through from this group – no doubt about that. I am looking forward to playing England. We need to have respect for them but not too much.'

## OLOF MELLBERG

Sweden defender, Olof Mellberg of Aston Villa, also claimed they would not be fazed by facing England. He said, 'It's not bad for us. I know we can beat England, and that's the most important thing. We know each other inside out.'

Mellberg, 28, will captain Sweden in the group game against the Three Lions in Cologne on 20 June. England have not beaten Sweden since 1968 but Mellberg said, 'With the players England have now got, they look stronger than they did at the last World Cup. We've had some good results against them but any game with England is tough.'

## HERNAN CRESPO

The Argentina forward scored the opening goal in the 3–2 defeat by England in the friendly in Geneva. Crespo, 30, has had limited opportunities since returning to Stamford Bridge from loan at AC Milan, but Argentina are warning his lack of match sharpness could threaten his World Cup hopes. He was limping heavily after he had to come off in the England friendly. Coach Jose Pekerman said, 'It's difficult to understand a world-class striker not playing very often. Of course I'd like to see him sharper and fitter in a World Cup. It was a strain injury to his calf. It came through not playing regularly, without a doubt. If he was fitter and playing regularly, that would not have happened.'

Crespo's first season at the Bridge, where he earns £97,000 a week, turned into a nightmare, but he seems to be back on track once more and scoring goals. English football has not had a high-profile player from Argentina since the days of Ossie Ardiles and Ricky Villa at Tottenham. Ardiles said at the time of Crespo's arrival, 'I rate Crespo very, very highly. He is one of the best strikers, right up there with van Nistelrooy, Henry, Raul and Ronaldo. He is a big, strong guy and he is a winner. He is aggressive, quick, good in the air and has a very nice touch. He is the No.1 striker for Argentina right now. The others, like Saviola and Aimar, play around him – that's how good he is.'

## NEMANJA VIDIC

Nemanja Vidic was Manchester United's £7m signing from Spartak Moscow in the January transfer window. He was seen as a prospective new partner for Rio Ferdinand in the centre of defence. Sir Alex Ferguson said, 'We've been watching him for some time and he's been very impressive. He's quick, he's aggressive and he's a good passer of the ball, with good physical attributes, so all the vital parts are there. What we have to do is give him a crash-course in English because his language is only limited.'

Vidic, 24, is a regular for his national team and the first player from Serbia & Montenegro to sign for Manchester United. He is the aggressive type of centre-half the club has been missing since Jaap Stam's departure. United had to fend off competition from several clubs, most notably Liverpool and Fiorentina, before securing the transfer. Liverpool's manager Rafael Benitez was bitterly disappointed to have missed out after United had desperately tried to keep the transfer quiet for fear of alerting Chelsea.

## EDWIN VAN DER SAR

Edwin van der Sar will retire from international football after the World Cup to prolong his playing career at Manchester United. The Dutch captain has turned 35 and, while not old for a goalkeeeeper, he admits that the demands of playing at Old Trafford are too great for him to carry on with his country.

His period with the club could, of course, have been prolonged further had Sir Alex Ferguson followed up his gut instinct and moved for him after Peter Schmeichel's departure in 1999. Instead, Ferguson let van der Sar make his ill-fated move to Italy, and Juventus. United ended up working their way through eight goalkeepers – from Fabien Barthez to Tim Howard – and £18.5m, only for each to fail to fill the void left by the imposing Dane. Finally the club returned to their first apparently unflappable 6ft 5in target last summer.

Van der Sar's confidence never dipped. He is the most experienced player for club and country. In European competition, he won the UEFA Cup with Ajax as long ago as 1992, and followed that three years later with the European Cup, beating Milan, before losing in the final the year after. He also has a European Super Cup medal. At United, only Sir Alex Ferguson can match those achievements. For Holland, that experience is a little more bitter. He has been a losing semi-finalist in major competitions three times – in the 1998 World Cup and the European Championships of 2000 and 2004.

With the appointment last year of Marco van Basten as the national coach, there has been a revolution in Dutch football. 'The effect he has had on the national team has been quite strong,' says van der Sar, who was made captain by the legendary striker. He is the only Dutch player actually to have faced van Basten on the field of play.

Van der Sar admits there is a concern that maybe the squad is too inexperienced this time. 'Yes, that's what I've been saying all along,' he explained. 'We are not as good as two years ago or even four years ago when we missed out on qualification for the World Cup. At that time we had a better team, better players. But, so far, this squad connects better than four years ago.'

### JENS LEHMANN

Jurgen Klinsmann has the problem of sorting out which keeper is his No.1, Oliver Kahn or Jens Lehmann. Such is the enmity between the goalkeepers that they cannot stand to be in the same room together, so Klinsmann has adopted a rotation policy, ensuring that his senior players are never in the same squad!

Having missed out against China, Lehmann was in goal at the Stade de France charged with keeping out his Arsenal team-mate Thierry Henry, as France hosted Germany in a pre-World Cup friendly. The game ended 0–0.

There is a fear in Germany that the ill feeling between the pair of goalkeepers could destabilise their World Cup campaign, but Klinsmann says the pair can co-operate. 'They have a huge rivalry and deal with things a certain way, but can spend six weeks together, no problem,' he said.

### PETR CECH

One player doesn't make a team, but a top goalkeeper makes a huge difference. In the season Chelsea first ran away with the Premiership, both Arsenal and Manchester United experienced crises at No.1, Chelsea had the best goalkeeper in the Premiership, 6ft 5in Petr Cech from the Czech Republic.

Cech became a Chelsea legend just seven months after signing for £7m from Rennes with a 1–0 win at Ewood Park, which marked their eighth successive Premiership victory along with eight clean sheets. Cech also set a new Premiership record for the most minutes without conceding a goal: 781, surpassing Peter Schmeichel's 1997 mark of 694.

Schmeichel was an early role model, but by no means the only one. The young man from the Bohemian brewing town of Plzen is quick to add that, in his formative years, he also looked up to, and learned from, Edwin van der Sar, in the Dutchman's Ajax days, and Gianluigi Buffon, the Italian regarded by many as No.1 in the world. 'I tried to take the best bits from each of them,' Cech said.

Schmeichel paid his own tributes to Cech, when he said, 'He is big and he has superb speed, both in terms of his ability to get around the box and his reactions. He can catch, he can dive, he can read the game, and his kicking is good enough to take the pressure off his defence. But forget all that. Any goalkeeper who has made it to Premiership level has most, if not all, of these attributes. What separates the best goalkeepers is the mental side of things, most notably their decision-making and concentration. Cech's concentration is fantastic.

'He's not yet 23 and, if he keeps playing the way he is over the next 10 years, he could become one of the all-time greats. Outfield, a Wayne Rooney comes along once in a generation. I wonder if, at Stamford Bridge, we're seeing the goalkeeping version.'

## JERZY DUDEK

Poland goalkeeper Jerzy Dudek thought about leaving Liverpool in January in search of first-team football to help him win back his international place before the World Cup finals. The 32-year-old, whose heroics in a penalty shoot-out against AC Milan won last year's Champions League final for Liverpool, began the next season playing second fiddle to Spain's Jose Reina on Merseyside. According to the *Gazeta Wyborcza* newspaper, Liverpool manager Rafael Benitez told Dudek, who joined Liverpool from Dutch side Feyenoord in 2001, that he wanted the Pole to stay with the European champions but would not play him unless Reina was ruled out by injury or a loss of form. 'I told him that solution does not interest me,' the paper quoted Dudek as saying. 'I don't want to be counting on an injury to a colleague and that places me in a tough situation. I played most of Poland's matches in qualifying for the World Cup, but if I don't play for my club I could wind up not going to the finals. For me, this would be a disaster.'

Artur Boruc drew wide praise when filling in for the injured Dudek in Poland's World Cup qualifiers in September and October. Most commentators think the Celtic goalkeeper is likely to be coach Pawel Janas's first choice for Germany.

## DIDIER DROGBA

Jose Mourinho convinced his record £24m capture from Marseille that signing for Chelsea would catapult him into an elite group alongside the Arsenal maestro Thierry Henry and Brazilian superstar Ronaldo.

That prediction struck a chord, because Drogba idolised the French striker and envied his love affair with the Highbury faithful. He was building up the same rapport with Marseille's supporters but recognised he needed a bigger challenge to emulate his hero. He explained, 'What Mourinho said was simple but very effective. Marseille were a good team, yet I had to think of winning trophies first. I had to contest the Champions League every year to make progress. He ended up saying, "For me, there is Thierry Henry, Ronaldo and you. You belong up there."'

Drogba had a slow start to his career, scoring just 15 goals in four seasons for Le Mans and Guingamp, but then he notched 17 goals in 34 games for French first-division club Guingamp in 2002–03, earning him a move to Marseille. Incredibly, one year before his move to Chelsea, Drogba signed for Marseille from Guingamp for £3m. He scored 18 goals in 30 starts for the former European champions, collected the French Player of the Year award and his bonus prize was the big-money move to the Bridge.

Mourinho said, 'I wanted to sign him two years ago for Porto but I couldn't afford him. Then I had to play against him in the Champions League and I had to watch him score against me. But I won.'

Drogba's incredible strength and speed made him the pivotal component of Mourinho's tactics of adopting a lone striker with two wingers in support. Drogba, though, had his setbacks with injuries but enjoyed playing at Stamford Bridge. 'I love the Premier League. What speed the game's played at and with what passion. I don't agree with those who devalue the English championship. I belong to a team with incredible talent who are at the top of the table.'

As his reputation grew, he reflected on his decision to choose the Ivory Coast over France. 'I have no regrets about not playing for France. I arrived in France at the age of five. I was always a fan of the team of Platini at the time of the 1986 World Cup, but I am proud to play for Ivory Coast and to have been born in Abidjan.'

## HARRY KEWELL

Rafael Benitez hoped his striker Harry Kewell responded to Australia's qualification for the World Cup finals by making up for lost time with his contributions at club level. Frequently injured, Kewell has mostly been a flop at Liverpool, but he finally came back to fitness if not his former sharpness.

Club managers normally view internationals as a necessary evil, but Benitez believes the prospect of Germany will spur a resurgence in form from Kewell which will secure his place in the Australian squad. 'There was a problem with Harry here but you expect that over the years as a manager,' Benitez said. 'We are now hoping that he can play more games for us than he has been doing. If he can play every week for the next three months, we will see a different player. He is still very talented, but he is much fitter now than he was.'

### LEE YOUNG-PYO

After seven seasons with championship-winning South Korean club Anyang, Lee followed the younger Park Ji-Sung to PSV Eindhoven and established himself there as an attacking left-back or midfield player. He has proved a popular and talented acquisition for Spurs. His bright start to the season and his new career in English football were rudely interrupted when he was left squirming in agony after an appalling tackle by Manchester City's David Sommeil, but he was soon back playing again.

## SOME WORLD CUP STARS FROM THE FOOTBALL LEAGUE

### CHRIS BIRCHALL

Chris Birchall is nicknamed 'White Boy' by his team-mates as he is the first Caucasian to play for Trinidad & Tobago for 60 years. Outside Staffordshire, he is unlikely to register on the global stage. Yet, 4,000 miles away in Trinidad & Tobago, the Port Vale midfielder has become a cult figure. He marked his 13th cap with a superb goal to salvage a 1–1 draw against Bahrain in the first-leg World Cup play-off at Port-of-Spain for the Soca Warriors.

A place in the World Cup finals for the first time in their history completed a whirlwind six months for Birchall, whose head must be spinning at his extraordinary journey from League One to Germany 2006.

Before the second leg of the play-offs, he was still rehearsing the national anthem for a place which he had not visited until he donned the national jersey for the first time in May 2005. 'It's gone remarkably quickly and it's just a big blur really,' said Birchall. 'I didn't expect the call-up but got one, didn't expect to get into the team but got there. I haven't had the time to sit down and think how well I and the team have done in the last six months.'

Birchall's call-up arrived in bizarre circumstances when Dennis Lawrence, Wrexham's 6ft 7in central defender, bounded over before a match last season and said, 'I hear you've got some Trini blood in you.' Lawrence, referring to Birchall's mother who was born in Port-of-Spain and lived there for 18 years, was acting on the instructions of Jack Warner. The FIFA vice-president and special adviser to the Trinidad & Tobago Football Federation had noted Birchall's parentage and, once Lawrence confirmed that the midfielder was interested, Warner wasted little time in arranging a trial.

Birchall, though, arrived unsure of how he would be received. 'I'll admit I was very nervous before I went over there to see how the people would take to me,' he said. 'I wondered if the players would think, "Who's this white lad trying to get in the team?" But because there are so many English-based players it made it a lot easier. As for the locals, they have always been great to me since I got there. After we beat Guatemala, we were out at a private party and someone tapped me on the shoulder,' Birchall recalled. 'I turned round and it was Brian Lara. I was gobsmacked. He's an absolute legend there and he put his arm around me and said, "You played well," and gave me a hug.'

There were plenty more hugs when they made it to Germany.

In 2002, Birchall cheered on England from his local, the Crown & Anchor in Stone. Now he could be lining up against Beckham and co in the World Cup finals.

## CARLOS EDWARDS

Trinidad & Tobago welcomed its heroes home after they had beaten Bahrain in a play-off to book a place at the World Cup. 'It was just a sea of red with so many people wearing the team shirt when we arrived back from Bahrain that morning, the greatest party you ever saw,' Carlos Edwards recalled after the World Cup draw had placed the Caribbean country with England in Group B. 'If we were to win the World Cup, the people couldn't be any more jubilant than they were that day. The feeling was magical, like no person there would have to worry another day in their life.' The journey from the airport, which normally takes less than half an hour, took six hours.

It was the reaction in Bahrain of the captain Dwight Yorke that brought home to Edwards what had been achieved. 'Dwight was in tears. He was so overcome. Looking into his face at that moment made me realise that we'd qualified for the finals of a major tournament, which for a little country like ours is phenomenal. When we get to Germany, we'll want to show we're a good team. I heard Jack Warner [the FIFA vice-president] say the other day, "Trinidad & Tobago will light up Germany, like no other country ever has or ever will." This is what we hope to do.'

Dutch coach Leo Beenhakker, whose former clubs include Real Madrid and Ajax, has made the team ambitious. 'We're an attacking team, an exciting team. Leo likes short passes and a high pace, plenty of running. Keeping possession, he always says, is the key,' said Edwards. 'We'll play against England just the same way. The World Cup, for a country like Trinidad & Tobago, will just be the greatest thing.'

Edwards is a 27-year-old midfielder or wing-back who is forging his career in the Championship with Luton Town. 'Eventually it has sunk in,' he says of qualification. 'But, yes, it did take a while. About a week and a half, I think.'

Edwards never expected to pursue his career in the UK, either. 'Joey Jones arranged a three-week trial,' Edwards said of his arrival at Wrexham five years ago after being spotted by the former Wales defender playing for the Trinidadian Defence Force team while doing national service. It took six months to get a work permit because, back then, he didn't have enough international caps. Now he has 40.

## STERN JOHN

Stern John warned England not to take Trinidad & Tobago lightly. The Coventry striker, currently on loan at Derby, leads the front line and he insisted, 'We're not going there just to enjoy the moment and make up the numbers – we are going there to have a real go. Although pundits have said we've no chance, who would have thought Northern Ireland could beat England? Football is about who wants it most on the day. If England think they can take us lightly, we are capable of turning them over. Most of our players play over here, so they are relishing the prospect of playing one of the favourites. England should have a chance of winning the cup or at least getting to the final. But, like I say, it's all about who wants it most on the day.'

## DENNIS LAWRENCE

Dennis Lawrence, the giant Wrexham defender, earned a place alongside Brian Lara and Hasely Crawford in the Trinidadian sporting pantheon when he scored the goal which put Trinidad & Tobago into the World Cup finals for the first time. Lawrence rose to head in Dwight Yorke's corner 49 minutes into the second leg of a play-off against Bahrain in Manama to secure a 2–1 aggregate victory for the Soca Warriors.

He said, 'We're a small nation and the win was for everyone. I've been getting phone calls from home and you can just hear the excitement in the background. But I have to be professional – my day job is with Wrexham. I've had texts off a lot of the boys to congratulate me. But I have to focus and that's why I am already starting to prepare my mind for Peterborough.'

The 31-year-old journeyman is now set to become the first-ever Wrexham player to appear at the finals, and there are other little-known players from the lower divisions who will join him there, such as Reading's Bobby Convey of the USA, Southampton's Kamil Kosowski (Poland) and Wigan keeper Josip Skoko (Australia).

## BRITISH-BASED PLAYERS LIKELY TO BE IN GERMANY 2006

(England not included)

### ARGENTINA

Hernan Crespo (Chelsea), Gabriel Heinze (Manchester United)

### AUSTRALIA

Mark Schwarzer (Middlesbrough), Lucas Neill (Blackburn), Tim Cahill (Everton), Tony Popovic (Crystal Palace), Harry Kewell (Liverpool), Brett Emerton (Blackburn), Mark Viduka (Middlesbrough), John Filan (Wigan), Stan Lazaridis (Birmingham), Craig Moore (Newcastle), Luke Wilkshire (Bristol City), Josip Skoko (Wigan)

### BRAZIL

Gilberto Silva (Arsenal)

### CROATIA

Dado Prso (Rangers), Ivica Mornar (Portsmouth)

### The Czech republic

Petr Cech (Chelsea), Milan Baros (Aston Villa), Jiri Jarosik (Birmingham)

### FRANCE

Djibril Cisse (Liverpool), Claude Makelele (Chelsea), William Gallas (Chelsea), Jean-Alain Boumsong (Newcastle), Thierry Henry (Arsenal), Mikael Silvestre (Manchester United)

### GERMANY

Dietmar Hamann (Liverpool), Jens Lehmann (Arsenal), Robert Huth (Chelsea)

## GHANA

Michael Essien (Chelsea)

## HOLLAND

Edwin van der Sar (Manchester United), Ruud van Nistelrooy (Manchester United), Mario Melchiot (Birmingham), Arjen Robben (Chelsea), Wilfrid Bouma (Aston Villa), Robin van Persie (Arsenal), Andy van der Meyde (Everton)

## IVORY COAST

Didier Drogba (Chelsea), Kolo Toure (Arsenal), Emmanuel Eboue (Arsenal)

## JAPAN

Junichi Inamoto (West Bromwich Albion), Hidetoshi Nakata (Bolton), Shunsuke Nakamura (Celtic)

## MEXICO

Jared Borgetti (Bolton)

## POLAND

Jerzy Dudek (Liverpool), Artur Boruc (Celtic), Kamil Kosowski (Southampton), Tomsaz Hajto (Southampton), Grzegorz Rasiak (Tottenham)

## PORTUGAL

Cristiano Ronaldo (Manchester United), Ricardo Cavalho (Chelsea), Paulo Ferreira (Chelsea), Luis Boa Morte (Fulham)

## SERBIA & MONTENEGRO

Zvonomir Vukic (Portsmouth), Nemanja Vidic (Manchester United)

## SOUTH KOREA

Park Ji-Sung (Manchester United), Lee Young-Pyo (Tottenham)

## SPAIN

Luis Garcia (Liverpool), Xabi Alonso (Liverpool), Fernando Morientes (Liverpool), Jose Reina (Liverpool), Albert Luque (Newcastle), Jose Antonio Reyes (Arsenal)

## SWEDEN

Olof Mellberg (Aston Villa), Freddie Ljungberg (Arsenal)

## SWITZERLAND

Philippe Senderos (Arsenal)

## TOGO

Emmanuel Adebayor (Arsenal)

## TRINIDAD & TOBAGO

Chris Birchall (Port Vale), Russell Latapy (Falkirk), Jason Scotland (St Johnstone), Stern John (Derby), Kenwyne Jones (Southampton), Kelvin Jack (Dundee), Marvin Andrews (Rangers), Dennis Lawrence (Wrexham), Carlos Edwards (Luton), Shaka Hislop (West Ham), Brent Sancho (Gillingham)

## TUNISIA

Hamed Namouchi (Rangers), Rahdi Jaidi (Bolton)

## UNITED STATES

Claudio Reyna (Manchester City), Brian McBride (Fulham), Carlos Bocanegra (Fulham), Bobby Convey (Reading), Tim Howard (Manchester United), Eddie Lewis (Leeds United), Jonathan Spector (Manchester United)

# TWELVE

**THE WORLD CUP DRAW:**

THE ROAD TO THE FINAL

Sven-Goran Eriksson was delighted with a seeding place, but let's not forget his side were ranked second by FIFA behind holders Brazil for the draw. Eriksson said, 'The news is excellent. I think it is right, too. We are one of the teams with the potential to do very well in Germany and we have some of the best players in the world. Finishing top of our qualification group with the second-best record in Europe was a big achievement and I'm sure that played a part in this decision.'

Being seeded meant England avoided Brazil, Argentina and hosts Germany in the group stage. England were not seeded in 2002 and went out to Brazil in the quarter-finals. They feared they would be ignored again because they are outside the top eight in the FIFA world rankings and not in the top eight based on recent World Cup performances. But, just as they did for the 2002 World Cup, FIFA decided to assess each country's ranking over the past three years and their performances in the last two World Cups.

Under this seeding system, Brazil had 64 points followed by England (51), Spain (50), Germany (48), Mexico (47), France (46),

Argentina (44) and Italy (44). The USA had 43 points and Holland 38. Under the new system, performances at the 2002 World Cup were given twice as much weight as in 1998, and the only surprise was that FIFA decided against using performances at the 1994 finals.

Eriksson travelled to Leipzig, where the draw was made, after watching the Champions League showdown between Benfica and Manchester United in Lisbon. He said, 'It's starting to get very exciting for everyone and I'm really looking forward to seeing who we are drawn to play against. There are many very good sides going to be in Germany, but I don't think too many will want to face England. The seeding is a big boost, but when the tournament starts we must show why we have been selected.'

Brian Barwick, FA chief executive, said, 'Coming on the back of our strong performance in qualification and, with the win over Argentina still so fresh in our minds, it puts us in good heart.'

Holland, who did not qualify for Japan, were not seeded, although Italy scraped into the top eight ahead of the USA. World Cup supremo Franz Beckenbauer reckoned everyone wanted to avoid Holland. The Dutch are not among the top seeds despite being third in the world rankings. Beckenbauer – a World Cup-winning captain for Germany in 1974 – was praying his country would not have to play them. 'The Kaiser' said, 'It's something we don't want. We hope not to draw them.' He believes any team who wants to lift the trophy will have to beat Brazil. 'At the moment, I'd say Brazil are playing the best football. They showed that at the Confederations Cup. Whoever beats Brazil has the best chance to be world champions. Germany have a chance with home advantage.'

In Japan, England were drawn against Argentina, Sweden and Nigeria. Eriksson admitted, 'It is about time we had a little bit of luck. We certainly didn't get any in Japan. I am not nervous about this World Cup draw, but in 2002 it was horrible. We were already drawn with Argentina and Sweden and I just knew the fourth country out would be Nigeria. It was exactly what happened. It was awful. Two years later, history repeated itself when we got France [at Euro 2004].'

Eriksson hoped to avoid Holland, Australia and the USA. He said, 'I remember when we lost to Australia 3–1 at West Ham, not understanding why they were so desperate to beat us. Then I watched the cricket in the summer and I discovered why. The reaction of the English crowds was amazing. I never knew about this rivalry.

'If I had known about the history between the two countries, I would have never arranged that game with Australia. It was supposed to be a friendly. It was nothing like it. They were more determined to beat us than almost any other team we have faced. That is why I hope we don't get them. In a way, it is the same with the USA. For English-speaking countries to beat us is a tremendous incentive – it will give a real boost to their game back home. The USA are very dangerous, anyway. No one talks much about their football and yet they are ranked eighth in the world, one above us. As for Holland, they are the best of the unseeded teams, a side I have never beaten in three games with England and full of players who know English football only too well. Can you imagine how much Ruud van Nistelrooy, Arjen Robben and Edwin van der Sar would want to beat us?'

Sweden? 'No,' he laughed, 'we don't want them, either!'

As for unknowns, Ivory Coast, Eriksson said, 'They are strong – half the team look like Didier Drogba!'

Conversely, few countries wanted to be drawn in the same group as England. He said, 'I'm quite sure most of the other coaches don't want us. We have so many players who can compete with the very best in the world. I know if our players hit top form, it will be very difficult for any team to beat us – even Brazil. Yes, we can win the World Cup. I have always believed that. We are stronger and far more experienced than we were in 2002 and much better technically than in the last two major tournaments. We don't have to be afraid of anyone. Absolutely not.'

Eriksson has high hopes for Wayne Rooney. 'He is a player who could be the difference between us winning the World Cup and not winning it. But he is not the only world-class player we have. Look at Michael Owen. He always produces when it matters – and he did it again when we played Argentina. You didn't see him and, suddenly, two goals in three minutes. But, like all teams, we need to have luck with injuries.'

Of the 24 teams that they could have drawn in the group stages, England have at some time in the past faced all but eight in either friendly or competitive fixtures. The emergent African nations represent the least well-known element of the draw with four out of the five – Angola, Ghana, Ivory Coast and Togo – never having faced England.

Eriksson still believes his side are one of five who could triumph in Berlin on 9 July. 'I think we showed in the last two tournaments that we are good,' he said. 'We didn't win them, I know. We only reached the quarter-finals. But how we went out of those tournaments – the difference was all or nothing. This time we have one week more of preparation, which I think will mean a lot more to the squad. The team is much stronger now than 2002 – much, much stronger, even than 18 months ago.'

Felipe Scolari, who was Brazil's coach when they won the 2002 World Cup, had hoped his Portugal side would meet England. 'If I had to choose a group in today's World Cup draw, I would like to be with England, Brazil or Germany – because they are strong teams and there are two qualifying places. So, it is not a single confrontation that would decide your fate in the tournament. There is still the possibility of getting through even if we lose to them. If you face them not in the group but in the knock-out stage, then it is a question of winning or going back home. Coming from the same group, we only meet them again in the final.

'England are top seeds but we can match them in all departments. Sven-Goran Eriksson has changed the way they play, adopting a "world style of football". By this, I mean you still keep a bit of the British way with the aerial game – their win against Argentina came thanks to two headed goals – but there is more work with the ball now, and the technique has improved quite a lot since 2002. I cannot talk much about weak links. Every time I've watched England, I've paid attention to the good things they do. I do not look much to the negative side. If I keep an eye on what they are doing well, I am able to find ways to counter them.

'The arrival of Wayne Rooney, Frank Lampard and Steve Gerrard, who were not at the 2002 finals and are among the best players in the world, is the main difference between the present England side and the one at the last World Cup. They have great technique, are very competitive and are excellent at shooting. They are the ones who make England play with the ball on the ground, and the team's firepower has increased considerably.

'I think England are among the four to six best teams in the world. They are doing very well, have tradition and history – qualities that generate respect from other nations. When you have experience, pedigree, good players, the others get a bit more worried and defensive-minded, opening opportunities to exploit. The Europeans outside the elite will be in the same pot, but I do not understand why Spain are among the top seeds. They were eliminated by Portugal at Euro 2004 and booked their place in the World Cup via a play-off, while we finished top of our group and were unbeaten in 12 matches.'

Hosts Germany and defending champions Brazil were named among the top eight seeds, along with England, Spain, Mexico, France, Argentina and Italy. FIFA decided the rest of the draw would group teams in pots according to their geographical locations rather than their current world ranking or previous World Cup performances. The USA and Holland both just missed out on being seeded.

The second pot contained Australia, the five African finalists – Ghana, Ivory Coast, Tunisia, Angola and Togo – plus the two lower-ranked South American teams, Ecuador and Paraguay. The third pot comprised eight European teams: Croatia, the Czech Republic, the

Netherlands, Poland, Portugal, Sweden, Switzerland and Ukraine. The fourth pot comprised four Asian teams – Iran, Japan, Saudi Arabia, South Korea – and the three remaining from CONCACAF – Costa Rica, Trinidad & Tobago and the USA.

A special pot contained only Serbia & Montenegro, the lowest-ranked European team, who were placed in a group including either Brazil, Argentina or Mexico. FIFA created the special pot, so they could avoid having any groups with more than two European teams.

Jim Brown, FIFA's director of competitions, explained, 'The seedings were based on FIFA rankings for the last three years and the last two World Cup finals. Germany will be seeded in slot A1 in the draw and Brazil in F1, and there were economic factors involved in this decision as those teams are guaranteed to play in larger stadiums.' One team from each pot was drawn into the eight groups for the first stage of the finals.

FIFA also confirmed the 23-man squads for the World Cup had to be submitted by 15 May and no player would be allowed to appear for their clubs after that. The only exception would be the Champions League final on 17 May. This meant World Cup players would not be allowed to take part in Football League play-off matches if their clubs were involved in those games after 15 May. FIFA general secretary Urs Linsi said, 'We do not want burned-out players coming to the World Cup. They have to have sufficient time to recover and to prepare with their national team. The 23 players on the list will not be available for any other competition after 15 May, apart from the Champions League final on 17 May.'

During the ceremony, the World Cup ball was unveiled, followed by a televised endorsement from David Beckham who praised it for going 'in the right direction'. The World Cup trophy was handed over by the Brazilian holders to the German hosts, having spent a short spell being cleaned in Milan. 'The Brazilians sprinkled *Caiprinhia* [Brazilian sugar cane spirit] on it,' FIFA's president Sepp Blatter joked.

In a rare serious note during proceedings, Blatter said he hoped the tournament would prove a platform for promoting peace. 'The world is crazy, aggressive,' he said. 'Let the positives of football be carried into the world to make the world a better place.'

Then came the draw. Would you believe it? Eriksson's home nation Sweden came out of the hat, along with Paraguay and Trinidad & Tobago. England thus avoided any of the potential big guns, apart from a country England have trouble beating, Sweden. England have not beaten the Scandinavians in 11 attempts but Eriksson concluded, 'It's a good draw. It is about time we beat Sweden and, hopefully, it will be this time.'

England could be on a semi-final collision course with holders Brazil. If England win Group B and the team of Ronaldinho and Adriano claim the high ground of Group F, they will share the same half of the draw and, if they both successfully negotiate subsequent knock-out ties, they will meet in Munich on 5 July for a place in the final.

England might therefore be better served finishing as runners-up to remove them from Brazil's side of the draw.

Eriksson knows the sort of gifted players who stand between his team and the World Cup. 'Ronaldinho is the best in the world,' said the Swede. 'If you give him space, he'll kill you. You have to pay him a lot of attention.'

'When you go to the World Cup, the pressure is on from the moment you get there,' he reflected. 'Football is never in the middle ground. You are either the best or the worst.'

Beckham sounded England's battle cry. 'We can win in Germany. We have the team and talent to beat anyone on our day. There are no easy games in a World Cup. But if everyone is fit – and we have a bit of luck – we have a genuine chance to bring the trophy back home. Watching the draw has already excited me as I start to think about the tournament ahead. We meet a familiar opponent in Sweden, one both the players and manager know well. I'm looking forward to playing my old Manchester United team-mate Dwight Yorke with Trinidad &

Tobago. Paraguay are an unknown quantity but we'll be prepared fully when we meet them.'

Eriksson added as if by way of confirmation, 'We'll now see about playing a friendly against a South American side.' [Reflecting the types of opponents they will face in Group B, the sides England will face in friendly matches before the World Cup finals are Hungary, Uruguay and Jamaica.]

England's players believe that winning their group and meeting Poland in the last 16 is as far as they should look ahead. 'You can start trying to second-guess where you might meet Brazil, but I think we just have to get on with trying to finish top of our group,' Michael Owen said. 'After the first couple of teams came out of the hat, I thought it could have been worse for us and, when Trinidad & Tobago were last out, I think everyone would say that our draw was better than average. You would expect Germany to win their group, but looking beyond that is making too many assumptions.'

If Brazil also live up to their billing, winning the group would almost certainly bring about a semi-final confrontation with the holders and favourites.

Even the surfeit of top-quality centre-halves will not persuade Eriksson to experiment with formations before June. 'We don't have enough time to practise a back three before the World Cup,' Eriksson said. 'It's too late to try something complicated.'

Plan B is the introduction of Ledley King in the holding role, with Joe Cole dropped and Steven Gerrard out on the left. It was not convincing against Argentina despite the 3–2 victory, but Eriksson will stick with the Tottenham captain. 'King can do it,' he said. 'He's showed it many times. Against Argentina it was not easy because they are technically very difficult but he did well and can do it. His only problem is that he doesn't play in that position for Tottenham.'

Sweden manager Lars Lagerback embraced his old pal Eriksson as the two bosses reacted with amazement when the draw pitched them together once again – just as it did in 2002 in Japan. On that occasion, they drew 1–1 and both qualified for the second stage at the expense of Argentina and Nigeria.

Eriksson said, 'It's something of a destiny for Sweden to come out from so many teams. You thought it would be any other team but them. Sooner or later we have to beat them. It's over 30 years since we won – and I know we don't have a good record against them. I spoke to Lars before the draw and we agreed we didn't want to see each other, but here we are again. I won't feel divided. Sweden is my country, it's my land. That's why I want them to go through just as I want England to.'

England got one of the easiest rides in Group B. Eriksson conceded, 'It could have been worse. What I said was to avoid Holland and Australia and we did that. I'm happy with the group. I saw part of Trinidad & Tobago's play-off game. They have a very good manager in Leo Beenhakker. I'm sure Dwight Yorke will do everything to try and beat England. We beat Paraguay 4–0 in a friendly at Liverpool before 2002, but I don't expect a World Cup game to be that easy.'

England must top their group if they are to avoid Germany at the first knock-out stage. He said, 'I had a quick look and probably Germany will win their group, so it's important to win our group otherwise we'll meet them very early. I'm always confident, but in a World Cup if you underestimate any team you could be out. I would have changed Sweden given the choice, but we could've met Holland and Australia. Sweden know us 100 per cent and we know them 100 per cent. We have met them many times.'

England No.2 Tord Grip, also Swedish, said, 'It is unbelievable. Sweden must have something special to do with England. We meet in our last game, so maybe we will have both qualified by then.'

Largerbeck added, 'I feel a little unhappy. We spoke before the draw and I never thought we could play each other again. At least we can't say it was surprising. It seems like an old love story. We played them in the Euro 2000 qualifiers too. England have had a lot of influence on Swedish football and we've had a lot of players playing in England. I think that's why we have such a good record against them. England are stronger than 2002. They have a very good balanced team now with some high-profile players.'

England kick off their campaign against Paraguay in Frankfurt on 10 June. The South Americans' boss Anibal Ruiz said, 'Once again we are in a very difficult group but I'm confident in our abilities. I'm not going to get tired of saying I have full confidence in the team.'

Sven's men then face Trinidad in Nuremberg on 15 June. Beenhakker, the former Ajax, Feyenoord and Holland coach, said, 'It's fantastic for us and great to play such a historic team. On paper we cannot win, but we don't play on paper we play on grass.'

Chris Birchall, the Port Vale midfielder, 21, helped the Caribbean country clinch a place at Germany and he cannot wait for the clash with Eriksson's side in Nuremberg. 'It is just the best possible draw. When the slip came out with Trinidad's name on, my mates said I am living the dream and I am. For the first 10 seconds I was running around the bar but it hasn't really sunk in yet. I will be lining up against the players I watch week in and week out in the Premiership.'

Birchall warned England they could be in for a big shock if they underestimate their opposition. 'It's the best possible group for us. No one knew anything about us before the draw for the qualifying group, but we caused a few upsets and we beat Mexico when they put out a full-strength side. We'll just go there to enjoy it and there will be no pressure on us.'

If you think the Brazilian fans are noisy, colourful and dress imaginatively, wait until you see the supporters of Trinidad & Tobago turn out against England. Many years ago, I ventured to Trinidad to watch their team fail narrowly to qualify for the World Cup for the first time against the USA. That morning tens of thousands created snakelike queues for miles waiting to gain entry for an afternoon kick-off. The music, the colours, the excitement they generated was awesome, and they are coming to Germany. On that day, unknown kids called Dwight Yorke and Russell Latapy were in tears over just missing out on the World Cup, but now both have come out of retirement to gain their day in the global spotlight. But, while no one expects England to slip up against the World Cup minnows from the Caribbean, it might not be so easy in the opening game against the South Americans, even if they are also regarded as no-hopers.

On the morning of the draw, Martin Peters leaned across and smiled mischievously to me when he predicted that England would be drawn against Sweden. 'The last time we beat Sweden I was playing in 1968!'

Suddenly, pundits were lining up to suggest how lucky Sven has been and how easy this qualifying group will be. They've all been leaping ahead of themselves, considering the possibility of meeting hosts Germany in the first knock-out stage, and eventually facing Brazil. Hold on a minute. Doesn't anyone recall how England have been notoriously slow starters in the World Cup? Well, I do. All the way back to Mexico in 1986 when I stayed in the England camp for weeks in the build-up to the opening game against a Portugal side so demoralised by weeks of wrangling over their bonuses that the squad refused to train and even threatened to go back home. Their camp was just across the road from England up in the hills, and it was a stroll to their location to witness first hand the complete disarray. What happened next? You've guessed it: Portugal beat England in the opening game.

With tensions mounting, nerves frayed and expectations reaching a crescendo that England have such a great chance of winning in Germany, it's Sod's Law that there will be some heart-wrenching shocks, bitter recriminations and enforced changes before England get their act together in the later stages. Then again, it could be the perceived cakewalk through the qualifying group. But don't count on it. With England in the World Cup, there is always a drama, and there will be nothing more mind-blowing than having to face a country England and Sven simply find impossible to beat, Sweden, in the final group game, and needing all three points to go through.

Terry Butcher observed, 'Overall, it's a great draw even though I was absolutely gutted to be paired against Sweden because our record against them is so poor. You wouldn't believe it's 37 years since we last beat them. The Swedes are our hoodoo team. Ideally I didn't want them and that will definitely be our toughest game in the group stages. The challenge for Sven-Goran Eriksson and his men is to make sure that, by the time we face the Swedes, we're already through to the last 16. By then, we should be sitting on six points, with England and Sweden certs to go through. Then it will be a case of deciding whether we want to qualify in first or second place and working out the best route through the knock-out stages. But first we have to deal with Paraguay. That match is critical. I can see Trinidad & Tobago making the same kind of impact as Jamaica at France 98 with their Reggae Boyz. They had a great time and the world smiled with them. Leo Beenhakker is a very experienced coach. The draw must have delighted the many lads from Trinidad & Tobago currently playing in Britain. For instance, they have Marvin Andrews up at Rangers. He's a born-again Christian. He has God on his side. He's a lovely man. I'll tell you this: he'll have the biggest smile at the World Cup.

'Sweden are a real threat as outsiders to win the tournament. You've got to respect them when they have goalscoring match-winners like Zlatan Ibrahimovic, Henrik Larsson and Freddie Ljungberg. I don't really want us to be facing Germany in the last-16 game. That would be difficult. But if we can get off to that vital flying start, we'll have the momentum to make a real impact.'

Frank Lampard believes England have a side packed with so much quality that they will be feared by even the strongest teams in Germany. 'We all know who the strong teams are and that it will be a very tough game if you play against them. We know where they are but we're not scared.'

Eriksson was bullish about England's chances of actually landing the biggest prize of all. He feels England have the look of champions as he argued, 'The quality of the players we have is very, very good. These players could play in any team in the world, in any club in the world. The quality is there, absolutely. Other countries will look at us and be very jealous.

'They can take our two centre-halves, whoever they are. They are very, very good. Our left-back [Ashley Cole] is second to none. Gary Neville? He can sell experience at this level of international football. Then if you talk about the three midfielders, they are big stars all of them – Lampard, Gerrard, Beckham. If they are in good condition in a World Cup, you know you have a good team. Up front you have the new star, Wayne Rooney. And you have the old star, who is only 25, in Michael Owen. So it's a good team, and we have Joe Cole getting better and better. He could be a world star by next summer. When we have all available, there's a balance in the team. We are good attacking and we are good defending. That's strange: we don't have any weak points.

'And on the list of best European players we had one second, one third, one number 10 and one at 20. I don't know when that has happened before, but it was great. It was European but that means the world because none of the best 20 or 30 is playing outside of Europe. This group of players are less and less concerned about who the opponent is. Today they are very confident. They think we can win it. They know as I know you need fit players and you need a little bit of luck. But they think we can win it. I always said we were going to qualify and that we are going to have a very good World Cup. And having a good World Cup means doing much better than we did the last time. I think we can do that and I still believe we are one of five who could win it. But injuries are the main problem. How many do we have in the middle of May? You can't do anything about it. For sure we have the best team since I came to this country, there's no doubt about that.'

Eriksson added, 'It was a good draw for us. Compared to the last World Cup, it's a much better draw. I think we'll go through. After England, I'd like Sweden to win the World Cup. But when England play them, I'm English not Swedish. We have been fighting very hard to have four weeks' preparation instead of three like the last World Cup. We've achieved that. We have one more week to rest and prepare and that's very important. It's difficult for me to say this group of players is the best chance England have had of winning a World Cup because

I've only been here five years. But, since I came to this country, I've never had such a good squad. If I had to pick the squad tomorrow, I would be pretty clear on who the 23 are. But the World Cup is still months ahead and some things can change – a young player can come through like Wayne Rooney did.'

Pele, who received a lifetime achievement recognition at the BBC Sports Personality of the Year awards, said, 'England winning it is difficult to say. But to be in the final in Germany? Yes, no doubt. I've seen nearly all their games in the last two years and England have improved very much. We are still seven months before the World Cup.'

Three-time World Cup winner Pele, 65, added, 'England can beat Brazil, but the World Cup is tough. Anything can happen in the final. If I have to pick a winner, then I'll go for Brazil. But I never feel comfortable as the favourite because they do not tend to win the World Cup. Brazil are the best team. They have two players in every position.'

Pele sounded a note of caution, however, when he suggested that England's aspirations were heavily reliant on the enduring fitness of all of their key players. 'Of course, we are still seven months from the World Cup,' he said. 'If no one gets injured and everyone has a chance to be there in shape, then I think two of England, Italy or Brazil should make the final.'

Pele, who scored 77 goals in 92 appearances for his country, even went so far as to suggest that 'Roonaldo', who lit up last year's European Championship until his untimely metatarsal injury, would make Brazil's starting XI. 'Probably on the left side,' Pele said. 'But it would be one more problem for Parreira. He would be yet another good player.'

Brazil's strength in depth is apparently Pele's major concern. Brazil coach Carlos Alberto Parreira has a vast array of attacking talent available to him. 'Today I think Brazil are the best team,' Pele said, 'but the only coach who has a problem is Parreira because he has too many good players in every position. He doesn't know what team he has to use.'

## GROUP A

A1: Germany
A3: Poland

A2: Costa Rica
A4: Ecuador

| Date | Venue | Teams |
| --- | --- | --- |
| Jun 9 | Munich | Germany:Costa Rica |
| Jun 9 | Gelsenkirchen | Poland:Ecuador |
| Jun 14 | Dortmund | Germany:Poland |
| Jun 15 | Hamburg | Ecuador:Costa Rica |
| Jun 20 | Berlin | Ecuador:Germany |
| Jun 20 | Hanover | Costa Rica:Poland |

## GROUP B

B1: England
B3: Trinidad & Tobago

B2: Paraguay
B4: Sweden

| Date | Venue | Teams |
| --- | --- | --- |
| Jun 10 | Frankfurt | England:Paraguay |
| Jun 10 | Dortmund | Trinidad & Tobago:Sweden |
| Jun 15 | Nuremberg | England:Trinidad & Tobago |
| Jun 15 | Berlin | Sweden:Paraguay |
| Jun 20 | Cologne | Sweden:England |
| Jun 20 | Kaiserslautern | Paraguay:Trinidad & Tobago |

## GROUP C

C1: Argentina
C3: Serbia & Montenegro

C2: Ivory Coast
C4: Holland

| Date | Venue | Teams |
| --- | --- | --- |
| Jun 10 | Hamburg | Argentina:Ivory Coast |
| Jun 11 | Leipzig | Serbia & Montenegro:Holland |
| Jun 16 | Gelsenkirchen | Argentina:Serbia & Montenegro |
| Jun 16 | Stuttgart | Holland:Ivory Coast |
| Jun 21 | Frankfurt | Holland:Argentina |
| Jun 21 | Munich | Ivory Coast:Serbia & Montenegro |

## GROUP D

D1: Mexico
D3: Angola

D2: Iran
D4: Portugal

| Date | Venue | Teams |
| --- | --- | --- |
| Jun 11 | Nuremberg | Mexico:Iran |
| Jun 11 | Cologne | Angola:Portugal |
| Jun 16 | Hanover | Mexico:Angola |
| Jun 17 | Frankfurt | Portugal:Iran |
| Jun 21 | Gelsenkirchen | Portugal:Mexico |
| Jun 21 | Leipzig | Iran:Angola |

## GROUP E

E1: Italy
E3: USA

E2: Ghana
E4: Czech Republic

| Date | Venue | Teams |
|------|-------|-------|
| Jun 12 | Hanover | Italy:Ghana |
| Jun 12 | Gelsenkirchen | USA:Czech Republic |
| Jun 17 | Kaiserslautern | Italy:USA |
| Jun 17 | Cologne | Czech Republic:Ghana |
| Jun 22 | Hamburg | Czech Republic:Italy |
| Jun 22 | Nuremberg | Ghana:USA |

## GROUP F

F1: Brazil
F3: Australia

F2: Croatia
F4: Japan

| Date | Venue | Teams |
|------|-------|-------|
| Jun 12 | Kaiserslautern | Australia:Japan |
| Jun 13 | Berlin | Brazil:Croatia |
| Jun 18 | Munich | Brazil:Australia |
| Jun 18 | Nuremberg | Japan:Croatia |
| Jun 22 | Dortmund | Japan:Brazil |
| Jun 22 | Stuttgart | Croatia:Australia |

## GROUP G

G1: France
G3: South Korea

G2: Switzerland
G4: Togo

| Date | Venue | Teams |
|------|-------|-------|
| Jun 13 | Stuttgart | France:Switzerland |
| Jun 13 | Frankfurt | South Korea:Togo |
| Jun 18 | Leipzig | France:South Korea |
| Jun 19 | Dortmund | Togo:Switzerland |
| Jun 23 | Cologne | Togo:France |
| Jun 23 | Hanover | Switzerland:South Korea |

## GROUP H

H1: Spain
H3: Tunisia

H2: Ukraine
H4: Saudi Arabia

| Date | Venue | Teams |
|------|-------|-------|
| Jun 14 | Leipzig | Spain:Ukraine |
| Jun 14 | Munich | Tunisia:Saudi Arabia |
| Jun 19 | Stuttgart | Spain:Tunisia |
| Jun 19 | Hamburg | Saudi Arabia:Ukraine |
| Jun 23 | Kaiserslautern | Saudi Arabia:Spain |
| Jun 23 | Berlin | Ukraine:Tunisia |